The Need for a European Contract Law

THE UNIVERSITY OF
WINCHESTER

Martial Rose Library
Tel: 01962 827306

To be returned on or before the day marked above, subject to recall.

Europa Law Publishing, Groningen 2005

The Need for a European Contract Law

Empirical and Legal Perspectives

Edited by Jan Smits

Europa Law Publishing is a publishing company
specializing in European Union Law and public
international law.
For further information please contact Europa Law
Publishing via email: info@europalawpublishing.com
or visit our website at: www.europalawpublishing.com.

Typeset in Scala and Scala Sans, Graphic design by
G2K Designers, Groningen/Amsterdam

NUR 828; ISBN 90-76871-35-3

British Library Cataloguing-in-Publication Data
A catalogue record for this book is available from the
British Library

Introduction

This book addresses an often neglected question in the field of European Private Law: to what extent is there a need for unification of contract law in Europe? The present debate on unification of private law within the European Union mainly focuses on *the way in which* unification or harmonisation should come about or to what extent it is actually *possible* to create uniformity in view of diverging national legal cultures. These are indeed important questions, but they should be preceded by the issue of the *need* for uniformity. This issue is now high on the political agenda: over the last few years, the European Commission issued three communications on European contract law. The view of the European Commission seems to be that diversity of law stands in the way of a proper functioning of the internal market, but this view does not seem to be shared by business: in the reactions to the Communication on European Contract Law (2001) it was striking to see that most companies do not consider the present diversity to be a true barrier to trade.

The aim of this book is to shed light on the question to what extent there is a need for uniform contract law in view of the (primarily) economic interests of the European Union. The approach adopted is an interdisciplinary one: in order to obtain a full picture of the research question, not only law, but also insights from economics and psychology are taken into account.

The book sets off with the economic arguments in favour of and against harmonisation. The first contribution, written by Gerhard Wagner, gives a balanced account of these arguments. In weighing up the costs and benefits of diversity on the one side and of unity on the other, Gerhard Wagner considers the arguments in favour of diversity to be stronger. He shows how competition of legal systems leads to better and more efficient law, notwithstanding the fact that it is impossible to give a quantitative analysis. His plea is supported by the economist Helmut Wagner, who discusses what economic science has to say about the need for uniformity. Helmut Wagner weighs the substantial costs that full harmonisation generates against the costs of legal uncertainty from the macro-economic perspective. In the end, both Gerhard Wagner and Helmut Wagner plead for a step-by-step approach. In Gerhard Wagner's view, this means the adoption of an optional contract code which would allow the parties to choose a neutral system. It provides a 'reality check' of the need for uniform law.

In a contribution that adopts the *meta*-perspective, Jaap Hage confirms the findings of Gerhard Wagner that a quantitative analysis to address this book's research question is impossible. He argues that economic analysis does provide tools to assess the need for unification of contract law, but falls short of making reliable judgments on the need for harmonisation. This is partly due to the fact that we lack information on how such a uniform law will look like. As it is impossible to foresee the contents of a European contract code and the way in which this code will be applied, it is also impossible to assess in advance the costs and benefits of unification. Indeed, this does not mean that economic analysis has nothing to say, but its importance should not be overstretched. Hage's conclusions, founded on a theory of qualitative comparative reasoning, remarkably coincide with those of Helmut Wagner and Gerhard Wagner.

Very much in line with the other contributors, Heico Kerkmeester finds that the arguments for a uniform contract law are outweighed by the arguments for diversity. His findings are (partly) based on behavioural law and economics. This relatively new discipline applies the insights of behavioural economics to the law, thus trying to obtain a more accurate understanding of behaviour and choice concerning legal rules. In Kerkmeester's view, the traditional argument of Tiebout that diversity of law enables people to satisfy their own preferences is reinforced by behavioural analysis. The case he makes against forced unification is not necessarily one against spontaneous (bottom-up) unification. However, it is interesting to note that because of the cognitive distortions that consumers may suffer from, a uniform level of consumer protection *is* appropriate from the behavioural perspective.

A related cognitive perspective is provided in the contribution of Jeffrey Rachlinski. Rachlinski distinguishes three different reasons for diversity of law: variations in cultural values, differential political power and differential cognitive error. Rachlinski's contribution focuses on the latter. He explains that mechanisms to resolve conflicts of law (caused by legal diversity) present an opportunity to reduce irrationality caused by cognitive error in legal regimes. Erroneous judgment of the legislator, public officials and judges leads to biases that produce undesirable legal rules. Rachlinski's main point is that the process of resolving conflicts between legal systems creates an opportunity for correcting laws that are produced by such cognitive error. If erroneous laws are the product of erroneous beliefs, another legal system is unlikely to duplicate the same error. If there is a mediating institution that can identify cognitive errors, this institution can correct the erroneous rule. Rachlinski emphasises the role of the courts that have to deal with conflicts of law in correcting such errors, but it is likely that the mere exercise of comparing legal systems with each other will also lead to adjustment of rules that are the product of cognitive error. In the concluding contribution, some of the biases distinguished by Rachlinski are applied to the decision making process of contracting parties.

While this book focuses on the main argument (the economic need for uniformity), also some other arguments in favour of and against unification are discussed. This is to some extent done by Jaap Hage, but in particular by Thomas Wilhelmsson. Wilhelmsson raises the question whether there is a need for uniform law in view of present-day society. In his view, the globalised late modern European society requires an experimental and learning law, a law that leaves space for contextually determined pragmatic moral reasoning. A general codification of private law would not do justice to these requirements. Pre-existing maps (like a systematic codification) would not help in making the decisions present society needs. Even with an optional contract code, the risk would be that the option becomes the general norm and that it would be difficult to improve and amend if necessary. Wilhelmsson therefore suggests a continuously renewable and 'perhaps semi-official' (re)statement of European contract law.

In the final contribution, an attempt is made to bring together the insights of law, economics and cognitive science regarding the need for uniformity in European contract law. This chapter is based on the findings of the other authors to this book, but it also adopts a broader view, for example by explaining to what extent there is actually diversity in European contract law. It makes clear that if economic science and psychology cannot explain whether uniform law is necessary, the best way to proceed is by taking small steps, moving slowly and gradually from one stage to the next.

Previous versions of the papers published in this book were presented at research seminars held at Maastricht University. The main seminar took place on 4 June 2004 and was part of a project funded by the SARO-scheme of the Netherlands Organisation for Scientific Research (NWO). The financial support of NWO, the Maastricht Faculty of Law and the Ius Commune Research School are acknowledged. The Ius Commune Research School also provided the inspiring atmosphere in which interdisciplinary projects like this are fostered. Thanks are due to Nicole Kornet for meticulous language editing and to Renske van Dijken for assistance in editing this volume. The seminar of 4 June benefited greatly from the organisational skills of Marjo Mullers.

Jan Smits
Maastricht, January 2005

Contents

CHAPTER 3   **Law, Economics and Uniform Contract Law: A Sceptical View**
Jaap Hage

CHAPTER 4   **Uniformity of European Contract Law; An Economic Study Between Logic and Fact**
Heico Kerkmeester

CHAPTER I

The Virtues of Diversity in European Private Law

Gerhard Wagner

I The Commission Action Plan

The Communication from the Commission to the Council and the European Parliament on European contract law of September 2001[1] has triggered an intensive discussion that is not supposed to come to an end for a number of years. In its Communication, the Commission sketched three options for further action in the area of European Contract Law, in addition to the possibility of remaining idle and doing nothing.[2]

In its Action Plan submitted in February of 2003 the Commission embraced a multi-layered approach, working on three different levels:[3]
- improvement of the coherence of the EC acquis in the area of contract law;
- promotion of the elaboration of general contract terms uniform across the Union;
- reflection on the advantages and costs of an optional instrument in the area of European Contract Law.

The discussion to follow confronts the subject on the basis of new comprehensive legislation at the EU-level. Quite obviously, this is the course of action reaching farthest because full harmonization of European contract law raises fundamental issues both of governmental federalism and of transactional efficiency.

II Harmonizing European Contract Law

Harmonization of European Contract Law would replace the 25 systems of domestic contract law with a single European Code. Obviously, such a sweeping measure would simplify a lot of things. All the courts within the European Union would apply the same legal rules, all the scholars would comment on the same text, and the parties would have to accept or contract around the same scheme of costs and benefits.

Why not embrace such a bold vision that would achieve in the area of law what the Euro did in the area of currencies? Before the introduction of the Euro, consumers as well as business enterprises had to change gear each time they crossed a border, exchanging one currency for another and paying a premium to the banks and bureaus that provided this service. The transaction costs associated with such manoeuvres were considerable, and the Euro worked to save them. In the same manner, one could argue that the transaction costs associated with the fragmentation of European law could easily be saved by introducing

---

[1] European Commission (2001) 1. See also Council of the European Union (2001); European Parliament (2001).

[2] European Commission (2001) 7 seq., no. 41 *et seq.*

[3] European Commission (2003) 2.

a single legal currency, a European Civil Code, replacing the several domestic systems.

It should not be disputed that a European Civil Code would produce considerable benefits, as it would work to save transaction costs. The crucial question is not whether this is so but what the costs of these savings are and whether the savings outweigh the costs or vice versa. However, many proponents of harmonization keep celebrating the virtues of a European Civil Code without ever acknowledging the price tag associated with these. On the other hand, it seems equally misguided to insist on legal diversity for the simple reason that diversity is always best, without acknowledging that diversity imposes costs on parties engaged in cross-border transactions. 19th century Germany with its fragmented map of jurisdictions is a good example for the proposition that there might very well be an overkill of diversity that imposes a tax on cross-border trade and therefore serves as an instrument of inefficiency. Thus, there is no point in continuing the debate on an abstract level by either ignoring the benefits of harmonization or by denying that these benefits come at a certain price. Instead of blinding oneself on one eye and focussing only on those aspects of the problem conducive to one's own position, one has to confront the difficult issue head on and to engage in a quantitative and even-handed analysis of both, the benefits and the costs of harmonization.

It needs no further explanation that a quantitative analysis that really deserved this name is impossible to come by. There is simply no way of measuring with some exactness the benefits and costs both of legal harmonization and of legal diversity in order to compare the two. However, the mere fact that it is impossible to come up with numbers must not foreclose the door to a more thorough analysis of the crucial issues. In particular, it should not spare us the task to investigate the costs and benefits to the fullest possible extent, and to engage in some sort of weighing up of advantages and disadvantages, costs and benefits of diversity on the one side and of unity on the other.

In the analysis to follow, I will first focus on the benefits of diversity. After these have been explored, we will turn to the other end of the balance, *i.e.* the promised savings in transaction costs. Finally, I will try to discuss some examples and cases in order to generate a sense of where the balance may be struck.

III The Virtues of Diversity

1 Party Autonomy

Looked at through the eyes of an economist, the obvious solution to problems of legal diversity is to let the parties make a choice. In fact, the conflicts rules of virtually all legal systems of the Western World currently accept the principle of party autonomy in international contract law, allowing them to choose the law applicable to their agreement. Within Europe, Article 3 of the Rome Convention on the law applicable to contractual obligations[4] does just that, and in doing so, it seems to put the whole issue of efficiency concerns in international contract law to rest.

Adding another well-received wisdom, economics also assumes that if every individual pursues her own interests, the result will be optimal not only for the individual in question but for society as a whole. The mechanism bringing about this miracle is the invisible hand of the market. This institution enjoys the virtue of aggregating the diverse and conflicting ends of the numerous individuals to a common good not because of some divine blessing but because of the workings of a very human characteristic, *i.e.* competition. Under perfect competition, no individual exercises power over the preferences of any other individual and over the ways and means these preferences are satisfied, such that prices reflect the 'true' values of the relevant commodities and the factors of production are channelled to their most productive uses.

Of course, markets do not function well in the state of nature but are in need of a legal framework, if only to guarantee that promises may not be broken with impunity. Such legal frameworks are the products of governments chosen by the people. In theory, private autonomy has a counterpart in public autonomy and the power of each individual to choose his contracting partner has a counterpart in the right of each individual to share an equal vote in the choice of its government. In this regard, the issue as to the appropriate institutional level of government activity becomes moot. In theory, optimal markets are protected by optimal governments, and the outcome, of course, is optimal as well.

2   Federalism

In order to transform these principles to a federal system of government, one would have to replace the individual with a particular member state. Communities of individuals entertain different sets of preferences just as individuals do. How does a political system reflect these parallels? This is precisely the question raised – and answered – by Charles Tiebout in his famous 1956 paper 'A Pure Theory of Local Expenditures', in which he reasoned that competition among local communities comprised of citizens with different preferences will yield allocative efficiency.[5] Competing jurisdictions will be forced to learn from each other, and the system with the most efficient legal structure will ultimately prevail.[6]

To illustrate, take two hypothetical communities A and B, with the people in A being enthusiastically interested in all sorts of sports and physical exercises

---

[4]   *OJ EC* 1998, C 27/34.

[5]   Tiebout (1956). See also Ogus (1999) 406 *et seq.*; Faure (2001) § 2 A; Tijong (2002) 70 *et seq.*

[6]   For an overview of current research see Cooter (2000) 127 *et seq.*; Inman and Rubinfeld (2000) 667 *et seq.*; Posner (1998) § 25.1, 695 *et seq.*

whereas the population in B prefers adventures and exercises of intellectual nature. On these facts, one would expect community A to build and operate a large number of sporting facilities, whereas community B will focus its resources on libraries, universities and the like. If movement between the two communities is possible at little or no cost, one would expect the intellectuals living in A to move to B where their preferences may be satisfied to a larger extent than in A, and the athletes of B would of course move to A where they will find the desired sports facilities.

The same reasoning may be applied to legislative powers, since from the economic standpoint legislation may be looked at as a public good to be provided by the government. In particular, statutory or other rules of contract law are goods of public nature, since everyone may use them, without each individual user diminishing the returns to any rival user of the good.[7] To illustrate Tiebout's reasoning with respect to the law of contract, imagine two different communities, with the people in A being merchant-minded, tending to enforce contracts as written and defending the principle of pacta sunt servanda. The people in B, however, place a high value on the protection of the consumer, they are strong supporters of the principle of good faith and fair dealing, they believe in the ability of public courts to achieve 'just' results and thus they are in favour of judicial control over contractual agreements in the interest of the protection of the supposedly weaker party. In a situation like this Tiebout's model yields the prediction that the people in A entertaining a set of preferences similar to those dominant in B will move to B, and vice versa.[8] As a result, people will 'vote with their feet', moving to the jurisdiction they like best.

Leaving the possibility of moving aside for a moment, this model seems to yield a quite accurate description of the real European landscape. Among the peoples of Europe, there is certainly no consensus on the proper scope of consumer protection. German law, for instance, although replete with tools that control the behaviour of the contracting parties, has never used the distinction between consumers and commercial men in its legal history until the European Union introduced its policy of consumer protection, following the French example. On the other hand, the Scandinavian countries are often quite discontent with the low level of consumer protection EU-law provides. They have a strong tradition of a far-reaching consumer protection, and they are very reluctant to give up a bit of it in the interest of European unity. Why should the majority of the states impose a certain level of consumer protection policy both on peoples which would rather have more and on those which would rather have less of it? Under the assumption that the level of consumer protection is a matter of political beliefs rather than 'objective truth' there is simply no point in harmonizing the laws of the member states on an intermediate level. Why not allow the Fins

---

[7] As to the concept of public goods see Cooter and Ulen (2000) 42 *et seq.*

[8] Tiebout (1956) 418.

to choose the level of consumer protection they like, and the English to do the same?

True enough, in the longer run it might turn out that community A, thanks to its strict contract law, is doing better than community B with its preoccupation with consumer protection. Assuming for purposes of illustration only that the average wealth of the people in A rises thanks to the strict contract law in force there and that the welfare of the people in B declines, that process in turn will induce people from B to move to A, either because they changed their preferences or because they awarded their preference for a high level of wealth priority over their taste in consumer protection. Thus, one would expect people to move to A, creating incentives for the government in B to change its policy in order to catch up with A and to stop the drain of human resources from B to A. In theory, competition between governments yields the efficient result.

IV   Questioning the Economics of Federalism

As most other economic theorems, the Economics of Federalism rest on a set of assumptions which might not be very realistic. In Tiebout's model the most important underlying assumptions are, as stated by the author himself:[9]

1) consumers and firms enjoy full mobility between communities at zero cost;
2) the citizens are perfectly informed about the differences of the public goods offered by rival communities competing to attract them, and they also know the costs and benefits associated with such differences;
3) there are a large number of communities among which consumers and firms can choose the one most attractive to live and work in.

As should be obvious from their mere formulation, these assumptions are anything but strong. Apart from this general observation their distance from the real world is much greater with regard to the European market than with respect to the American scene.

i   The Assumption of Complete Information

In order to vote by his feet on a rational basis, the consumer or business enterprise has to be perfectly informed about the properties of the public goods on offer within each of the communities competing for it to take his residence or seat within its borders. Applied to the issue of harmonization of legal rules, this assumption presupposes that people in A not only know about

---

[9] Tiebout (1956) 419.

the properties of their own set of legal rules, but also about the legal system in B. In addition, in order to make a rational choice, the citizens would also have to realize how different legal standards affect the performance of the economies in both A and B.

In reality, these assumptions will hardly ever be born out in full. However, hard facts about these parameters are typically unavailable.

2 The Costs of Moving

Things do not improve much when we now turn to the second critical assumption of the Economics of Federalism, which is full mobility at zero cost. *Tiebout* himself was fully aware of the fact that the costs of moving prevent competition among communities to yield efficient outcomes: 'The higher this cost, *ceteris paribus*, the less optimal the allocation of resources.'[10]

Of course, in the context of the EU it is highly unlikely that someone would move from one member state to another only because she prefers the legal system or even the contract law of the state winning her as a citizen. Even if people were fully informed about the differences in the several contract laws and were able to identify the state with the best, *i.e.* most efficient system, it would be plain nonsense to believe that the gain to be earned by moving would be anywhere near the cost of such an enterprise. The decision to move one's residence to a different state cuts deeply into everyday life and will not be made lightly. That is true even within a given nation like Germany where, for example, people from regions with little industry and high unemployment prefer to commute long distances or spend the whole week away from their families to moving themselves and their home to another German region. Within the European context the forces of immobility are much stronger, the most important reason being the diversity of languages. With the exception of a relatively small élite, people are not familiar with the languages spoken in neighbouring countries. The diversity of European languages in turn preserves the relatively deep differences in the culture and lifestyle among the states of Europe. In this respect, the United States of America fare much better since the American people share a common language and, in spite of regional differences, a quite homogenous culture.[11] For these reasons, 'voting by feet' is not an option for most European citizens and firms.

However, these attitudes may change. Among business leaders in Germany there is already a discussion about the alleged fact that the country suffers a 'brain drain' caused by the poor performance of its economy during the last few years and the lack of a vision how things could turn to the better. Of course it is

---

[10] Tiebout (1956) 422.

[11] Neuman (1996) 576.

impossible to link this trend – if it exists – to any particular feature of German law, let alone contract law. But still, it sure may count as a vote against the inflation of the welfare state, against tight regulation of the labour market through means of private law and so on. People may still be able to turn away from a community that adheres to political and legal principles they dislike.

3   Is Voting an Option?

In a similar vein, it will readily be acknowledged that the democratic process does not excel when it comes to issues of private law.[12] These matters are usually far too complex to capture the public eye. Lacking any public apprehension, politicians do not really care either, as long as there are no pressure groups who push their particular concerns. Thus, to suggest that 'the people' would vote a government out of office for the reason of it inaugurating an inefficient contract law or leaving such inferior law in place is simply absurd.

On the other hand, one would be hard-pressed to deny that private law issues may occasionally be thrust into the spotlight of public discourse, usually in the aftermath of a legislative move or court decision arousing the public interest. Moreover, the overall 'mood' or atmosphere is subject to changes, and with due lag of time, these changes also affect the behaviour of parliaments and courts. If certain aspects of German labour law were to be introduced today, it is far from clear whether they would win a majority in parliament, a majority they easily won during the booming fifties and sixties.

In addition, one has to remember that, of course, the same failures the democratic process might suffer from in the area of private law on the national level also affect policy making at the European level. And not only that, the legislative process in Brussels suffers from a deficit in democratic participation and is much more opaque than the processes at national levels, with the impact of interest groups weighing even heavier.

4   Comparative Law as a Mechanism of Competition

Even if the political process may be inapt to foster legislative competition in the area of private law, that is not to say that competition for the best legal solution has not been occurring in Europe. No-one will be prepared to defend the proposition that the existence of the several European laws of contract has not had any beneficial effect on the development of each of these systems. In most cases, however, the beneficial legal interplay between one jurisdiction and another has not been the work of an invisible hand but rather of the very visible writings of great scholars who were impressed by the blessings of a foreign legal rule. But still, if one admits – as one must – that there have

---

[12] Cf. O'Hara and Ribstein (2000) 1160 *et seq.*

been such beneficial spillovers between 'competing' European legal systems, then one has also acknowledged what harmonization would destroy.

In the particular case of Germany, the legal system as a whole was inspired by the reception of Roman law, *i.e.* a 'foreign' legal order available only in books and writings. In the 19th century, German civil procedure received repeated injections of fresh ideas and institution from France, particularly since the Rhine territories decided to retain the Ancien Code de Procedure Civile even after Napoleon's defeat. The modern law of products liability would be unthinkable without the groundbreaking work of English and American courts, which handed down decisions like *Donoghue* v. *Stephenson*[13] or *Escola* v. *Coca-Cola Bottling Co. of Fresno*[14] for being studied by German scholars.

Legal history of the several European states is replete with similar examples. A most recent one is the replacement of the principle, long enshrined in German law, restricting compensation for non-pecuniary loss to extra-contractual and fault-based liability. For more than 100 years, damages for pain and suffering were neither available for breach of contract nor in cases of strict liability. When this principle was discarded in 2002,[15] it certainly was of tremendous help that the civil servants in the ministry of justice were able to point to other European jurisdictions which had followed the opposing principle for centuries without encountering any difficulties. Had these jurisdictions not existed, it would have been easy to denounce the reform as a sinful departure from the right track.

The adherents of harmonization usually counter this train of reasoning with the argument that the European systems of private law have had their competition for 2000 years such that there is very little – if anything – that can be expected to gain from further competition in the future. This argument misses the point completely. The concern is not with the variety of solutions and doctrines the now existing systems of contract law have developed for traditional and current legal problems. It may very well be that a benign lawmaker, harmonizing these systems will be able to pick the 'best' solution offered. However, even under this optimistic assumption, the argument may be torn apart easily. It would be naïve to believe that legal history has come to an end now in the sense that we now have all the good solutions in our toolbox. Quite the contrary, legal history shows that every generation has to cope with utterly new problems and has to come up with creative solutions to solve them. It is the competition for the best answer to new challenges that harmonization would destroy. Strange to think that at the same time that European lawyers move together again in order to compare their ideas and to discuss the solutions they have developed, the call

---

[13] *Donoghue* v. *Stephenson* [1932] A.C. 562.

[14] *Escola* v. *Coca-Cola Bottling Co. of Fresno*, 24 Cal.2d 453, 150 P.2d 436 (Cal. 1944).

[15] Zweites Gesetz zur Änderung schadensersatzrechtlicher Vorschriften (Second Tort Law Reform Act), BGBl. 2002 I, 2674. Cf. Wagner (2002) 2053 *et seq.*

for harmonization surfaces that tries to bring this dialogue to an end as quickly as possible.

V   Examples of Competition at Work

Perhaps it serves to provide some examples for the abstract plea in favour of legal diversity.

1   European Family Law

Take for instance the development of family law. If the northern, protestant countries had not moved ahead with the liberalization of divorce, the southern and catholic countries would certainly not have moved either. Even more to the point, it seems a fair guess that in a Europe with a single code of family law, the transformation of family law that occurred during the second half of the 20th century would have proceeded at a much slower pace. The same phenomenon may be observed today with respect to the recognition of same-sex marriages. If no jurisdiction in Europe had the authority to move ahead and to prove to the attentive states that the world does not fall apart if homosexuals are allowed to marry, then it would be much more difficult to promote law-reform in this area.

The history of family law clearly supports an argument in favour of legal diversity. Diversity allows 'avant-garde' jurisdictions to boldly move ahead and prove to the others that it is safe to follow. That is not to say that it is desirable that the Irish live under the same legal regime of family law as the Dutch or the Swedish. If the Irish people prefer a more conservative model of marriage and family they should be free to opt for one and to keep living under it. I see no benefit in forcing them to comprise with the Swedish, just as the Swedish should not be forced to comprise their model of family law with the ideas prevalent in Ireland.

2   European Corporate Law

a)   Regulatory Competition at Work

Currently, one of the most interesting and dynamic areas of European legal integration certainly is corporate law. In a series of decisions, beginning with the judgment in the *Centros* case, continuing with the *Überseering* case and coming to a preliminary end with *Inspire Art* the ECJ broke up the national systems of corporate law and allowed foreign corporations the freedom of movement in the same way as natural persons.[16] Although the ECJ

---

[16]   ECJ Case C-167/01 *Inspire Art* [2003] ECR I-10155; ECJ Case C-208/00 *Überseering* [2002] ECR I-9919; ECJ Case C-212/97 *Centros* [1999] ECR I-1459.

has shunned away from confronting head on the 'real-seat'-theory dominating the German international law in the area of corporate law for decades, it is clear that this theory is in shambles. In light of the guarantees of the EC Treaty this destiny is anything but surprising. The real-seat-theory was designed from the start not as a purportedly 'neutral' way of identifying the law governing a corporate entity but as a legal iron-curtain protecting the domestic market against the influx of companies incorporated under foreign law. It is this curtain that the ECJ has torn apart in the interest of freedom of movement within the European internal market.

How does real life react to the newly gained freedoms? What the switch to the place-of-incorporation-theory effectively does is to allow the founders and shareholders of a corporation to choose the law applicable to their creation from the menu of European company laws. At this present time, there is a heated debate among German corporate lawyers on how to advise German companies with respect to the new choices.[17] Is the English Limited Company to be preferred to the German GmbH or the Dutch Besloten Vennootschap? At present, it is hard to tell whether the GmbH will lose more than a minimal share of the German corporate market to the Limited or the Besloten Vennootschap. What has become apparent beyond any reasonable doubt is, however, that competition works very well once the parties are allowed to choose the law applicable to their relationship. Almost instantly, the parties concerned start to compare the advantages and disadvantages of different legal regimes in order to opt for the one they consider best. Moreover, this competition also affects the lawmaking process and thus the arena of regulatory law. The civil servants in the German ministry of justice in charge of corporate law have already taken off their jackets and gotten down to work, devising various schemes of how to reform German corporate law, particularly with an eye towards the GmbH in order to make it more attractive to domestic and foreign investors.

The recent history of European corporate law works like a live demonstration of the workings and virtues of competition in the legal field. The opening of the German borders to foreign corporate entities has thrust principles of German corporate law into question which have been worshipped for decades and which would still be standing there like holy truisms if the ECJ had not intervened. A pertinent example is the requirement that in order to obtain the privilege of limited liability the founders of a GmbH have to supply the corporation with a minimum amount of capital, currently set at 25.000 Euros.[18] The English Ltd. may be brought to life without paying up such a sum, and thus may be more attractive for investors. Thus, the principle of minimal capital in German corporate law may have to go.

---

[17] Cf. Lutter (2003) 7; Lutter (ed.) (2005); Eidenmüller (ed.) (2004).

[18] Sect. 5 par. 1 GmbHG (Limited Liability Company Act).

As the example of corporate law shows, voting with one's feet, *i.e.*, moving one's place of residence to a different territory, or voting one's government out of office may not be necessary in the first place in order for regulatory competition to work. It is enough if the individual has the power to choose the law applicable to his own affairs from the menu of legal systems within the Union.

b)   The Race to the Bottom

It should not go unnoticed that the whole rationale of the economic analysis favouring federalism, by embracing competition among jurisdictions, not only accepts but supports a process that those of us holding sceptical views about markets and laissez faire have pejoratively labelled 'the race to the bottom'. The underlying idea is that competition among jurisdictions will drive social, environmental, cultural and what-have-you-else standards down, down to the level at which no further degradation is possible. The current focus of this argument is international corporate law, namely the authority of corporate entities to choose their corporate law by incorporating in the state of their choice while having their headquarters in another state – and doing business anywhere.[19] In the United States, such a rule has resulted in a strong concentration of charter business in one particular state of the Union, *i.e.* Delaware: Over 40 per cent of the companies whose shares are traded at the New York Stock Exchange are incorporated in this particular state.[20]

To be sure, even the proponents of competitive federalism allow for uniform rules, but only if unification is commanded by compelling reasons. The hallmark of such reasons is that local rules would create an incentive for the relevant communities to externalise costs caused by domestic activities on others, people outside the community.[21] The most obvious cases of such externalities in the context of corporate law are takeover bids as well as negative externalities created for external creditors in general, and involuntary creditors such as tort-victims in particular, further rules regulating corporate disclosure and the responsibility of corporations towards the public at large.[22] Under these objectives it may readily be explained that, even in the United States, the leeway for competition between states in corporate law is not without limits but embedded in an environment of federal law and regulation of capital markets, *i.e.* the federal laws governing securities transactions, and a strong regulatory agency – the Security

---

[19] Cf. only Bebchuk (1992) 1442 *et seq.* with further reference.

[20] Historical accounts of the development leading to the dominance of Delaware, instead of New Jersey as the initial front runner in the charter business market are presented by Charny (1991) 427 *et seq.*; Bebchuk (1992) 1443 *et seq.*; Barnard (2000) 59 *et seq.*

[21] Tiebout (1956) 423; in the context of corporate law see Easterbrook and Fischel (1991) 221 *et seq.*

[22] For such an approach, going much further than orthodox proponents of federalism see Bebchuk (1992) 1485 et seq.

Exchange Commission – charged with enforcing them. In the context of torts a pertinent example for federal or supranational interference with local law-making is the case of trans-border pollution of air, soil or water, explaining the need for federal environmental law. But even here, the case for federalization is not uncontested, with a number of commentators claiming that regulatory diversity in the field of environmental law has resulted in a 'race to the top' rather than one for the bottom.[23] And as far as corporate law is concerned, it is even less clear whether the so-called Delaware-effect has really caused more harm than good to the American economy.[24]

3   Lessons for Contract Law

What lessons can be learned for contract law from the example of corporate law?

a)   Allowing for Choice of Law

The first conclusion to draw from the area of corporate law is to broaden the scope of choice of law. Choice of law works as a low-cost substitute for moving physically and thus holds much more potential for regulatory competition.

To be sure, the Rome Convention already allows for a choice of law, without requiring one or both parties to make a physical move. The parties have the power to opt out of an inefficient municipal contract law by simply choosing the law of a rival jurisdiction to govern their contract.[25] In this sense, the authority of the citizens to choose the law governing their transactions works as a 'virtual' substitute for the 'physical' exit otherwise necessary to avoid the application of inefficient laws. Thus, one might think that competition among the several jurisdictions of the Union might work here.

Unfortunately, freedom of choice of law, even under the Rome Convention, is subject to serious constraints. First of all, the parties lack the authority to contract out of a legal regime they both are strongly connected with. Pursuant to Article 3 para. 3 of the Rome Convention, if the case is connected with the law of one member state only, the parties may not derogate from mandatory provisions of such state.[26] Thus, for domestic transactions there simply is no

---

[23] Paul (1995) 41 et seq., 57 et seq.; Faure (2001) § 3 B.

[24] For a balanced account of the issue see Bebchuk (1992) 1448 et seq.; more pronounced Romana (1999) 370 et seq.; Barnard (2000) 73 et seq; O'Hara and Ribstein (2000) 1162 et seq.

[25] Kobayashi and Ribstein (1999) 331 et seq.; O'Hara (2000) 1555 et seq.; O'Hara and Ribstein (2000) 1155, 1163 et seq.; Ogus (1999) 408.

[26] For a similar provision prevalent in the United States see Sect. 187 par. (2) (a) of the Restatement (Second) of Conflict of Laws (1971); for an overview of cases under this rule see O'Hara (2000) 1563 et seq.

freedom of choice in the sense of choice between legal systems. People who wish to escape the inferior but mandatory rules of their domestic contract law really have no other choice than to move physically, *i.e.* to take their place of residence to a member state with a 'better' law. What is required to foster competition in the area of contract law is not harmonization, however, but allowing the parties more leeway to choose the applicable law. Thus, the remedy would be to strike out the limitation of Article 3 para. 3 Rome Convention and to allow for choice of law also with respect to purely domestic transactions.

Another serious constraint for choice of law is Article 5 Rome Convention, which guarantees to the passive consumer who does not leave his home country the protection of the laws of his state in favour of consumers. In this area it is unlikely that the member states favouring a strong policy of consumer protection would be willing to allow their businesses to opt out of this policy by choosing a foreign contract law providing a lower standard of consumer protection.

b) The Race to the Bottom

If business enterprises within the Union were allowed to choose the appropriate standard of consumer protection, this would again raise the issue of a race to the bottom, already familiar from the area of corporate law.

First of all, the dangers inherent in choice of law must not be exaggerated. As long as the laws of a particular state governing private transactions are the same for everyone engaging in such transactions, the risk that the level of consumer protection will decline drastically is only slight. After all, the parties may only choose a system of contract law one member state is subjecting its own citizens to.

Secondly, it must be borne in mind that large parts of the law of consumer protection have already been harmonized through the many directives the Commission has introduced during the last decades. At best, the fear of a race to the bottom justifies the harmonization of the law of consumer protection, but not of contract law as a whole.

4   Conclusions

The lesson to be learned from the preceding analysis is twofold:
- There is no need for harmonization of municipal contract laws across the board;
- What is needed instead is a policy of fostering competition rather than killing it off. In light of the experiences made recently within the area of corporate law, the parties should be entitled to opt for another law even with regard to purely domestic transactions. For this purpose, Art. 3 par. 3 Rome Convention needs revision.

Competition among the domestic systems of the Union will always be fraught with the problem that these systems are of national origin such that the parties would have to opt in favour of a 'foreign' law. This stain could be removed by the introduction of an optional European Civil Code, which would allow the parties to choose a 'neutral' system as the law governing their relationship. In addition, the existence of such a code would place the domestic systems of contract law under even more pressure to reform themselves and to strive for the 'better' solution. In turn, the co-existence of these national systems would prevent the European Code from becoming an abstract, academic enterprise as it would have to prove its superiority to any domestic system in daily practice. Such a regime of co-existence would place the belief of many English lawyers that the common law is superior to other systems of contract law under some sort of reality check. If it then turned out that the common law actually fares better, it would be in the interest of the particular parties, and of the European people, to retain it and not to supplant it with a Uniform Civil Code.

VI The Transaction Costs Argument

As has been indicated at the beginning, the central argument for going further than an optional code is one saving transaction costs. If the contract laws of Europe were merged into one, consumers and business would stand on uniform ground and would not need to change gear when moving across the border.

1 Legal Diversity as a Tax

The proliferation of legal rules under the current system of legal diversity imposes serious costs on enterprises doing business in more than one member state because they have to comply with the rules of a number of legal systems. In the case of contract law, an enterprise competing in every single member state of the current Union has to comply with no less than 25 municipal laws, each harbouring its own rules on issues of form, duress, and unconscionability, on the proper balance between the power of the court to review standard contract terms and party autonomy, and a whole maze of provisions on problems sometimes even trivial in theory but highly relevant for the outcome of a particular case. Thus, the proper time limit to bring a particular claim may be set at one, two or three years from the date of accrual of the claim, with good reasons counselling for each of the three solutions. An enterprise doing business in the Union might not bother if the time limit is set at one, two or three years but it will be very interested in a uniform rule since it would make it possible to run its claims management and debt collection procedures on a uniform basis.

In fact, the legal diversity just described forces the European multina-tional enterprise to devise a different contract for each member state, or, more precisely, to change its whole way of doing business when crossing each border, developing different business practices for each municipal market. It should be obvious that such a state of affairs places additional costs on the dealings of a truly European enterprise marketing its goods and services in every jurisdic-tion of the Union. This burden will loom particularly large if the goods supplied are not chattels but services like an insurance policy because such products are 'created' by the law, in the sense that the core of the obligation of the supplier may not be identified without reference to the applicable legal regime.[27] Espe-cially under the conditions just described, but also in general, it is no exag-geration to say that legal diversity places a tax on European business, a tax that creates no benefits either for firms or for consumers but only benefits for lawyers. Therefore, the Commission is correct in placing the objective to reduce transaction costs at the centre of its reasoning concerning the harmonization issue.[28]

2   Legal Diversity as Barrier to Entry

Having started with the issue of transaction costs, one must not stop at noting that goods and services are expected to be more expensive in a system of legal diversity than they would be in a Europe of legal unity. Large, multinational enterprise will not be deterred by the need to adapt to local rules from entering each domestic market and competing for customers there. Such enterprises know how to cope with legal diversity, and they do so by hiring local lawyers to steer their business operations through the pitfalls of the legal system foreign to the managers of the enterprise. Usually, the firm will incorporate a subsidiary in the foreign state which has to and will be playing by the local rules from the start.

With small and medium-size enterprises the matter will be different. For them, it is not worth it to set up a shop in neighbouring countries or even to hire expensive lawyers as counsel in each case of a cross-border transaction. Take the case of a mid-sized construction firm thinking about competing in the bidding process for a foreign construction project. Such a firm would have to make an investment not only in calculating its bid but it would also be compelled to hire a lawyer for advice on the relevant legal issues. Thus, it would have to incur considerable expenses without being able to count on being successful in the competition for the contract on offer. As can be seen easily in examples like this, high transaction costs create barriers to entry of rival firms into a given market.

---

[27] Cf. Wulf-Henning Roth (1993) 133.

[28] European Commission (2001) I, par. 31 et seq.

However, it is doubtful whether such barriers, erected in theory, also exist in reality. In the south of Germany, for instance, there is a high concentration of small and medium-size firms, each highly specialized in some field of engineering and catering to the world market. These enterprises face tremendous legal diversity because they have to deal with contract laws not only of European origin but of any nation on earth, including those of Asia and of developing countries. Quite obviously, however, these firms remain undeterred by legal diversity; in fact, they represent one of the backbones of the German export industry. It will be granted immediately that this is only anecdotal evidence, but as of yet, nobody has come up with hard facts suggesting any other state of affairs that the one just described. Quite to the contrary, during the consultation process on the Commission Communication on European Contract Law, business associations representing small and medium-size enterprises have rejected the idea that full harmonization was necessary to foster competition within the common market.[29]

3   Consumer Behaviour

However, the expectations raised by the perspective of harmonization reach farther than that. The objective is to stimulate cross-border shopping by consumers, which in turn should lead to intensified competition within the common market.[30] But is it realistic to believe that the average European consumer will consider buying a car abroad once he may be sure that the foreign seller has to play by the same legal rules as his local dealer? Intuitively, one might answer the question in the affirmative. Upon closer consideration, however, the matter looks more complex. It bears remembering that the consumer protection branch of contract law has already been the subject of extensive harmonization. Thus, even without any further advances on the harmonization front, the European consumer may be assured that he does not forgo the protection accorded him by local law once he goes on a shopping trip to another member state.

Even more important, the Regulation on Jurisdiction and the Recognition and Enforcement of Judgments in Civil and Commercial Matters[31] guarantees

---

[29] Cf. generally the summary prepared by the European Commission of the reactions to the Communication on European Contract Law; available at www.europe.eu.int/comm/consumers/policy/developments/ contract_law/comments/summeries/sum_en.pdf, under 4.4.2; see e.g., Verband Deutscher Maschinen- und Anlagenbau, Stellungnahme zur Mitteilung der Kommission zum europäischen Vertragsrecht, p. 2; Zentralverband Deutsches Baugewerbe, Stellungnahme zur Mitteilung der Kommission zum Europäischen Vertragsrecht, p. 1.

[30] European Commission (2001) 5, no. 30 et seq; see also introductory consideration no. 4 to Directive 1999/44 on certain aspects of the sale of consumer goods and associated guarantees, OJ EC L 171/12.

[31] Council Regulation 44/2001 on Jurisdiction and the Recognition and Enforcement of Judgments in Civil and Commercial Matters, OJ EC L 12/1.

that the passive consumer-buyer, entering into contracts with foreign sellers, always enjoys the advantage of a *forum actoris*. In international cases, he may sue and be sued in the courts of his home country, not being subject to litigation in a foreign court. As regards the active consumer, his main problem will certainly be the fact that he is forced to litigate any dispute he might have with his seller or other contract partner in a foreign court. If I bought a household appliance in Maastricht and cared to think about the legal position I would find myself in should a dispute arise, my main concern would be the venue, not the law. Given that the court at my home town in Bonn would be competent, I would not feel uneasy about it applying Dutch contract law. On the other hand, I would regard it as a serious handicap if I had to travel to Maastricht for my day in court, even if the substantive law to be applied were of my home-grown variety.

VII Balancing Costs and Benefits

1 Contract Law in General

As has been indicated already, it is virtually impossible to calculate the costs and benefits of harmonization. However, it helps to put the relevant question in precise terms. It has to be asked whether the savings in transaction costs, understood to include any benefits from the removal of barriers to entry, are greater or lesser than the losses caused by the termination of competition within the legal systems of Europe.

The example of the U.S. suggests that with respect to the particular case of contract law, the balance may be struck in favour of harmonization, given the fact that the municipal laws of sale have been replaced by the Uniform Commercial Code. This example is particularly impressive, as adoption of the UCC has been brought about by a spontaneous and voluntary process involving each and every of the United States. A further aspect to note is that the ambit of the UCC is limited to the law of sales and does not extend to contract law in general, but does include a framework for security interests in moveable property. This choice of topics suggests that the real-life interests of the business community may differ from the interests of academics who tend to favour coherency and systematic clarity.

2 Consumer Law in Particular

The first of the projects under the Action Plan of the Commission is the improvement of the coherence of the EC *acquis*,[32] which is by and large equivalent to the directives on consumer protection. The serious draw-

---

[32] European Commission (2003) 2.

backs and difficulties associated with the incremental approach the Commission has followed in the past are rightly emphasized in the Action Plan. Examples included the different modalities concerning the right of withdrawal in the Directives on Doorstep Selling,[33] Timesharing,[34] Distance Selling[35] and Distance Selling of Financial Services,[36] in particular the divergent duration and methods of calculation of the withdrawal periods.[37] Other examples concern inconsistent approaches regarding information requirements between the E-commerce Directive[38] and the two Directives on Distance Selling or divergent information requirements in different consumer protection directives as far as contract law is concerned.[39]

The divergences in the several directives just mentioned impose serious costs both on domestic lawmakers and on the private parties concerned. Domestic lawmakers usually have no other choice but to transpose the directive into national law more or less in the same shape and language it is written in, creating a series of legal instruments. The judge hearing the case, in turn, must consult various acts in order to patch together the legal framework applicable to the case at bar. The parties, finally, have difficulties in foreseeing the controlling legal standard and to comply with divergent and sometimes contradictory legal requirements.

The jurisprudence of the ECJ in the matter of *Heininger*[40] has highlighted the difficulties inherent in a style of legislation that is piling instrument on instrument without paying too much attention to the coherence of the underlying principles. Every judge or lawyer will be hard pressed to explain why the Consumer Credit Directive[41] does not apply to agreements to grant credit for the purpose of acquiring property rights in land (Article 2(a)) whereas the Doorstep Selling Directive (Article 3(2)(a)) does not cover contracts for the construction, sale and rental of immovable property or contracts concerning other rights relating to immovable property. Interpreting these provisions, the ECJ has held that

---

[33] Directive 85/577 to protect the consumer in respect of contracts negotiated away from business premises, *OJ EC* 1985, L 372/31.

[34] Directive 94/47 on the protection of purchasers in respect of certain aspects of contracts relating to the purchase of the right to use immovable properties on a timeshare basis, *OJ EC* L 280/83.

[35] Directive 97/7 on the protection of consumers in respect of distance contracts, *OJ EC* L 144/19.

[36] Directive 2002/65 concerning the distance marketing of consumer financial services and amending Council Directive 90/619 and Directives 97/7 and 98/27, *OJ EC* L 271/16.

[37] European Commission (2003) 7.

[38] Directive 2000/31 on certain legal aspects of information society services, in particular electronic commerce, in the Internal Market ('Directive on electronic commerce'), *OJ EC* L 178/1.

[39] European Commission (2003) 7.

[40] ECJ Case C 481/99 *Heininger* [2001] ECR I-9945.

[41] Directive 87/102 for the approximation of the laws, regulations and administrative provisions of the Member States concerning consumer credit, *OJ EC* L 42/48.

a credit agreement secured by means of a charge on immovable property comes within the scope of the Doorstep Selling Directive but not within the ambit of the Consumer Credit Directive.[42] That may be the correct result in terms of interpretation, as the court has always stressed the rule that derogations from the Community rules for the protection of consumers must be interpreted strictly.[43] A sensible reason to define the scope of the two directives differently can hardly be made out, however.

In this sense, the co-existence of the several directives burdens European businesses with additional costs for the procurement of legal advice and for hedging legal uncertainty.

3   Procedural Issues

I would like to close my contribution with another case that has been decided by the ECJ quite recently. In the matter of *Freiburger Kommunalbauten GmbH* v. *Hofstetter,* the court was called upon to examine a contract for the purchase of a parking space in a multi-story car park.[44] Under the boiler plate contract terms, the buyers were liable to pay the contract price up front, before completion and acceptance of the building, in exchange for a bank guarantee covering any warranty claims brought against the seller. As the German law of construction contracts includes the reverse rule of payment upon completion and acceptance, the buyers thought the clause to be ineffective under the directive on unfair terms in consumer contracts.[45]

The ECJ neither enforced the clause nor invalidated it, but refused to answer the question posed to him by the German *Bundesgerichtshof.* As the ECJ rightly stressed, a thorough evaluation of the issue of unfairness requires 'that consideration be given to the national law' in addition to the nature of the goods or services for which the contract was concluded, all the circumstances attending the conclusion of the contract as well as the consequences of the incriminated term.[46] It will readily be granted that these tasks would be made easier to perform if the ECJ could refer to a Uniform Civil Code but even then the effort would be great indeed. The interpretation of a European Civil Code would require a European Civil Court, *i.e.* a forum that is familiar with private law and its methodology, with the workings of different markets and with some expertise and experience as to which practical consequences different legal rules might have. The ECJ seems to consider itself not to be such a forum. Until it has been established, harmonization would work more evil than good.

---

[42] ECJ Case C 481/99 *Heininger* [2001] ECR I-9945, par. 40.

[43] ECJ Case C 481/99 *Heininger* [2001] ECR I-9945, par. 31

[44] ECJ Case C 237/02 *Freiburger Kommunalbauten GmbH,* OJ EC, C 106, 30.04.2004, 12.

[45] Council Directive 93/13 on Unfair Terms in Consumer Contracts, OJ EC L 95/29.

[46] ECJ Case C 237/02 *Freiburger Kommunalbauten GmbH,* OJ EC 2004, C 106/12, par. 21.

References

BARNARD (2000)
K. Barnard, "Social Dumping and the Race to the Bottom: Some Lessons for the European Union from Delaware", 25 *European Law Review* (2000) 57-78

BEBCHUK (1992)
L.A. Bebchuk, "Federalism and the Corporation: The Desirable Limits on State Competition in Corporate Law", 105 *Harvard Law Review* (1992) 1435-1510

CHARNY (1991)
D. Charny, "Competition among Jurisdictions in Formulating Corporate Law Rules: An American Perspective on the 'Race to the Bottom' in the European Communities", *Harvard International Law Journal* (1991) 423-456

COOTER (2000)
R.D. Cooter, *The Strategic Constitution* (Princeton, N.J.: Princeton University Press 2000)

COOTER AND ULEN (2000)
R. Cooter and T. Ulen, *Law and Economics*, 3rd ed. (Reading, Mass.: Addison Wesley 2000)

COUNCIL OF THE EUROPEAN UNION (2001)
Council of the European Union, *Council Report on the need to approximate Member States' legislation in civil matters*, DGH III 13017/01, 16.11.2001

EASTERBROOK AND FISCHEL (1991)
F.H. Easterbrook and D.R. Fischel, *The Economic Structure of Corporate Law* (Cambridge: Harvard University Press 1991)

EIDENMÜLLER (ED.) (2004)
H. Eidenmüller (ed.), *Ausländische Kapitalgesellschaften im deutschen Recht* (München: Beck 2004)

EUROPEAN COMMISSION (2001)
European Commission, *Communication from the Commission to the Council and the European Parliament on European Contract Law*, COM (2001) 398 final

EUROPEAN COMMISSION (2003)
European Commission, *Communication from the Commission to the European Parliament and the Council. A More Coherent Contract Law – An Action Plan*, COM (2003) 68 final

EUROPEAN PARLIAMENT (2001)
European Parliament, Committee on Legal Affairs and the Internal Market, *Report on the approximation of the civil and commercial law of the Member States*, A 5-0384/2001 Final: European Parliament resolution on the approximation of the civil and commercial law of the Member States, Rapporteur Klaus-Heiner Lehne

FAURE (2001)

M. Faure, "The Possible Contribution of Law and Economics to Harmonization of Tort Law in Europe", paper presented at the 28th Tagung für Rechtsvergleichung, Hamburg, 22.9.2001, forthcoming in: R. Zimmermann (ed.), *Harmonization of Tort Law in Europe*

INMAN AND RUBINFELD (2000)

R. Inman and D. Rubinfeld, "Federalism", in: B. Bouckaert and G. de Geest (eds.), *Encyclopedia of Law and Economics, Volume V* (Cheltenham: Elgar 2000) 661-691

KOBAYASHI AND RIBSTEIN (1999)

B. Kobayashi and L. Ribstein, "Contract and Jurisdictional Freedom", in: F. H. Buckley (ed.), *The Fall and Rise of Freedom of Contract* (Durham: Duke University Press 1999) 325-349

LUTTER (2003)

M. Lutter, "'Überseering' und die Folgen", 58 *Betriebsberater* (2003) 7-10

LUTTER (ED.) (2005)

M. Lutter (ed.), *Europäische Auslandsgesellschaften in Deutschland*, forthcoming

NEUMAN (1996)

G.L. Neuman, "Subsidiarity, Harmonization, and their Values: Convergence and Divergence in Europe and the United States", 2 *Columbia Journal of European Law* (1996) 573

OGUS (1999)

A. Ogus, "Competition Between National Legal Systems: A Contribution of Economic Analysis to Comparative Law", 48 *International and Comparative Law Quarterly* (1999) 405-418

O'HARA (2000)

E.A. O'Hara, "Opting Out of Regulation: A Public Choice Analysis of Contractual Choice of Law", 53 *Vanderbilt Law Review* (2000) 1551-1604

O'HARA AND RIBSTEIN (2000)

E.A. O'Hara and L. Ribstein, *"From Politics to Efficiency in Choice of Law"*, 67 *University of Chicago Law Review* (2000) 1151-1232

PAUL (1995)

J.R. Paul, "Free Trade, Regulatory Competition and the Autonomous Market Fallacy", 1 *Columbia Journal of European Law* (1995) 29-62

POSNER (1998)

R.A. Posner, *Economic Analysis of Law*, 5th ed. (New York: Aspen 1998)

ROMANA (1999)

R. Romana, "Corporate Law as the Paradigm for Contractual Choice of Law", in: F. H. Buckley (ed.), *Fall and Rise of Freedom of Contract* (Durham: Duke University Press 1999) 370

TIEBOUT (1956)

C. Tiebout, "A Pure Theory of Local Expenditures", 64 *Journal of Political Economy* (1956) 416-424

TIJONG (2002)

H. Tijong, "Breaking the Spell of Regulatory Competition: Reframing the Problem of Regulatory Exit", 66 *Rabels Zeitschrift für ausländisches und internationales Privatrecht* (2002) 66-97

WAGNER (2002)

G. Wagner, "Das zweite Schadensersatzrechtsänderungsgesetz", *Neue Juristische Wochenschrift* (2002) 2049-2064

WULF-HENNING ROTH (1993)

Wulf-Henning Roth, "Das Allgemeininteresse im europäischen Internationalen Versicherungsvertragsrecht", *Versicherungsrecht* (1993) 129-139

CHAPTER 2

Economic Analysis of Cross-Border Legal Uncertainty

The Example of the European Union

Helmut Wagner

Introduction

Demands for a more comprehensive harmonization of law between legal areas are based on the assumption that legal diversity causes transaction costs and lowers economic trade and welfare, in particular by creating legal uncertainty. For example, in its Communication to the Council and the European Parliament on European contract law of September 2001, the EU Commission argued that legal diversity within the European Union (EU) increases the transaction costs of cross-border contracting and discourages consumers and small entrepreneurs from engaging in such transactions. Consumers as well as producers tend to refrain from contracts in foreign legal systems if the costs of information (about the law, about administrative procedures, about competent legal advice) and/or the costs of enforcement (by way of litigation or alternative forms of dispute resolution) seem too high or unpredictable. This unpredictability or uncertainty about the costs of cross-border transactions may stem from the diversity in the formal legal system or diversity in judicial administration across the individual member countries.

The purpose of this contribution is to make some basic considerations on the macroeconomic costs of legal uncertainty, particularly on the effects of cross-border legal uncertainty[1] on economic performance, and to ask whether legal harmonization could be an appropriate solution to this problem, or why not. As will be argued, full harmonization may (at first sight) seem to be an adequate instrument for reducing the costs of cross-border legal uncertainty; however, full harmonization itself tends to imply high economic costs, so that it is not generally recommendable. Nevertheless, a gradual (partial) harmonization process could, in some circumstances, be beneficial in the European Union.

The structure of the chapter is as follows. Section 2 starts with a methodological introduction of the concept of legal uncertainty and of an estimation of its costs and continues with an elaboration of the advantages of a reduction of cross-border legal uncertainty by means of harmonization of law within in the EU. This is done by focusing on the macroeconomic effects of legal uncertainty, particularly on economic growth, both theoretically and empirically. In section 3, the advantages and the disadvantages or costs of full harmonization of law, which is often propagated as a mechanism for reducing legal uncertainty, are worked out. In section 4 we argue that/why some groups may have a stronger interest in an international governmental-institutionalized harmonization of law than other groups. Section 5 concludes.

---

[1]   With 'cross-border legal uncertainty' I mean uncertainty concerning cross-border transactions.

1 The European Union and the Role of the Legal System

The European Community is first of all an economic community (currently an economic union of 25 member states, and a monetary union
of 12 member states). Sometimes it is also called a 'community of Law' (*e.g.*
Mock 2002). However, so far, Europe has no definite and precise constitutional
status. The legal regime in the European Community builds upon a number of
Treaties forming a compact that defines the European legal order. This set of
treaties cannot be considered as a constitution itself.

The European Community does not aim (any more) at the creation of one
European Law in contrast to the laws of its, currently 25, member states.[2]
Instead, the European Community aims at harmonizing the national legal
systems only to the extent that is required for the functioning of the Common
Market (Article 3(1)(h) EC Treaty).[3] In other words, harmonization of national
legal systems in the European Community is not an end in itself or an ultimate
goal but plays a functional role. This role is to foster the interplay of the numerous national (goods, labor, and financial) markets and thereby to raise the overall economic utility in the European Community. Hence, the main task in the
EU is to find an optimal degree of international (partial) harmonization between
the 25 national legal systems.

The legal system is one of the most important institutions of a society.[4]
Following North (1994), 'institutions' are understood here as formal and informal mechanisms, which control social interaction in some form or other and
in this way shape restrictions for individual behavior so that negotiation and
coordination costs are reduced. The sum of governmental-institutionalized rules
is defined as the 'legal system' of a country or union. It symbolizes 'rules of the
game', which place limits on the leeway available to actors in the same way as
technological restrictions. During the last decades, much greater attention has
been paid in economics, and in macroeconomics as well, to such institutions.

---

[2] Originally, the EC's integration concept aimed at widespread harmonization of regulations in its
member states. However, in the 1980s there was a clear reversal of direction in the Community's integration strategy (for details see section 3 below).

[3] This is also the basis of the 'subsidiarity principle', introduced in 1990, which implies that competition
between legislators is the rule and centralized governance or harmonization (unification) the exception.
However, this principle does not cover the full scope of EC policy fields, for instance it does not cover
agricultural policy, external commercial policy, and parts of competition policy.

[4] 'A reliable legal system adds credibility to private economic exchanges, enforces contracts, protects
economic freedoms and reins in arbitrary state power' (Pitarakis and Tridimas (2003) 361). The 'vigor'
of markets 'may depend on the establishment of an environment in which legal rights, especially
property and contractual rights, are enforced and protected' (Posner (1998) 1). 'A modernizing nation's
economic prosperity requires at least a modest legal infrastructure centered on the protection of property and contract rights' (ibid).

Not only is the actual existence of institutions regarded here as being important, but also, and above all, their stability. On the one hand are those institutions that are stable in themselves, because participants feel themselves bound to them either for traditional, religious or ethical/moral concepts, or because all deviations would result in an intimidating sanction contained in the rule itself. On the other hand are those rules that do not contain this type of stimulus, which itself leads to the danger of individual deviation so that the institutions are not *a priori* stable. The state can only protect such rules by means of its monopoly of force, by determining these rules to be a legal system. Securing the stability of such a legal system is among the most important tasks of a government, since the instability of this type of legal system, or 'legal uncertainty', hinders growth and the stability of an economy.[5] The dominating argument here is that legal uncertainty represents an investment risk for both domestic and foreign investors. Legal uncertainty can be caused not only by imperfect national legal systems, but also by the different natures of legal systems in the international spectrum.

Law is a fundamental instrument of all transnational economic integration. Different legal systems within an integration area increase transaction costs in cross-border business, because, on the one hand, costs occur through the provision of information about, and adapting to, the respective national regulations, and, on the other hand, the great number of legal provisions and processes increases the uncertainty which adheres to individual cross-border transactions.

The European Commission already noticed this danger in the middle of the 1990s.[6] At that time, legal uncertainty was regarded by the European Commission as the main reason for the fact that the economic dynamics triggered by the process of European integration in the early nineties developed more slowly than expected and desired.[7]

---

[5] The modern transformation and development economics provide unequivocal evidence for this (see, *e.g.*, Chong and Calderón (2000), or Knack and Keefer (1997)).

[6] Cf. Sutherland (1992) and Freyhold, Gessner, Vial and Wagner (ed. 1995).

[7] To be more precise, the hopes with regards to economic growth expressed in, and in connection with, the Cecchini Report in the context of the completion of the Single Market were not realized completely. The Cecchini Report (Cecchini 1988) was the central study for preparation of the Single European Market, which was (formally) completed in 1992. In this report the growth effects were overestimated, among other things because insufficient light was thrown on implementation problems in a single market program which (may) come into existence as a result of institutional asymmetries and insufficiencies of information. This was, for example, later criticized in the Sutherland Report (1992).

2   Costs of Legal Uncertainty[8]

The supposed advantages of a harmonization of law are derived in part from the costs of legal diversity and the legal uncertainty that possibly results from it for particular groups. Before turning to the costs of legal uncertainty, we first want to outline the term and the cornerstones of an estimation of the costs of legal uncertainty.

2.1   On the Term 'Legal Uncertainty'

Legal uncertainty always occurs when individual actors are uncertain of the effects of the provisions of the dominant legal system on the results of their actions. In the wider sense, the term covers both 'subjective' and 'objective' legal uncertainty.

2.1.1   Subjective Legal Uncertainty

The term 'subjective legal uncertainty' refers here to the subjective assessment of marginal costs and marginal utility, which differs from individual to individual. Subjective legal uncertainty can also be referred to as 'uncertainty as to what the law is'. Because an improvement in individual knowledge of the law is bound up with, in part, considerable information and transaction costs, it is irrational to want to do away with complete legal uncertainty. With increasing marginal costs of acquiring information and the sinking marginal utility of additional legal knowledge, individual economic subjects will only spend so much on information and transactions until marginal costs and marginal utility are equal. Ignorance beyond this will remain in existence so that decisions will continue to be taken in uncertainty.

2.1.2   Objective Legal Uncertainty

'Objective legal uncertainty' describes an objective reality that has to be accepted to an equal extent by all involved. It is found where statutory regulations for certain sets of facts are either non-existent or do not form a reliable basis for decisions. Examples are:
- 'Absence of law': this term applies to areas for which there are (as yet) no statutory rules and regulations, *e.g.* areas not subject to national sovereignty, such as the seabed, space, the environment (with cross-border air pollution), and legal areas which have not yet been determined, such as in some transformation and developing countries.
- 'Legal instability': this type of legal uncertainty occurs where regula-

---

[8]   Sections 2 and 3 draw closely on Wagner (1997a, 1995).

tions are unstable over and beyond consumption or investment periods, because amendments to statutes are frequent and unforeseeable, so that even experts are not clear about the current legal position and the continuance of subjective claims.
- 'Denial of justice': this is understood to be the obstruction or prevention of the enforcement of legal rights by state authorities or employees.

In the following we will assume a very broad meaning for legal uncertainty, one which includes all the aspects referred to. We will restrict ourselves here to an analysis of the costs of legal uncertainty with reference to cross-border transactions, because we have in particular the effects on European integration in view.

2.2   Theoretical Derivation of the Costs of Legal Uncertainty

On a plausibility level, 'static costs' can be easily derived from legal uncertainty. Static costs are understood to mean a one-off loss of welfare or income as against the reference case with legal certainty. Some essential effect mechanisms are shown in section 2.2.2. In this way it can be shown that legal uncertainty generates a lower level of trade and a persistently lower level of income as against the reference case of legal certainty. This type of one-off fall in national income is a short-term negative growth effect. It is difficult to derive persistent growth effects in the meaning of a permanent loss of income with traditional macroeconomics.[9] Only a more recent theoretical branch of macroeconomics, the so-called 'new' or 'endogenous' growth theory, provides a microeconomically founded set of analytical instruments for the explanation of this type of dynamic costs. Section 2.2.3 will contain sketches[10] of what possible reasons for the long-term growth effects of legal uncertainty in the framework of the new growth theory could be. However, section 2.2.1 will first introduce some brief explanations of the costs generated by legal uncertainty.

2.2.1   Types of Costs Caused by Legal Uncertainty

Legal uncertainty generates the following transaction costs: (a) costs of collecting information, (b) costs of legal disputes, (c) costs of setting incentives for pushing through legal claims, and (d) other transaction costs. As explained above, it is obvious that costs are higher in international transactions than in domestic trade, and I will take this as given on the following pages.

On (a): Lack of knowledge of foreign statutes prevents international purchases or leads to the necessity of more or less expensive information collection.

---

[9]   For the fundamental difficulties, cf. *e.g.* Wagner (1997b), Chap. 2. See Klump (1995) for an attempt to derive growth effects from institutions within the traditional neo-classical growth model.

On (b): In the event of international legal disputes the costs are much greater than in the case of a domestic legal dispute (cf. Freyhold, Gessner, Vial and Wagner (eds.) 1995, Part II).

On (c): This includes private attempts to speed up approval procedures, and legal procedures in the broadest meaning of the term. As is known, 'beneficial charges', which include bribes or pay-offs, represent an important cost factor for multinational corporations. (This applies in particular in developing countries.) No small part of this is probably the result of having to deal with legal uncertainty or legal instability.

On (d): The difficulties involved in complaining about goods, in making warranty claims, and in exchanging goods, should probably prove to be much greater in the case of international purchases in comparison with domestic purchases. The associated costs, including travel expenses, time spent (opportunity costs), and annoyance (negative utility), are then correspondingly higher, in particular if law suits are the consequence.

2.2.2 Static or Level Effects of Legal Uncertainty

Static or level effects of legal uncertainty occur above all in the form of trade and income effects. The derivation of trade and income effects is based on the following presumed causal chain: legal uncertainty implies higher transaction costs. These are reflected in higher prices or in reduced revenues or benefits for the entrepreneur or consumer. Both lead to lower investment, lower consumption and lower national income.

I will now provide some detailed explanations of this presumed causal chain. (The individual causal chains are also summarized in the Appendix in a figure.)

Even the expectation of the costs sketched in section 2.2.1 can lead to consumers and entrepreneurs to pull back from international transactions. For consumers, greater legal uncertainty in international purchases means that foreign goods bring them fewer benefits. For entrepreneurs, on the other hand, these additional costs reduce profits. (The reduction in profits is caused not only by higher transaction costs but also by higher risk premiums.[11]) They have to increase prices in order to prevent a reduction in their return on capital in

---

[10] Detailed theoretical analyses of this type of static, and of dynamic, effects can be found in Wagner (1995) and in Wagner (ed. 1995).

[11] As noted above, it is not individually rational for economic subjects to eliminate all legal uncertainty by collecting information and setting incentives. Therefore, 'real' uncertainty remains, and this is taken into account in the calculation of profits in the form of an uncertainty or risk deduction. Some of the risk cover can be provided by internal reserves and by means of a risk pool in the scope of an insurance policy covering the consequences of legal uncertainty. But the latter also results in costs that are passed on in the price. It is impossible to be insured against all risks; and even if this were possible, a rational actor would not do it for cost reasons (see above).

international transactions.[12] Both, *i.e.* price increases and a fall in the return on capital, lead from the point of view of the economy as a whole to a reduction of international transactions and thus to a fall in international trade.

Lower levels of international trade usually mean that existing price diffe-rences – because of legal uncertainty in this case – are not fully utilized. This means that the price level (with a given demand) is higher than would be the case with more international trade (*i.e.* with legal certainty). Income-reducing effects can be derived from this, in certain circumstances intensified by capital effects and so-called Keynesian effects.

There is yet another impact channel through which legal uncertainty has an income-reducing effect. Legal uncertainty may simply lead to waiting. Wait-ing is a rational strategy, if imperfect information impairs the decision-making capability of the actors and at the same time either additional useful information can be expected in the following period, or legal uncertainty will be reduced (*e.g.* through unification of law).[13] This aspect can be made clear with the help of the theory of options. From the point of view of this theory, legal uncertainty delays individual economic decisions and in this way reduces international supply and demand for consumer durables in particular. Put another way, legal uncertainty reduces international trade and thus leads to aggregate losses of income as well (as explained above).

2.2.3   Dynamic or Growth Effects

In order to be able to assess the consequences of legal uncer-tainty in international transactions for the growth dynamics of a national econ-omy, we have first of all to be clear about the factors that determine these growth dynamics. In the theory of growth, 'technical progress' is regarded as the central engine for economic growth; in the traditional neo-classical theory according to Solow this progress was exogenous, whereas in the modern approaches of endogenous growth models an attempt is made to explain technical progress endogenously.

---

[12] Because/if cross-border legal uncertainty applies to all countries of an integration area, it is a general phenomenon and, therefore, causes a general extra charge on import goods which, nevertheless, differs from country to country. From an analytical point of view this legal uncertainty can be seen as a general (non-tariff) trade barrier. In this article we concentrate on trade effects. However, the argument is also transferable to movements of factors of production.

[13] The introduction of waiting as a possible reaction to legal uncertainty already presupposes a dynamic balancing of possibilities by the actors involved. Seen statically, legal uncertainty leads simply to trans-actions not being carried out. Whether this can be interpreted as a final decision or as waiting can only be decided in a dynamic approach. In so far, this aspect might also be placed in the following section on dynamic effects. However, it is mentioned here for reasons of content systematizing.

We can differentiate as follows between endogenous growth models depending on how the growth engine is modelled.

The *first class of models* is concentrated on the accumulation of capital (Romer 1986) or human capital (Lucas 1988) as the driving force in the process of growth, or regards the provision of state productive inputs as essential for long-term growth (Barro 1990). These models build on the assumption of perfect competition. In these models it is assumed among other things that investment (often) accompanies the production of additional new knowledge. Knowledge is regarded here as the central input in the production of technical progress. The conclusion can be drawn from this that lower investment levels are also combined with lower levels of technical progress and therefore with lower growth rates within the national economy. Alternatively, reductions in national incomes can be regarded as the reason for loss of growth, if less national income induces lower infrastructural investment, as is assumed in other branches of the new theory of growth, and a positive correlation can be assumed between infrastructure investment and technical progress.[14]

The *second class of models* stresses the research and development of companies as the driving force behind growth. An attempt is made to make a model of Schumpeter's conception of the process of innovation. In these models, companies can either diversify existing consumer products or intermediate products with constant quality, or improve the quality of a constant number of products, whereby these may be investment or consumer goods. These innovation-driven models, which have been developed above all by Grossman and Helpman (1991) and by Aghion and Howitt (1992), abandon the assumption of perfect competition in favor of an oligopolistic market structure. Innovations can namely only be accounted for in a state of imperfect competition, because innovations are only carried out with appropriate (monopoly) profit expectations. And investment in research and development is worthwhile for companies for as long as the costs of an additional investment correspond to its expected yield.

For practical purposes, a difference should be made between two model types. *One type* assumes a closed economy. Legal uncertainty can be introduced here through the assumption of a risk surcharge. Since/if companies cannot pass this risk surcharge on fully in their prices, net profits fall. As a result, company profits are reduced, which itself leads to less investment in research and development. Less research and development reduces the rate of innovation, and this is accompanied by a reduction in the long-term growth rate of the economy. The *other type* assumes an open economy and combines aspects of the theories of endogenous growth and foreign trade.[15] A multi-country model with

---

[14] See also Wagner (2002).

[15] Foreign trade can strengthen growth in different ways: by avoiding double R&D activity, through the diffusion of knowledge, and by the use of comparative advantages based on different factor productivities.

different factor productivities appears to be particularly suitable for an analysis of legal uncertainty in an economic structure such as the EU.

To sum up, it can be stated that several effective channels can be derived from the approaches shown here for endogenous growth models through which legal uncertainty can have a negative impact on economic growth.[16] Firstly, efficient use of existing capital is impeded because of reduced marginal yields, so that there is less knowledge-creating investment, innovative research is inhibited and state infrastructure is only insufficiently available. And secondly, international trade exchanges are obstructed, so that the knowledge incorporated in traded goods does not spread as rapidly and the deficient use of comparative advantages leads to the waste of innovative potential. This results in reduced growth dynamics not only for an economic area such as the European Union but also for individual states.

2.3   Empirical Analyses

Empirical research on the effect of legal uncertainty on economic trade and growth suffers from the difficulty of measuring the degree of legal uncertainty. Most studies derive legal uncertainty from factors such as political instability, juridical incredibility or a lack of civil liberty (see below). They concentrate on explaining cross-country variations in growth due to differences in legal uncertainty within a country in world wide samples or for developing economies[17]. But there are only very few studies that analyze the effect of legal uncertainty in such a broad way as I have done in this article and between developed countries alone.

A *first approach* of measuring the quality of (legal) institutions uses easily observable characteristics of formal institutions such as written law. De Long and Shleifer (1993), for example, show that in medieval times western European cities that were under absolutist regimes (interpreted as being associated with high legal uncertainty because of insecure property rights) experienced a stronger retardation of their city growth than cities with other forms of political regimes. La Porta et al. (1999) discover that formal legal protections for investors correlate with the size and depth of capital markets and hence with investment levels. Another recent study by Feld and Voigt (2003) concentrates on a crucial aspect of the rule of law, namely judicial independence, which is meas-

---

[16] Beyond that, we can try to introduce legal uncertainty endogenously. This aspect of endogenization can be treated analytically by means of the theory of time inconsistency. For reasons of space we have left this out here. For an endogenous introduction of legal uncertainty in the framework of a model of this kind cf. Wagner (ed. 1995), Chap. 5.

[17] Studies of these kinds mainly applied the method of Ordinary Least Squares (OLS) regressions and hence suffer the problems of mutual dependency and reverse causality due to the endogeneity of the institutional variable independently of how it is measured.

ured by (i) a *de iure* indicator based on the legal foundations as found in legal documents, and (ii) a *de facto* indicator 'focusing on the factually ascertainable degree of judicial independence' (p. 1), *e.g.* the factual average term length of the members of the highest court or the number of judges. Their results show that the *de iure* judicial independence does not have an impact on economic growth, but there is a positive relationship between *de facto* judicial independence and real GDP growth per capita.

However, this approach has its limitations because it cannot capture the role of informal institutions nor take possible interdependencies with formal institutions into account. This may distort the findings.

Therefore, *another approach* uses proxy variables that measure the quality of institutions indirectly. For example, an often quoted study by Barro (1991) uses the number of revolutions and coups per year as well as the number of political assassinations as proxy variables for political – and hence legal – stability. Both variables are significantly negatively related to economic growth. A related study by Alesina et al. (1996) confirm that countries with less political and legal stability grow less. The quality of this approach clearly depends on the quality of the proxy chosen. It has to be guaranteed that the proxy variable does not influence the dependent variable through another channel it stands for. This sensitivity analysis is mostly missing in each of these studies.

A *third approach* in the empirical literature on the impact of legal uncertainty or institutions on economic growth is based on surveys of country risk experts or foreign and domestic investors. These surveys cover a series of questions about the business environment.

An early attempt stems from Knack and Keefer (1995) who take the data from the International Country Risk Guide and analyze the relationship between institutions and economic performance in a cross-country-regression with 111 countries. The data covers five categories for measuring the quality of institutions: the rule of law, the corruption in government, the quality of the bureaucracy, the expropriation risk, and the reliability of the government in complying with agreements, which includes the risk of changes to agreements following a change of government. They find that institutions that protect property rights are crucial for economic growth and investment. Differences in institutional quality account for a major share of cross-country growth differences. Here the rule of law variable seems to be the most important determinant of cross-country variations.

In a more recent study, the IMF (2003) finds a strong positive relationship between indicators of governance and economic performance. The IMF augments the institutional indicators corresponding to six fundamental governance concepts, used by Kaufmann, Kraay and Zoido-Lobatón (1999),[18] and proves their relevance in a global cross-country regression.

---

[18] The two additional aspects were: the extent of legal protection of private property and how well such laws are enforced; the constraint on the executive, reflecting institutional and other limits placed on political leaders.

This third approach is not undisputed either. Rodrik (2004), for example, notes that the survey data used in this approach raises two difficulties. First the survey data is highly subjective and may depend upon other aspects than the actual institutional environment (*e.g.* investors may value the institutional quality highly when there is an economic upswing in the relevant country). The second difficulty is that this kind of data gives no policy guidelines because the results say nothing about which institutional design is superior but just that it is important to make investors feel save.[19]

Apart from these studies, there are also a few studies that explicitly analyze the effects of *cross-border* legal uncertainty. De Sousa and Disdier (2002), for example, examine the influence of different measures of the legal framework quality in Central and Eastern European countries on international trade. They assume that a weak legal framework limits contract enforcement by acting as an informal trade barrier. They find 'that legal framework quality appears as a strong determinant of export decisions of EU producers. (...) In the opposite, the CEFTA producers seem less affected by this quality in their trade decisions' (p. 16).

De Groot et al. (2004) investigate the effect of institutional differences on bilateral trade flows within an augmented gravity model in a broad sample of more than 100 countries.[20] They find that the quality of institutions (measured by the updated index of Kaufmann et al. (2002)) has a remarkable significant effect on bilateral trade volumes. They further test whether institutional homogeneity is a significant determinant of bilateral trade patterns, too. They find that only really large differences in the quality of institutions have a significantly negative impact on trade. These results confirm the earlier findings of Anderson and Marcouiller (1999), who build upon a structural model of import demand and estimate a 4% increase in import volume for a 10% rise in the index of enforceability of commercial contracts.

3   Disadvantages of Full Harmonization of Law

There is a more or less widespread amount of legal uncertainty inside each country that is expressed in a lack of clear, unambiguous and stable legislation and/or in (expected or feared) realization problems. However, even

---

[19] These difficulties should also be a warning that a 'panacea' for the 'right' institutional design of an economy does not exist. For this reason 'transferring the formal political and economic rules of successful Western economies to third-world and Eastern European economies is not a sufficient condition for good economic performance' (North 1996).

[20] The gravity model was originally developed by Tinbergen (1962) and assumes that bilateral trade volumes decrease with the geographical distance between the two countries and increase with national income levels.

more extensive problems occur in international transactions. There are legal
trade or transaction barriers in the form of a lack of knowledge of the legal situation in foreign markets and in the form of uncertainty regarding the interpretation or the stability of legal regulations abroad. We have argued in section 2 that
these barriers imply costs which are reflected in higher prices and lower output,
and, possibly, in lower growth rates as well.

The European Union is faced with this problem. Along with 25 national legal
systems there exists the extensive and complicated set of rules and regulations
of community law, with the constituent treaties, regulations and directives, so
that the individual economic actor is often overstrained when it comes to finding out and understanding the regulations governing an individual case. Even
where it is clear that a harmonized community regulation is to be applied to a
defined case, implementation of the regulation is usually the obligation of the
national authorities in the 25 member states. Different societal standards and
practices will probably prevent objective legal certainty being achieved throughout the EU even in the long term.

The question arises whether there is any possibility of removing/reducing
legal uncertainty without leading to new losses of growth or efficiency on the
other side. One answer to the problems of legal uncertainty and lack of legal
knowledge discussed might be to demand complete harmonization of national
legal systems within the EU. With the achievement of uniformity of laws within
the EU, transnational legal uncertainty would seemingly be impossible, because
there would now only be EU law, and the complexities of 25 different legal
systems would be reduced to a single uniform system. The question then arises
whether this is really (a) desirable, and (b) practicable.

(a) Desirability

When economic policy conclusions are drawn, attention should be paid to
more than just the costs of legal uncertainty. The (transaction) costs of eliminating legal uncertainty (*i.e.* pushing through a common alternative institutional regulatory framework) also have to be taken into account, if a balanced
cost-benefit analysis is to be carried out. Scientific costs analyses can easily be
ideologically misused without this type of consideration of both sides.

From an institutional economics point of view, the above problem might be
formulated as follows: a comparative institutional analysis must not estimate
the costs of legal barriers only. The reference situation for this is implicitly a
'Nirvana'. The costs of legal uncertainty play an important role even in national
transactions; in so far, a comparison situation free of transaction costs is not
realistic. Even on a national level, not all disposal rights have been clearly
defined and are clearly executable, and in most cases safeguards going beyond
contractual relationships will be looked for (family ties, reputation, etc.). The
new institutional economics contradicts the widespread impression that production costs are legitimate and transaction costs superfluous. Transaction costs

play an important part in the economics of modern societies and are just as difficult to avoid as 'regular' production costs. In addition, it is often very difficult to differentiate between production and transaction costs (cf. *e.g.* Furubotn and Richter 1991).

In so far, precise institutional scenarios (*e.g.* harmonization of civil law, etc.) must be used to examine which costs can definitely be saved in individual sectors. In doing this, non-formal, socio-cultural restrictions must also be taken into account. The residual potential benefits must be contrasted in the first place with the costs of political decision-making. In addition there is even the danger that the result of the political process will not correspond to the original intentions, because lobbies are tempted to represent their intentions incorrectly to enable them to participate in public goods with as few costs as possible. Furthermore, the costs of the effective realization of the reforms must also be considered. If a positive benefit remains in this overall survey, a comparative institutional analysis comes to the conclusion that a planned reform is reasonable.

There is a good deal of evidence that complete harmonization would lead to substantial costs. These include not only direct costs for developing new bureaucracies or demolishing old structures, but also costs arising from the renouncement of the *advantages of system competition*, which appear in

(i)   an adaptation to the variety of preferences;
(ii)   efficiency advantages of regulative competition;
(iii)   the minimization of 'rent-seeking' costs caused by bureaucrats/
        politicians.

On (i): economic structures in different countries are not identical. However, legal systems must in a sense 'harmonize' with the respective economic and social conditions in a country. This means that not every legal system 'fits' into a country; put another way, because of its structural peculiarities, each country needs a special legal system as well.[21] For this reason alone, harmonization of the legal system in an integration area with heterogeneous countries would not be appropriate. Implementation of perfect harmonization would not be politically possible, because it is at variance with the preferences and cultural habits of the respective countries, or of their populations. The central argument as far as economic systems are concerned is therefore: variety of regulations or laws reflects variety of preferences.

In other words: If states compete with their legal systems, more preferences may be satisfied. Consumers and firms in different countries may 'vote by feet' (Tiebout 1956) and choose the jurisdictions that in their views offer the best sets of laws. Furthermore, with such a competition between legislators, individu-

---

[21]   Individual institutions or regulations are part of a mature system with its specific requirements for
       consistency and stabilizing traditions; cf. Streit (1996) 7, as well.

als could choose the legal rules that most efficiently regulate their problems by moving to the jurisdiction that offers laws best suitable to their preferences.[22]

On (ii): In addition, variety of regulations also means competition among rules and therefore represents a process for discovering the regulations that fulfill the desired purpose with the lowest costs (Hayek 1968). Diversity in laws enables states to experiment in their search for efficient and workable rules of law.[23] Competition between legislators may generate a learning process. Exaggerated harmonization would prevent such experiments and learning processes from arising and transaction costs from being lowered. Market integration would be inhibited. Moreover, dynamic competitive processes between legislators may produce voluntary harmonization (see section 5 below).

On (iii): Not only market failures, but also regulatory failures are possible. Bureaucrats/politicians serve their self-interest, too, by maximizing their budget or increasing their status and improving their working conditions. Competition is the most efficient mechanism to control politicians and to restrain their rent-seeking activities. In contrast, harmonization in a union can be considered as a restriction of competition analogous to a cartel, where non-member countries are outsiders.

With this in mind, there was a clear reversal in the integration strategy of the European Community in the 1980s (cf. European Commission 1985). While the Community's integration strategy was previously aimed at widespread harmonization of regulations in member states,[24] under the new strategy only particularly important regulations were to be harmonized, and there was otherwise to

---

[22] National governments exposed to system competition are subject to constant control by the owners of mobile factors in that the latter are able to evade the sphere of influence of a government by moving to that of another government. This is also linked to the hope that system or regulation competition can reduce the influence of lobbies to eliminate welfare state incrustations or 'institutional sclerosis' (Olson 1982). However, it must be taken into account that international legal uncertainty limits system competition (Wagner 1997a).

[23] If the possibility of a faulty or unsuitable statutory provision is considered, competition between systems of rules permits a relatively low-risk and low-conflict method of correcting errors, compared with harmonized policies. The controlling effect of competition arises from private agents being able to compare different institutional attempts at solving problems and to sort out inferior ones. There does not necessarily have to be an exchange of the legal system itself, but there may also be, corresponding to the cultural peculiarities, efficient institutional innovations within the prevailing legal system.

[24] The governing principle was that national regulations were to be replaced as far as possible by uniform regulations so that basically the same provisions applied everywhere. This approach failed because of technical problems and above all because of the political resistance of member states to a waiver of sovereignty in the legal sector. Since 1990, the subsidiarity principle has therefore been applied. The 'subsidiarity principle' states that the Community may only intervene if the aims of the treaty and the aims of individual measures 'cannot be adequately achieved at the level of member states and can therefore be better achieved at Community level because of their range or their effects' (Art. 3b of the ECT).

be joint stipulation of minimum requirements. Central regulations covering the whole of the EU are therefore only necessary where market integration would be hampered without them. The latter would be the case if transnational external effects were not allocated in accordance with their causes and collective goods were not offered in sufficient amounts and at reasonable prices.[25]

(b) Feasibility (The chances of success of a strategy for full harmonization)
Neverthless, attempts towards a broad harmonization of law are still under way (within the EU Commission as well). To justify unification or harmonization, the European Commission often argues that diverging legal rules create unequal conditions of competition within the Single Market, and that such differences should be minimized in order to create a 'level playing field' for industry. Another argument is that as long as Europe has not achieved a single legal system, economic interaction in the area is severely hampered. As argued above, transaction costs either increase the price level of exchanges of goods and services or hinder economic actors from taking advantage of markets in all member states. Economic actors – providers of goods and services as well as consumers – refrain from contracts in foreign legal systems if the costs of information (about the law, about administrative procedures, about competent legal advice) and/or the costs of enforcement (by way of litigation or alternative forms of dispute resolution) seem too high or unpredictable.

A further argument for legal harmonization is that interjurisdictional competition may lead to a lowering of standards to the detriment of citizens in need of protection against abuses (workers, consumers) or degrade important standards (environmental conditions, protection of health).[26]

But an argument against fighting legal uncertainty by full harmonization says that only formal law can be adapted through a forced harmonization of legal systems. Harmonization of behavioral structures, and therefore of the forms of realization of formal law, cannot be ordered from above simply through a formal decree. In other words, uniformity of law cannot be created by just imposing rules through public policy. Compliance with the law requires more than just rules; it must match the (legal) culture of a country. But this is the real problem

---

[25] However, this approach by the Commission was pushed into the background again by the Single European Act, which came into effect in 1987. 'Under pressure from highly-regulated member states, basic harmonization had to make space for harmonization 'at a high protection level' for the protective aims of health, security, the environment and consumer interests (Art. 100a Section 3 EC Treaty). In addition, even higher levels of protection were permitted as exceptions (Art. 100a Section 4 EC Treaty)' (Streit 1996, p. 19, translation by H.W.).

[26] A good example for this is the current attempts in the European Community to harmonize company taxation. It is argued that tax competition leads to a vicious circle or is ruinous, insofar as it has detrimental effects on other countries or regions. For a critical analysis of this argument see, *e.g.*, Wagner (2004). Another example is labor co-determination; see Gerum and Wagner (1998).

of reservation in the face of foreign transactions. General uncertainty regarding behavioral structures and their stability, which express 'legal uncertainty in the narrow sense', and the connected fear of the arbitrary implementation of regulations by the state or public authorities is (to a certain extent) ever-present, both nationally and internationally. But uncertainty, and the fear connected with this, is usually much greater with regard to transnational transactions. This hampers international trade. Formal harmonization decrees can only reduce this to a certain extent. A further reduction can only be achieved through 'experienced integration' (by gradually overcoming ignorance and prejudice). This also includes a thorough reform of the European system of civil justice and of judicial administration in civil matters.

4 Politico-economic Aspects

In the introduction to this book there is the following statement:

'The view of the European Commission seems to be that diversity of law stands in the way of a proper functioning of the internal market, but this view does not seem to be shared by business: in the reactions to the Communication on European Contract Law (2001) it was striking to see that most companies do not consider the present diversity to be a true barrier to trade.'

This may be regarded as an astonishing discovery; however, it can easily be explained, at least for the large companies. In contrast to small companies and to consumers, large companies have the advantage of lower information and coordination costs per unit of output due to economies of scale when doing transborder business. In particular, they can more easily organize or coordinate their common interests. Insofar, it is easier (and/or less costly) for them to reduce legal uncertainty by privately organizing common rules or standards. For example, in an open market such as the European Single Market, product standards will likely be shaped by the activities of international coalitions of firms. Therefore it is sometimes argued that harmonization will occur 'from the bottom', through the coordinated actions of private firms operating across borders, more quickly than through international treaties and bureaucrats' interventions. Even where national governments must give the final approval, business groups will lobby their respective national authorities to support the privately developed international standards' (Casella 2001, p. 244). Because of the international nature of the business interests directly affected by the standards, business groups are willing to take upon themselves the costs of standards development and certification. Standards, as well as other legal rules, are public goods improving the functioning of the market. Two of the most important functions that they fulfill are providing information and compatibility. By sharing a common standard, anonymous partners in a market can communicate at all, and can develop common expectations on the performance of each other's products. Hence, standards as well as legal rules are necessary for the efficient functioning of a market. As long ago as 1991, the OECD stated that '[r]ecent trends in all (OECD) countries seem to converge towards a greater emphasis on self-regulation and non-mandatory standards...[This] introduces an element of flexibility into national safety systems which may become more open to international harmonization' (OECD 1991, p. 55). Hence, it may be concluded that, contrary to the common view, the 'problem is not how to orchestrate harmonization through government treaties; it is how to create the appropriate regulatory structure to prevent and if necessary discipline anti-trust violations in international markets' (Casella 2001, p. 262).

The above finding is typical for large companies. However, this finding cannot be simply applied to consumers, not even to small companies. Higher information costs and higher coordination costs of organizing their common interests may prevent consumers (and even small companies) from organizing efficiency-increasing standards or rules themselves (Olson 1965).[27] Thus, while large companies may largely be able to help themselves in reducing legal uncertainty by creating desired harmonization on their own, consumers and small companies cannot do this to the same extent.[28] Therefore, it is the task of the governments to help consumers and small entrepreneurs particularly to reduce legal uncertainty in transborder exchanges through searching for and implementing/harmonizing the right standards or rules. However, because of the costs of full harmonization described above, the level of harmonization should be limited.

---

[27] Similarly it can be argued that '[t]he single market is indeed an opportunity for larger enterprises which are able to reduce legal transaction costs by establishing stable relationships across European borders. The risks of breaking contracts are small in this kind of repeated exchange. The situation is different in anonymous markets with small enterprises and consumers. They need institutions to defend and protect their property rights. The European Single Market has been conquered by these actors only to a limited degree due to a deficient institutional infrastructure of law enforcement' (Freyhold, Gessner, Vial and Wagner (1995), Part A, p.5).

[28] Nevertheless, during the consultation process on the Commission Communication on European Contract Law, business associations representing small and medium-size enterprises spoke against full harmonization being necessary to foster competition within the common market. However, as is known, the fact that particular interest groups reject reforms does not mean that reforms cannot be welfare-enhancing on an overall (macro)economic level.

5 Conclusion

Legal diversity within an economic union such as the European Union usually goes along with legal uncertainty. The reason is that legal diversity there implies:
- additional costs for acquiring the information needed to write a particular contract in other legal areas;
- higher costs for litigating issues under various contracts governed by different legal regimes;
- costs of instability due to the fact that several contracts are subject to subsequent changes in the law;
- diversity in judicial administration across the different member countries.[29]

As not all of the individual consumers and entrepreneurs are able or willing to pay these costs, however all of them are subject to the (unstable[30]) diversity of legal administration within the economic union, they have to act under increased uncertainty if they want to do transborder transactions.

Legal uncertainty, however, raises costs. Legal uncertainty can be regarded as a non-tariff trade barrier. It generates a lower level in trade and in income against the reference case of legal certainty, because some of the cross-border transactions cannot be done, or are done inefficiently, since the individuals have to act under increased uncertainty.

But from this it does not follow that full harmonization is necessary, because harmonization itself generates substantial costs. These include not only direct costs for developing new bureaucracies or demolishing old structures, but also costs arising from a loss of the advantages of system competition, the advantages being an adaptation to the variety of preferences, efficiency advantages of regulative competition, and the minimization of 'rent-seeking' costs caused by bureaucrats/politicians. Nevertheless, from the point of view of the economy as a whole, welfare gains could possibly be realized through more harmonization.

Correspondingly, the EU could adopt a step-by-step approach. It could start with harmonization of contract law for international (transborder) transactions. This would give individuals time to get acquainted with the new regime and to evaluate it. A step-by-step approach would also allow the correction of errors at an early stage. Against the background of the experience gathered, the EU could then turn to a more comprehensive harmonization at a later stage if this then is assessed as being desirable. However, legal harmonization in the EU only makes

---

[29] See Wagner (2002), p. 1014, as well. For a detailed analysis concerning the nature of such costs see, for example, Ribstein and Kobayashi (1996).

[30] 'Unstable' here means that the diversity of legal administration within the union is not stable over time, because procedural law in the single countries may change unexpectedly.

sense if it is accompanied by a thorough reform of the European system of civil justice and a harmonization of procedural law.

REFERENCES

ANDERSON AND MARCOUILLER (1999)
J.E. Anderson and D. Marcouiller, "Trade, Insecurity, and Home Bias: An Empirical Investigation", *NBER Working Paper*, No. 7000 (Cambridge: National Bureau of Economic Research 1999)

ALESINA, OZLER, ROUBINI AND SWAGEL (1996)
A. Alesina, S. Ozler, N. Roubini and P. Swagel, "Political Instability and Economic Growth", 1 *Journal of Economic Growth* (1996) 189-211

AGHION AND HOWITT (1992)
P. Aghion, and P. Howitt, "A Model of Growth through Creative Destruction", 60 *Econometrica* (1992) 323-351

BARRO (1990)
R. Barro, "Government Spending in a Simple Model of Endogenous Growth", *Journal of Political Economy* (1990) 103-125

BARRO (1991)
Barro, R. (1991), "Economic Growth in Cross Section of Countries", 106 *Quarterly Journal of Economics* (1991) 407-443

VAN DEN BERGH (2002)
R. van den Bergh, "Regulatory Competition or Harmonization of Laws? Guidelines for the European Regulator", in: A. Marciano and J.-M. Josselin (eds.), *The Economics of Harmonizing European Law* (Cheltenham: Edward Elgar 2002)

CASELLA (2001)
A. Casella, "Product Standards and International Trade. Harmonization through Private Coalitions?", 54 *Kyklos* (2001) 243-264

CECCHINI (1988)
P. Cecchini, *The European Challenge 1992. The Benefits of a Single Market* (Aldershot: Wildwood House 1988)

CHONG AND CALDERÓN (2000)
A. Chong and C. Calderón, "Empirical Tests on the Causality and Feedback Between Institutional Measures and Economic Growth", 12 *Economic and Politics* (2000) 69-81

DE GROOT, LINDERS, RIETVELD AND SUBRAMANIAN (2004)
H.L.F. de Groot, G.-J. Linders, P. Rietveld and U. Subramanian, "The Institutional Determinants of Bilateral Trade Patterns", 57 *Kylos* (2004) 103-124.

DE LONG AND SHLEIFER (1993)
J.B. de Long and A. Shleifer, "Princes and Merchants: European City Growth before the Industrial Revolution", 36 *Journal of Law and Economics* (1993) 671-702

DE SOUSA AND ANNE-CÉLIA D. (2002)
J. de Sousa and and Anne-Célia D., "Legal Framework as a Trade
Barrier – Evidence from Transition Countries: Hungarian, Romanian
and Slovene Examples", *HWWA Discussion Paper*, No. 201 (Hamburg:
Hamburgisches Welt-Wirtschafts-Archiv 2002)

EUROPEAN COMMISSION (1985)
European Commission, Completing the Internal Market: White Paper
from the Commission to the European Council, COM (85) 310

FELD AND VOIGT (2003)
L.P. Feld and S. Voigt (2003), "Economic Growth and Judicial
Independence: Cross Country Evidence Using a New Set of
Indicators", *CESifo Working Paper*, No. 906 (München: CESifo GmbH
– Munich Society for the Promotion of Economic Research 2003)

VON FREYHOLD, GESSNER, VIAL AND WAGNER (EDS.) (1995)
H. von Freyhold, V. Gessner, E.L. Vial and H. Wagner (eds.), *Cost of
Judicial Barriers for Consumers in the Single Market, A Report for the
European Commission* (Brussels:DG XXIV; AO-2600/94/00103)

FURUBOTN AND RICHTER (1991)
E.G. Furubotn and R. Richter, "The New Institutional Economics:
An Assessment", in: E.G. Furubotn and R. Richter (eds.), *The New
Institutional Economics* (Tübingen: J.C.B. Mohr 1991), 1-31

GERUM AND WAGNER (1998)
E. Gerum and H. Wagner, "Economics of Labor Co-Determination in
View of Corporate Governance", in: K.J. Hopt, H. Kanda, M.J. Roe, E.
Wymeersch and S. Prigge (eds.), *Comparative Corporate Governance
– The State of the Art and Emerging Research* (Oxford: Clarendon Press
1998)

GROSSMAN AND HELPMAN (1991)
G.M. Grossman and E. Helpman, *Innovation and Growth in the Global
Economy* (Cambridge: MIT Press 1991)

HAYEK (1968)
F.A. von Hayek, "Der Wettbewerb als Entdeckungsverfahren", *Kieler
Vorträge*, N.F. 56 (1968)

IMF (2003)
IMF, "World Economic Outlook – Growth and Institutions", April
2003 (Washington: International Monetary Fund)

KAUFMANN, KRAAY, AND ZOIDO-LOBATÓN (1999)
D. Kaufmann, A. Kraay, and P. Zoido-Lobatón, "Governance matters",
World Bank Policy Research Working Paper, No. 2196 (Washington:
World Bank 1999)

KAUFMANN, KRAAY, AND ZOIDO-LOBATÓN (2002)
D. Kaufmann, A. Kraay, and P. Zoido-Lobatón, "Governance matters
II – Updated Indicators for 2000/2001", *World Bank Policy Research
Working Paper*, No. 2772 (Washington: World Bank 2002)

KLUMP (1995)
R. Klump, "On the Institutional Determinants of Economic Development. Lessons from a Stochastic Neoclassical Growth Model", 46 *Jahrbuch für Wirtschaftswissenschaften* (1995) 138-151

KNACK AND KEEFER (1995)
S. Knack and P. Keefer, "Institutions and Economic Performance: Cross-Country Tests Using Alternative Institutional Measures", 7 *Economic Policy* (1995) 207-227

KNACK AND KEEFER (1997)
S. Knack and P. Keefer, "Why Don't Poor Countries Catch Up? A Cross-National Test of an Institutional Explanation", 35 *Economic Inquiry* (1997) 590-602

LA PORTA, LOPEZ-DE-SILANES, SHLEIFER AND VISHNY (1997)
R. La Porta, F. Lopez-de-Silanes, A. Shleifer and R.W. Vishny, "Legal Determinants of External Finance", 52 *Journal of Finance* (1997) 1131-1150

LUCAS (1988),
R.E. Lucas, "The Mechanics of Economic Development", 22 *Journal of Monetary Economics* (1998) 42

MOCK (2002)
S. Mock, "Harmonization, Regulation and Legislative Competition in European Corporate Law", 3 *German Law Journal* 2002, *Available in www-format: URL <http://www.germanlawjournal.com/ article.php?id=216>*

NORTH (1994)
D.C. North, "Economic Performance through Time", 84 *American Economic Review* (1994) 359-368

NORTH (1996)
D.C. North, "Economic Performance Through Time: The Limits to Knowledge", *Available in pdf-format from Economics Working Paper Archive at WUSTL: URL <http://econwpa.wustl.edu:8089/eps/eh/papers/ 9612/9612004.pdf>*

OECD (1991)
OECD, *Consumers, Product Safety Standards and International Trade* (Paris: Organisation for Economic Co-operation and Development 1991)

OLSON (1965)
M. Olson, *The Logic of Collective Action: Public Goods and and the Theory of Groups* (Cambridge: Harvard University Press 1965)

OLSON (1982)
M. Olson, The Rise and Decline of Nations: *Economic Growth, Stagflation and Social Rigidities* (New Haven, CT: Yale University Press 1982)

PITARAKIS AND TRIDIMAS (2003)

J.-Y. Pitarakis and G. Tridimas, "Joint Dynamics of Legal and Economic Integration in the European Union", 16 *European Journal of Law and Economics* (2003) 357-368

POSNER (1998)

R.A. Posner, "Creating a Legal Framework for Economic Development", 13 *The World Bank Observer* (1998) 1-11

RIBSTEIN AND KOBAYASHI (1996)

L.E. Ribstein and B.H. Kobayashi, "An Economic Analysis of Uniform State Laws", 25 *Journal of Legal Studies* (1996) 131-199

RODRIK (2004)

D. Rodrik, "Getting Institutions Right", *CESifo DICE Report*, No. 2 (München: CESifo GmbH – Munich Society for the Promotion of Economic Research)

ROMER (1986)

P.M. Romer, "Increasing Returns and Long-run Growth", in: *Modern Business Cycle Theory*, edited by R.J. Barro (Cambridge: Harvard University Press 1986)

STREIT (1996)

M.E. Streit, „Systemwettbewerb und Harmonisierung im europäischen Integrationsprozeß", in: *Entstehung und Wettbewerb von Systemen: Schriften des Vereins für Socialpolitik, Band 246*, edited by D. Cassel (Berlin: Duncker & Humblot 1996) 223-244

SUTHERLAND (1992)

P. Sutherland, "The Internal Market after 1992: Meeting the Challenge", *Report to the EEC Commission by the High Level Group on the Operation of the Internal Market*

TIEBOUT (1956)

Ch. Tiebout, "A Pure Theory of Local Expenditures", 64 *Journal of Political Economy* (1956) 416-424

TINBERGEN (1962)

J. Tinbergen, *Shaping the World Economy: Suggestions for an International Economic Policy* (New York: Twentieth Century Fund 1962)

WAGNER (1995)

H. Wagner, "Macroeconomic Analysis of the Cost of Judicial Barriers in the Single Market, Part III", in: H. von Freyhold, V. Gessner, E.L. Vial and H. Wagner (eds.), *Cost of Judicial Barriers for Consumers in the Single Market, A Report for the European Commission* (Brussels: DG XXIV; AO-2600/94/00103)

WAGNER (ED.) (1995)

H. Wagner (ed.): Supplement volume *Bericht zur ökonomischen Analyse der Kosten rechtlicher Hemmnisse für die Verbraucher des Binnenmarkts – Globalanalyse (makro-ökonomischer Ansatz)*, Hamburg, European Commission DG XXIV

WAGNER (1997A)

H. Wagner (1997a), *"Rechtsunsicherheit und Wirtschaftswachstum",* in: S. Behrends (ed.), *Ordnungskonforme Wirtschaftspolitik in der Marktwirtschaft,* Festschrift für Hans-Rudolf Peters (Berlin: Duncker & Humblot 1997) 227-253

WAGNER (1997B)

H. Wagner, *Wachstum und Entwicklung: Theorie der Entwicklungspolitik,* 2nd ed. (München: Oldenbourg 1997)

WAGNER (2002)

G. Wagner, "The Economics of Harmonization: The Case of Contract Law", 39 *Common Market Law Review* (2002) 995-1023

WAGNER (2002)

H. Wagner, "Growth Effects of 'Heterogenous' Economic Integration: The Example of EMU-Enlargement", 17 *Journal of Economic Integration* (2002) 623-649

WAGNER (2004)

H. Wagner, "Fiscal Issues in the Central and Eastern New EU Member Countries: Prospects and Challenges – Analytical Background," *project study conducted for the IMF, forthcoming 2004 as an IMF Working Paper*

APPENDIX

Figure 1: Table of effects of legal uncertainty (macroeconomic costs)
(on the explanation of single effects see Wagner (1995, 1997a))
Source: Wagner (1995)

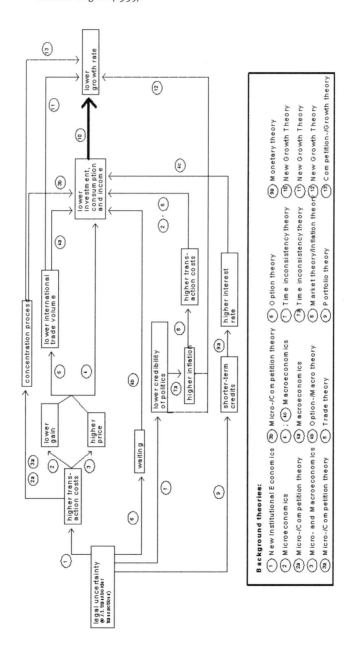

CHAPTER 3

Law, Economics and Uniform Contract Law: A Sceptical View

Jaap Hage*

1 Introduction

It goes without saying that the Dutch meteorological service is more competent than the author of the present paper to predict the weather in the Netherlands. So, when the question arises whether the temperature on August 8th, 2030 in Maastricht will be 30 degrees Celsius, it seems at first sight obvious that it is better to consult the Dutch meteorological service than the present author. On closer inspection, however, this becomes less obvious. Not because the author happens to know more about the weather than a layman, but because the meteorological service, despite its superior knowledge, probably cannot do better than a layman. There are many factors that are relevant for a precise weather prediction, however, the values of many of these factors are/remain unknown. Consequently, the meteorological service can do no more than forecast that, given the time of year and the development of temperatures over the last few years, there is a fair chance that the temperature will be 30 degrees Celsius. However, another temperature is more probable, if only because there are more other temperatures. In other words, the considerable superiority of the meteorological institute with respect to relevant knowledge is negligible in comparison to the large amount of possibly relevant information.

It is one of the main tenets of this paper that Law and Economics is in a similar position with regard to the issue whether European contract law should be unified. The knowledge that Law and Economics has to offer is in principle relevant, but hardly scratches the surface of all the information that could be relevant. The use of Law and Economics for answering the question whether European contract law should be harmonised is therefore limited to an extent that makes it almost irrelevant. Before I can draw this conclusion, I will have to say more about the Law and Economics approach and its role in theorising about the law.

2 Two Functions of the Law and Economics Approach

The Law and Economics approach has at least two functions with regard to the law. One is to explain existing law, the other to evaluate actual and possible law. A legal arrangement, such as the presence of a legal institution (*e.g.* private property), or a particular regulation, can be explained by pointing out that it is efficient. Such a functional[1] explanation can only be plausible on

---

* The author wishes to thank Jan Smits, Remme Verkerk, Nicole Kornet and Gerrit de Geest for useful comments on a draft of this paper.

[1] An explanation is functional if a phenomenon is explained by pointing out that it performs a useful function. Functional explanations play in particular a role in psychological, sociological and evolutionary settings. Cf. Rosenberg (2000) 455.

the assumptions that efficient[2] arrangements have a better chance of being introduced, or – even more importantly – of being maintained over the course of time. Whether these assumptions hold good, depends on a number of conditions, such as whether the efficiency of the arrangement is recognised as such, and whether there are other factors (for instance, ideological[3]) which make that less efficient institutions or regulations survive in the battle for existence.[4]

A second function of Law and Economics is to contribute to the evaluation of actual or possible legal arrangements. This is the function that is at stake in the discussion whether Law and Economics can help answer the question whether European private law should be harmonised, because this question deals with the desirability of a possible legal arrangement.

A rational evaluation of anything, including legal arrangements, requires two kinds of entities. One kind comprises factual characteristics of the item being evaluated, including facts that do not belong to the item proper, but which are relevant for its evaluation. For instance, a relevant characteristic for the evaluation of the desirability of harmonisation of European contract law is that the harmonisation will lead to uniform contract law in the European Union (to the extent that it participates in the unification). Additional facts may be relevant for the evaluation of a particular instance of harmonisation. For instance, for the hypothetical harmonisation promoted by the European Commission that should be finished in 2030, facts such as the political climate at the time that major steps towards harmonisation are made, are also relevant.

The other relevant entities are the standards by means of which the evaluation is made. An overly simple example of such a standard would be that harmonisation is good (should be brought about)[5], if the total economic production of the participating countries increases as a consequence of the harmonisation. A value judgement is the result of applying the standards to the facts about the harmonisation.

Law and Economics can contribute to the evaluation of the harmonisation of European contract law, both by bringing relevant facts to light and by contributing standards for the evaluation of the relevant facts. These two contributions are not independent. The standards used to evaluate the harmonisation determine which facts are relevant. A standard that mentions the total economic

---

[2] Presently, I leave the issue what efficiency is deliberately open. A brief discussion of different economic notions of efficiency can be found in Cooter and Ulen (2004) 16.

[3] I will not discuss the issue whether ideological considerations play a role in determining efficiency.

[4] Discussions of the (continued) existence of social phenomena in evolutionary terms can be found in, amongst others, Dawkins (1989) 189 and Dennett (1995) 335. A different evolutionary perspective is sketched in Smits (2002) and Smits (2003).

[5] In this paper I ignore the difference between evaluation and prescription and simply assume that the best legal arrangement is the one that should be brought about. This close relation between evaluation and prescription is quite often assumed, but should be scrutinised in a more extensive study.

production of the participating countries as being a relevant factor, makes facts about economic production relevant. A standard that refers to the political climate makes the political climate relevant. Note that this logical relation between the adopted standards and the relevance of facts does not imply that the standards are established first and are subsequently used to determine which facts are relevant. It is also possible that some facts are recognised as relevant and that this perceived relevance is generalised into a standard that attaches a value judgement to the presence of these facts.[6]

3 The Material Aspect of the Law and Economics Approach

How can Law and Economics provide standards for the evaluation of the harmonisation of European contract law and the identification of relevant facts? It is characteristic of the Law and Economics approach that it operates in terms of costs and benefits.[7] Law and Economics can point to the costs and benefits of harmonisation, and help balance them. In fact, these two possible contributions represent two distinct aspects of the Law and Economics enterprise. The identification of the costs and benefits of an arrangement is what might be called the 'material' aspect of Law and Economics, because it deals with the material aspects of the choice. The theory about how costs and benefits are to be balanced represents the formal aspect of the Law and Economics approach, because it abstracts from the material aspects of a particular choice and deals only with a general theory of rationality.[8]

The material aspect is not without complications. Are the costs and benefits to be understood broadly to include all disadvantages and advantages of an arrangement? In that case, the evaluative Law and Economics approach would be nothing more than the theory that those legal arrangements are good (to be introduced or maintained), which have more advantages than disadvantages. If there are several possible arrangements, it would lead to the theory according to which the legal arrangement with the greatest advantage-disadvantage difference is the best, or should be adopted. From this perspective, it is unclear what the specific role of economics would be, unless economics is to be understood broadly as the theory of advantage-disadvantage analysis.

---

[6] This kind of generalisation is discussed in Hare (1963) 7.

[7] This is another way of stating that the method of economics is a rational choice approach. Cf. Kerkmeester (1999) 384. The connection between rational choice and cost/benefit analysis is the assumption that the rationality of a choice depends (solely) on the costs and benefits connected to this choice (in relation to its alternatives).

[8] The relativity of this distinction between formal and material aspects of a discipline and more in particular between form and content in logic, is discussed in Hage (2001a).

It is also possible to understand costs and benefits more strictly. A natural interpretation would be to equate them with monetary costs and benefits.[9] The link with economics would then be obvious, but at the cost of disregarding everything that is not (or cannot?) be evaluated in terms of money. For instance, if the harmonisation of European contract law has monetary benefits because it diminishes transaction costs[10], and there are no important monetary costs involved, the verdict would be that from a Law and Economics perspective, harmonisation is a good thing. The loss of cultural identity that may result from harmonisation is disregarded because it is not expressed (and – arguably – not capable of adequately being expressed) in monetary terms.

Another way of dealing with this complication is to explicitly relativise the Law and Economics judgement/view/evaluation of legal harmonisation to the economic point of view, thereby leaving the balancing of economic and non-economic aspects of harmonisation out of consideration. For instance, Law and Economics would consider harmonisation of contract law to be desirable *from the economic point of view*, because it diminishes transaction costs, while there are no important monetary costs involved. Other advantages and disadvantages of harmonisation, not expressed in monetary terms, are not taken into account in giving this judgement from the economic point of view.

There is nothing wrong with evaluating harmonisation from a purely economic point of view, where this point of view is limited to monetary costs and benefits. However, this approach would disregard a useful aspect of Law and Economics. Since balancing economic and non-economic aspects of harmonisation is just another case of balancing advantages and disadvantages, these tools would also be useful in this context. Leaving non-monetary aspects out of the discussion means that a seemingly highly relevant instrument of (Law and) Economics (the theory of balancing) is not used.

It seems possible to take an in-between approach by replacing monetary costs and benefits with individual preferences.[11] Preferences are a common phenomenon in economic analysis, and they play a role in issues where other than purely monetary considerations are relevant. It is for instance possible to address the question whether harmonisation of contract law is in accordance with individual preferences if it involves both monetary benefits and costs with regard to cultural identity. Is harmonisation to be preferred because of its monetary advantages, even though it involves a loss of cultural identity?[12]

---

[9]   According to Kerkmeester (1999) 387, this approach is chosen by Coase and Posner.

[10] Cf. for instance Lando (1992).

[11] An efficient arrangement would then be an arrangement that has the highest utility, meaning that it leads to the highest preference satisfaction. Cf. Kerkmeester (1999) 386.

[12] In this paper I take a psychological approach to preferences. It is possible to translate preferences in the psychological sense into numeric values by the introduction of a so-called *utility function*. (See Cooter and Ulen (2004) 23). The introduction of such a utility function is not a way to deal with the issues discussed in this section, but rather *presupposes* that there is a way to deal with them.

The replacement of monetary considerations with preferences leads, however, to new complications. Let us assume that monetary costs and benefits are an objective matter, and that value judgements based on monetary considerations are *in this respect* objective. Actual preferences are objective too, but they can be the outcome of false beliefs, or malevolent indoctrination. Suppose, for instance, that most inhabitants of the European Union prefer not to harmonise contract law, because they fear the loss of their cultural identity. Suppose, moreover, that this preference is the outcome of active campaigning by nationalist groups, supported by national defence industries which hope to gain from nationalist sentiments and the call for armament that results from it. Should such preferences be allowed to play a role in the evaluation of legal arrangements? If not, which demands should be made on the preferences that are taken into consideration? Only preferences that are rational? If actual preferences are replaced with rational preferences, subjective values will be introduced in the form of standards for the rationality of preferences. Viewing costs and benefits as respectively disadvantages and advantages does not overcome this difficulty. On the contrary, identification of particular facts about a legal arrangement as advantages or disadvantages of the arrangement presupposes evaluative standards which are just as subjective as standards for rationality.

To summarise this section: the material aspect of the Law and Economics approach has two 'problems'. One problem has to do with the interpretation of 'costs' and 'benefits'. If they are understood broadly, the typical economic aspect of the Law and Economics approach is lost. If they are restricted to typical economic characteristics of an arrangement, the restriction seems to be arbitrary, or the resulting judgement must be relativised – without good reasons – to the economic point of view.

The second problem is that the identification of costs and benefits threatens to be subjective and possibly prone to error, in particular if they are defined in terms of actual preferences, or in terms of advantages and disadvantages that are perceived as such. This subjectivity can be avoided by defining costs and benefits in 'objective' terms, such as monetary costs and benefits, but then the question is how such costs and benefits can lead to value judgements about legal arrangements. If it is shown that the purely monetary costs of harmonisation of contract law exceed the purely monetary benefits, it does not follow automatically that harmonisation should be rejected. This conclusion only follows provided additional premises are made that these purely monetary costs are the only relevant factors that should be taken into account and that the net balance of these costs and benefits determines whether harmonisation should be accepted or rejected.

4 The Formal Aspect of the Law and Economics Approach

The formal aspect of the Law and Economics approach concerns the line of reasoning by means of which costs and benefits (or their replacement categories) are weighed. If the Law and Economics approach is confined to monetary aspects of legal arrangements, the line of reasoning are quite simple. There are two kinds of questions that play a role. One is whether a particular legal arrangement is good. This can be established by determining whether the benefits, expressed in some monetary unit, exceed the costs as expressed in the same monetary unit. To put it bluntly and apply it to the harmonisation question: Are the profits of the harmonisation of European contract law, as expressed in Euros, greater than the costs, also expressed in Euros? If the costs and benefits are uncertain, this should be taken into account by multiplying the costs or benefits with the probability (on a scale from zero to one) of their occurrence.[13]

The other kind of question is when there are several alternatives under consideration, and the issue is which of the alternatives should be adopted. Then the line of reasoning that should be followed is to determine for each alternative the net benefits (which may be negative), and to choose the alternative with the highest benefits.[14]

It is important to note that these simple lines of reasoning are only available if all the costs and all the benefits of an arrangement can be expressed on a common scale which allows mathematical operations (subtract the costs from the benefits), and negative numbers (if the costs exceed the benefits). If everything that is relevant can be expressed in monetary terms, this condition is satisfied, but the demand that everything relevant is expressed in monetary terms is quite demanding, to state it modestly.

If it is not possible to represent all the costs and benefits on a common scale that allows calculations, the line of reasoning that is required to make justified/ reliable judgements about legal arrangements becomes more complicated. There are several issues that must be dealt with. One is the absence of a numerical scale, or at least a scale that allows calculations. Another is that different types of costs and benefits cannot be represented on a common scale, which has led some authors/scholars to develop the theory that they are incommensurable.[15] There are, however, theories that deal with reasoning on the basis of factors that are not numerical and that cannot be represented on a common scale.[16] These theories are less powerful than the calculation of costs and benefits represented

---

[13] Cf. Keeney and Raiffa (1993) 5. This book also discusses more complex techniques of decision making.

[14] The first kind of question can be treated as a question of the second kind, if one treats adopting and rejecting an arrangement as the only two alternatives under consideration.

[15] See Chang (1997) for a general discussion of the problems.

[16] Verheij (1996), Hage (1997) and Hage (2001b).

in terms of monetary units, but have the advantage that their scope of application is much broader.[17]

In combination, the theories about quantitative and qualitative comparative reasoning provide a general framework that can be applied to choices between alternatives. If the costs and benefits of the alternatives can be represented on a common scale that allows calculation, the more powerful quantitative techniques should be applied. If this is not possible, one must be satisfied with qualitative comparative reasoning.

5   Limitation to Foreseeable Costs and Benefits

The costs and benefits of some action such as the harmonisation of European contract law consist of the costs and benefits of bringing this action about and the costs and benefits that are consequences of this action. These costs and benefits are always costs and benefits of a concrete action, which actually took place.[18] Hence, to determine the costs and benefits of harmonising European contract law, the relevant costs and benefits will (need to) be attached to the harmonisation as it actually takes place. These costs and benefits are not available in advance when one is merely considering whether to harmonise the law. In advance, it is only possible to speculate about the actual costs and one is confined to the costs and benefits of actions in general that involve the harmonisation of European contract law. All details of the practical implementation must be left out of consideration.

Let me be more concrete. In order to determine the costs and benefits of harmonisation, the only thing that is known about the action in question is that it involves harmonisation. The only consequences that can be taken into account are consequences that are related to harmonisation in general. These consequences are probably limited to the result that European contract law will be uniform, *and nothing else*. In particular, it is not given that the transaction costs involved in studying the law of foreign countries will disappear, for instance because it is not given that the new uniform law will be published. Clearly this is a counterfactual hypothesis. If European contract law will be harmonised, this will probably be accomplished through the introduction of uniform legislation that will be published. However, if this natural assumption is made, the arrangement that is evaluated is no longer the harmonisation of European contract law in general, but the harmonisation through published legislation. Let us therefore assume that the issue is reformulated in terms of the desirability of harmonising European contract law by means of uniform legislation that

---

[17] The appendix gives a first impression of what such a theory looks like.

[18] In the terminology of Von Wright (1963) 36, consequences are tied to *individual acts* (act tokens) and not to *generic acts* (action types).

will be published. Then it seems safe to assume that at least one of the benefits will be the avoidance of transaction costs.

Yet, this assumption is not safe at all. Maybe the uniform legislation will contain many open norms, which will be filled in differently in different countries. This possibility can be taken away by making still additional assumptions, for instance that there will be few open norms and that there will be a common supreme court that takes care of legal unity in the interpretation of the remaining open norms. On this assumption the legal arrangement to be evaluated is not merely the harmonisation of European private law, but the harmonisation by means of uniform legislation that contains few open norms and that is kept uniform by a common supreme court … etc.

As these examples illustrate, the determination in advance of the costs and benefits of a legal arrangement requires many details of the arrangement to be specified in advance, because only then can the consequences of the arrangement be taken into account.

It will be clear, however, that it may be possible to make proposed legal arrangements to some extent concrete, but that it is impossible to make them so concrete that *all* relevant costs and benefits can be determined in advance. The best possible approach is to specify in advance all details that are relevant for the determination of *foreseeable* costs and benefits and to evaluate the resulting proposal on the assumption that the remaining costs and benefits will be relatively unimportant. In the context of the harmonisation of European contract law this means that it is necessary to specify in advance all the factors that might be relevant for determining the costs and benefits of harmonisation. Then a possible course of action should be formulated, in which all these relevant factors are specified. For instance, it is necessary to consider that the harmonisation of European contract law will be by means of centralist European legislation containing many open norms referring to local standards, that a European court that has the task to look after the progress of the harmonisation will be established, and that the members of the European Union are free to determine whether they will participate in the harmonised law. In this way, it is possible to achieve at least some certainty about the consequences of the proposed arrangement, which makes the presupposition more realistic that the costs and benefits that were not taken into account would not tip the balance of costs and benefits.

The same point can be made in a different way. To evaluate a legal arrangement, ideally all its consequences should be known. Since these consequences relate to the actual implementation (or maintenance) of the arrangement (the implementation token), and the only thing we know is what kind of arrangement will be implemented (the implementation type), there is a problem. The best way to overcome this problem is to specify the type of arrangement as much as possible, in order to make it possible to determine as many of its consequences as possible in advance. On the basis of these foreseeable consequences, the implementation of the arrangement should be evaluated in terms of costs and benefits. On the basis of this evaluation, a decision about implementation can be made, under the assumption that the costs and benefits that were not foreseeable and were therefore not taken into account, would not tip the balance of costs and benefits.

6   The Role of Uncertainty

This leads me to the issue with which I started this paper. Is it a realistic assumption that we can specify a way to harmonise European contract law in such a way that it is possible to predict a significant amount of the costs and benefits in order to make a useful evaluation possible? Or is it in practice impossible to adequately foresee many of the relevant consequences, and can we only make estimates of the costs and benefits that we know beforehand to be insufficiently exhaustive. Is the harmonisation of European contract law comparable to predicting the precise temperature in Maastricht on August 8th, 2030? In the end, this question is unanswerable, because to answer it we not only need to know which consequences are foreseeable, but also which consequences will actually occur. Although we can know which consequences are foreseeable (that is precisely what makes them foreseeable), we cannot know which consequences will actually occur, because actual consequences belong to actual harmonisation and actual harmonisation will not have taken place yet when the desirability of harmonisation is being discussed.

The best approach in this context therefore seems to be to look at a hypothetical example. Suppose that the diminution of transaction costs is the main foreseeable benefit of the harmonisation of contract law and that this gain turns out to be relatively unimportant. In fact, it turns out to be less important than the cost of uniform law that the possibility/need to compare possible legal solutions for contract law issues and to choose between them, disappears.[19] Should we then draw the conclusion that harmonisation is not attractive and should not be brought about? No, because there is a (very) small possibility that the harmonisation of contract law contributes to the public feeling of belonging together and thereby prevents a war between European Union countries. This possibility is far-fetched and therefore I have assigned it a (very) small possibility. However, the consequences of such a war would be tremendous to an extent that they can hardly be estimated, if at all. Since the relevance of such a war for the desirability of harmonisation consists of the product of its costs and its probability, the smallness of its probability is counterbalanced by the size of its costs. So maybe this factor should be taken into account.

---

[19]   Cf. Smits (2002) and Smits (2003) and Wagner (2002) 1001.

But is that possible? Can we, if only by approximation, estimate the probability that harmonisation of contract law will prevent a war that would otherwise have occurred, or the costs of such a war if it would occur? In my opinion we cannot, especially not as far as the probability of (the avoidance of) war is concerned.[20] And this leads me to the conclusion that the harmonisation of European contract law is comparable to the long term prediction in detail of the temperature in a particular city: there is relevant information available but there is so much relevant information that is not available, that the value of what is available is limited.

7 A Possible Objection

It might be argued that the above line of reasoning leads to the unacceptable conclusion that, with regard to many crucial decisions, we should abandon all hope and refrain from deliberating about future actions because we cannot (be certain to) acquire all the relevant information. Clearly an argument with that conclusion must be wrong. However, this should not be the conclusion of the argument. When deciding what to do, the best (most rational) approach is to work on the basis of all the relevant information that is available, *while remaining aware of the fact that all the available information may not contain everything that is relevant*. To state it somewhat paradoxically:

Rational action takes into account that it is incompletely rational.

This was already known to Karl Popper, who drew from this insight the advice of *piecemeal engineering*.[21] Changes to social institutions (including the law) should take the form of small adjustments and re-adjustments *which can be continually improved upon*. This last phrase is in my opinion crucial and indicates that institutional changes should be made in such a way that the possibility of continuous monitoring and re-adjustment is so to speak built into the changes.[22] In the case of legal harmonisation this might, for instance, take the form of no changes at all, or small harmonisations (*e.g.* harmonisation of limited parts of contract law), or locally restricted harmonisation (start with a few countries and extend if possible).

---

[20] To state this in technical terms, we live under uncertainty in the sense of Knight (1921) 20, concerning the probability of a war in both the absence and presence of harmonization.

[21] Popper (1957) 66. A similar idea was promoted by Lindblom (1980) under the name of incrementalism.

[22] In this connection abstaining from change counts as a kind of 'change' too. The idea of piecemeal engineering is that any action should be taken under the recognition that it may be based on incomplete or even wrong information. Therefore the decision not to make changes at all is also subject to revision in the light of additional information, and should be taken with this limitation in mind.

8 Summary

Let me summarise the above. Law and Economics provides relevant information for the decision whether European contract law should be harmonised. This relevant information can be divided into material and formal information. Materially, Law and Economics can help decide which facts about harmonisation are relevant to determine whether harmonisation is desirable. There are some complications involved, concerning the subjectivity of the standards for determining what is relevant, but in my opinion these complications are involved in all evaluative enterprises. Formally, Law and Economics provides tools to determine, given the relevant facts about harmonisation, whether harmonisation is desirable. These tools can be quantitative, but often it will be necessary to fall back on tools for qualitative comparative reasoning. The usefulness of these formal tools is independent of the complications on the material side.

Although Law and Economics provides relevant information, both on the material and on the formal side, the question remains whether this information makes reliable judgments concerning the desirability of harmonisation possible. In this context, the parallel with weather prediction plays a role. If one has some relevant information, but lacks a lot of other relevant information, a well-founded judgement is not possible. A meteorological institute cannot, for this reason, predict the precise temperature 25 years from now. By means of an example about the prevention of war, I have tried to show that the harmonisation issue is in this respect similar: there may be many or important potentially relevant things that we do not know, that it is not possible to make reliable estimations about the desirability of harmonisation.

However, this does not mean that we should abandon hope and act at random because the issue cannot be solved rationally. Rationality in complex social issues requires taking into account that much relevant information is lacking and that we must take decisions under uncertainty. Popper's advice of piecemeal engineering is based on precisely this insight. With regard to the harmonisation of European private law, this suggests that harmonisation, if it is undertaken, should proceed in small steps and that the continuation and the precise form of the process should be adapted to the findings underway.

Appendix: Qualitative Comparative Reasoning[23]
Suppose that one must choose between buying a Volvo and buying a Mercedes and that there is no quantitative scale available by means of which these two alternatives can be compared. A rational theory about decision making

---

[23] This appendix is drawn from the paper *Qualitative comparative reasoning*, which is part of my book *Studies in Legal Logic* that will be published in 2005.

should then operate on a qualitative basis. Such a qualitative theory about the comparison can be developed on basis of the notions of reasons pleading for and against alternatives.

A Volvo has – let us assume – two reasons in its favour, namely that it is a safe car and that there is a Volvo dealer next door. It has the disadvantage that it is an expensive car. A Mercedes is also expensive, but has (in this example) only one advantage, namely that it is a safe car. There happens to be no Mercedes dealer in the neighbourhood. Under these circumstances, everything that argues for a Mercedes also argues for a Volvo, but a Volvo has an additional reason in its favour, namely the availability of a dealer nearby. Moreover, a Volvo and a Mercedes have the same reason against it, namely that they are expensive. It seems, therefore, that a Volvo is preferable to a Mercedes. This is a reasonable conclusion, even in the absence of any information concerning the (relative) weight of the reasons that the cars are safe, that there is a Volvo dealer nearby and that the cars are expensive. Analogously, it is reasonable to conclude that a Mercedes is preferable to a Porsche, if a Mercedes and a Porsche have the common advantage that they are German cars (for those who like German cars) and they also share the disadvantage that they are expensive, while a Porsche has the additional disadvantage that it liable to be stolen. In general, alternative A is preferable to alternative B if either:

1. the set of reasons for A is 'stronger' than the set of reasons for B, while the set of reasons against A is not 'stronger' than the set of reasons against B; or
2. the set of reasons against B is 'stronger' than the set of reasons against A, while the set of reasons for B is not 'stronger' than the set of reasons for A; or
3. both 1 and 2 hold.

A similar approach can be used to determine whether one set of reasons is 'stronger' than another set, because that is also a matter of comparative reasoning that may have to be dealt with in a qualitative fashion.

REFERENCES

CHANG (1997)

R. Chang (ed.), *Incommensurability, Incomparability, and Practical Reason* (Cambridge: Harvard University Press 1997)

COOTER, R. AND T. ULEN (2004)

R. Cooter and T. Ulen, *Law and Economics*, 4th ed. (Boston: Pearson 2004)

DAWKINS (1989)

R. Dawkins, *The Selfish Gene*, 2nd ed. (Oxford: Oxford University Press 1989)

DENNETT (1995)

D.C. Dennett, *Darwin's Dangerous Idea* (London: Penguin 1995)

HAGE (1997)

J.C. Hage, *Reasoning with rules* (Dordrecht: Kluwer Academic Publishers) 1997

HAGE (2001A)

J.C. Hage, "Legal logic. It's existence, nature and use", in: A. Soeteman (ed.), *Pluralism and law* (Dordrecht: Kluwer Academic Publishers) 347-374

HAGE (2001B)

J.C. Hage (ed.), "Formalizing legal coherence", in: *Proceedings of the 8th International Conference on Artificial Intelligence and Law* (New York: ACM) 22-23

HARE (1963)

R.M. Hare, *Freedom and Reason* (Oxford: Oxford University Press 1963)

KEENEY AND RAIFFA (1993)

R.L. Keeney and H. Raiffa, *Decision with Multiple Objectives. Preferences and Value Tradeoffs*, 2nd ed. (Cambridge: Cambridge University Press 1993)

KERKMEESTER (1999)

H. Kerkmeester, "Methodology: General (0400)", in: B. Bouckaert and G. de Geest (eds.), *Encyclopedia of Law and Economics* (http://encyclo.findlaw.com (1999)

KNIGHT (1921)

F.H. Knight, *Risk, Uncertainty and Profit* (Boston: Hart, Schaffner and Marx 1921)

POPPER (1957)

K.R. Popper, *The Povery of Historicism* (London: Routledge and Kegan Paul 1957)

LANDO (1992)

O. Lando, "Principles of European Contract Law", 56 *RabelsZ* (1992) 261-273

LINDBLOM (1980)

C. Lindblom, *The Policy-Making Process* (New York: Prentice Hall
1980)

ROSENBERG (2000)

A. Rosenberg, "Philosophy of Social Science", in: W.H. Newton-Smith
(ed.), *A Companion to the Philosophy of Science* (London: Blackwell
2000) 451-460

SMITS (2002)

J.M. Smits, "The Harmonisation of Private law in Europe: Some
Insights from Evolutionary Theory", 31 *Georgia Journal of International
and Comparative Law* (2002) 79-99

SMITS (2003)

J.M. Smits, "De missing link in het debat over unificatie van
privaatrecht: het evolutionair perspectief", 20 *Nederlands Tijdschrift
voor Burgerlijk Recht* (2003) 241-246

VERHEIJ (1996)

Bart Verheij, *Rules, Reasons, Arguments. Formal studies of
argumentation and defeat*, thesis Maastricht University 1996

WAGNER (2002)

G. Wagner, "The Economics of Harmonization: The Case of Contract
Law", 39 *Common Market Law Review* (2002) 995-1023

WRIGHT (1963)

G.H. von Wright, *Norm and Action* (London: Routledge and Kegan
Paul 1963)

CHAPTER 4

Uniformity of European Contract Law

An Economic Study Between Logic and Fact

Heico Kerkmeester

In this contribution I examine whether a relatively new branch of the economic analysis of law, called behavioural law and economics, supports the case for a uniform European Contract Law. Traditional law and economics pretends to be able to identify those legal rules that are efficient. It does not make a distinction as to cultural differences. This in itself pleads for uniformity. Moreover, regardless of the specific legal rules chosen, a uniform European Contract Law saves on transaction costs.

Behavioural law and economics adds an element to the analysis by taking the results of empirical studies of human behavior into account. I will contend that these empirical data show that an endeavor to impose a European Contract Law *top-down* is unlikely to satisfy individual preferences in an optimal way. Generally speaking, behavioural law and economics stresses differences and therefore does not contribute to the case for uniformity. However, in a number of cases behavioural law and economics could well contribute to *bottom-up*-processes of harmonization.

In the first paragraph I will define the terms *law and economics* and *behavioural law and economics*, recognizing that the distinction between both is not razor-sharp. In paragraph 2, I make the argument that law and economics as it has developed over the past few decades is a science of logic, rather than one of facts. In spite of its empirical pretenses, the strength of traditional law and economics lies in providing a coherent model for a logical approach to the law. If law and economics is regarded in this way, it strongly supports the idea that efficient rules can be determined, that those rules are similar everywhere and hence that developing a uniform European Contract Law is essentially a matter of translating the economic recommendations into legal terms. Paragraph 3 presents behavioural law and economics as a contrasting approach in which empirical results prevail over logic. Laboratory experiments show systematic deviations from the rational behavior that is expected on the basis of the assumptions underlying traditional economics. Scholars applying these results to legal issues have come up with recommendations with regard to the design of legal rules, thereby pretending to enrich the existing economic analysis of law. In paragraph 4 my point is that opting for an ideal economic approach is not choosing between either logic or fact, but rather looking for a synthesis. The facts of behavioural law and economics might well support the logic of the traditional approach. I present the conclusions of this paper in paragraph 5.

1 Defining the Terms: (Behavioural) Law and Economics

When I write about *law and economics* or *traditional law and economics*, I hereby refer to the mathematical, model-based approach that is founded in neo-classical economics and is predominant in leading journals like *The Journal of Legal Studies* and the *International Review of Law and Economics*.

On the basis of a number of assumptions a mathematical model is developed from which conclusions can be drawn as to the efficiency of a proposed legal rule. A typical representative is Steven Shavell of Harvard Law School, a mathematical-economist who in quite a few articles developed a detailed mathematical approach to several fields of law.[1] The central assumption is that 'economic man' chooses rationally. The meaning of this concept of rational choice – as well as its limitations – will be explored in paragraph 3.1.

Behavioural law and economics has its roots in psychological research by in particular Amos Tversky and Daniel Kahneman on cognitive distortions such as heuristics and biases in judgments on uncertainty.[2] It also derives its ideas from experimental economics.[3] In empirical research under laboratory conditions people showed behavior that differed from the rationality assumptions that were commonly made in economics. It also turned out to be the case that these deviations were not random, but occurred in a systematic way. That existing models allegedly had been wrong in the sense that they yielded inaccurate predictions does, therefore, not imply that people's behavior ipso facto is unpredictable. The empirical findings from psychology and experimental economics can be used to develop theories that take the systematic deviations from economic rationality into account.

The agenda for applying the insights of the so-called *behavioural economics* to law has been set by Cass Sunstein, who thereby developed behavioural *law and* economics.[4] This field pretends to bring a more accurate understanding of behaviour and choice concerning legal rules.

However useful for the purposes of this contribution, it should be noted that the sharpness of the distinction should not be overrated. A number of insights from behavioural law and economics have already invaded the domain of traditional law and economics and proven to be valuable. Since Robert Ellickson seminal fieldwork on social norms in Shasta County,[5] it has been recognized by a number of law and economics scholars that individual behavior is not only determined by rational choice.[6] Even the above-mentioned Steven Shavell sometimes takes the existence of cognitive distortions into account, for example in his analysis of the unforeseeability doctrine in tort law, recognizing that individuals may not be able to assess the risk of unlikely losses.[7]

---

[1]   E.g. Shavell (1987) on tort law and Shavell (2003) on contracts.

[2]   Some of the classical studies by these authors are Kahneman and Tversky (1972); Kahneman and Tversky (1973) and Tversky and Kahneman (1973).

[3]   See for an overview of the relevance of experimental economics to law and economics Hoffman, McCabe and Smith (1998).

[4]   Sunstein (2000).

[5]   See Ellickson (1991).

[6]   Witness Conference Proceedings (1998).

[7]   See Shavell (1987) 130.

Indeed, it will turn out that a synthesis of insights from traditional law and economics as well as from behavioural law and economics is quite useful for an economic approach to European Contract Law.

2   The Logic of Law and Economics

In spite of its pretenses, law and economics is not an empirical science. The presumption is that of a *positive* law and economics, explaining and/or predicting the effects of legal rules.[8] Following the well-known methodology of Milton Friedman,[9] the realism of assumptions like rational behavior is not relevant. What counts is whether the predictions derived from the theory are in accordance with empirical observations. According to Friedman it is even desirable that assumptions are *un*realistic, because the simpler the model the more general it is and the better, therefore, the predictions it yields.

Nevertheless, empirical testing of the models of law and economics is limited, although admittedly *The Journal of Law and Economics* is increasingly devoted to empirical studies. Moreover, much of law and economics – particularly the type of analysis that found its way into the *Law Reviews* – is normative rather than positive. The aim is not so much to give empirical proof of the efficiency of a legal rule, as well as arguing that a particular rule is desirable and invoking arguments of efficiency in supporting this point. Anyway, the enormous success of law and economics in legal debates, particularly in the United States, cannot be explained just on the basis of its proven ability to demonstrate the efficiency of legal rules.[10]

In spite of Milton Friedman's claim, the reason for making assumptions that are abstracting from reality and therefore unrealistic does not seem to be an increase in predictive power. These assumptions find their reason for existence rather in their tractability in mathematical models. Mathematics is not an empirical science, but a useful tool in deriving conclusions from assumptions. It is a science of logic, not one of fact.

At first sight, it would seem that without empirical support the results of mathematical models would not be convincing for lawyers, who are generally not gifted in mathematics. On second thoughts, however, an approach focusing on logic rather than facts is not so remote from traditional legal approaches. Of old, in accepting legal theories lawyers have not so much been persuaded by empirical fact as well as by power of reasoning. Compared to non-mathematical theories that found their final judgment in the authority attached to the author,

---

[8]   This obviously holds for the economists among the law and economics scholars, but even for a lawyer like Richard Posner. See Posner (1998) 17-19.

[9]   Friedman (1953) 3-43.

[10]   As to the topic of contract law, Eric Posner has demonstrated this in a review article. See Posner (2003).

the mathematical approach of law and economics has the advantage that an objective judgment of the correctness of the approach can be made, albeit it not lawyers but editors of law and economics journals – who are usually economists – perform the required tests.

It goes without saying that the choice for simplifying assumptions has systematic consequences for the outcomes of the models. A typical simplification is the abstraction from cultural differences. If economic man is thus supposed to be a universal phenomenon, then law and economics provides a universal framework. In that case it can be applied without regard to (legal) culture. Moreover, in spite of the influence of the above-mentioned Robert Ellickson a legal-centralist approach is common. This implies that law and economics focuses on state-based legal norms rather than on social norms, which might differ within the state's jurisdiction.

The results of the starting points just mentioned are recommendations as to efficient rules that are supposed to hold everywhere. Which rule is efficient is generally not regarded as depending on contingencies as peculiarities of a legal culture, prevailing social norms or differences in attitudes. The efficient rule is derived instead from a framework that is assumed to be relevant for all legal communities. A clear example is the economic theory of efficient breach of contract.[11] This theory is based on the common law that knows damages as the principal remedy, while continental law allows the debtor the choice between damages and specific performance. Even law and economics scholars from continental legal systems do not seem to bother about this difference in legal culture.[12]

If the economic analysis of law is based on a framework that is regarded to have universal applicability, this clearly supports a top-down approach to European Contract Law. Centralized lawmaking allows for thorough research for the efficient rules. Those rules can then be imposed everywhere, lowering transaction costs.

3 The Facts of Behavioural Law and Economics

There is no doubt that, unlike traditional law and economics, behavioural law and economics finds its lifeline in empirical research. The typical behavioural law and economics paper is devoid of mathematics. It is either an account of an experiment or an effort to apply to results of an experiment to a legal issue.

It is not the aim of this paper to give a complete overview of behavioural law and economics' findings, but in paragraph 3.1 a broad indication will be given.

---

[11] E.g. Shavell (1980).

[12] Compare the leading Dutch textbook on law and economics Holzhauer and Teijl (1995) 89-117.

In paragraph 3.2 I provide some illustrations of the implications of behavioural law and economics for the design of rules of contract law. In paragraphs 3.3 and 3.4 behavioural law and economics will be related to European Contract Law. I will first discuss arguments for uniformity, and thereafter the prevalent arguments against.

3.1 The Results of Empirical Research: A Brief Overview

As indicated in paragraph 2 a crucial assumption in traditional law and economics is that individuals make rational choices. Characteristics of rational economic man are that he has stable preferences, acts in accordance with these preferences, is furthering his self-interest and is able to make correct probability estimations if he has to take decisions under risk. Behavioural law and economics casts doubts on all these assumptions. I will illustrate these doubts on the bases of a number of examples and experiments. It should be noted that in the original studies accounting for those experiments, the experimenters took care that alternative explanations for the behavior found could be eliminated.

Instability of preferences
According to the assumptions of rational choice theory an individual who has to choose between different items will compare their value and opt for the item with the highest value. The preferences with regard to these items are not depending on whether the individual owns the item or not.

It turns out, however, that in experiments individuals have a preference for the existing allocation, a phenomenon known as the *endowment effect* or *status quo bias*.[13] For example, the amount of money that an individual requires in order to part with a good (*willingness to accept*) tends to be higher than the amount he is prepared to give in order to acquire it (*willingness to pay*).

A well-known experiment illustrating the endowment effect involved coffee mugs bearing the logo of Cornell University.[14] A random division was made between the participants in the study and half of them were given the mugs. The participants could then bargain over the mugs, so that the owners of the mugs could sell them to the others. On the basis of economic rational choice theory, it was expected that half of the mugs would trade. Given the random division of the mugs over the participants, the preferences of owners and non-owners with regard to the mugs were expected to be similar. The reason that in reality only few mugs were traded could be found in the noted difference between willingness to accept and willingness to pay. The median owner required $ 5,25 to agree with the sale of his mug, while the median buyer was

---

[13] See Curran (2000).
[14] See Arlen (1998) 1771.

willing to pay only about $ 2,50. Apparently, ownership of a mug strongly influenced one's preferences for it.

Not acting in accordance with preferences

The assumption that individuals act in accordance with their preferences implies that they are able to determine these preferences. They appear to have difficulties, however, with valuations of non-marketable assets, such as the value of a life, or in cases in which emotions play a role.[15]

The clearest examples of acting against one's preferences are probably cases of compliance with customs or traditions, or cases of addiction. Someone who prefers the shortest route to his work might yet take another one, since he is used to do so. A peculiar problem with addictions is that the addicted person prefers to act differently, but the very fact that he acts in violation of his preferences intensifies his behavior. Someone prefers not to smoke, but because he nevertheless does so, his dependence on nicotine increases.

Besides the issues just mentioned, weakness of the will is regarded to be an important phenomenon in behavioural law and economics. A person attempts to lose weight but simply cannot resist the temptation of eating a pizza.

Deviations from self-interest

In some contexts, human behavior cannot be explained on the basis of the assumption that individuals are furthering their individual interests. A well-known example is the so-called *ultimatum game*.[16] The ultimatum game is a simple bargaining game in which two players are involved, say player A and player B. Player A is asked to propose an allocation of a sum of money between himself and player B. Player B then has the choice between accepting the amount offered by player A and rejecting the offer, in which case both players get nothing. The game is structured in a way that reputations and the possibility of future retaliation are eliminated as factors.

It is in the self-interest of player B to accept every amount offered by player A, however small. Knowing this, player A could further his self-interest by keeping as much as possible for himself, for example by offering B only 1 euro in a game in which 100 euro is at stake. This is not the way the game usually is played, however. Players who have the choice between accepting and rejecting, typically reject offers that amount to less than 20 percent of the amount available. In anticipation of this response the players who are in the position to offer, typically offer an amount of between 40 and 50 percent of the sum. Apparently norms of fairness play a role and these norms induce players towards a 50/50-division. Behavior that deviates from these norms is punished, even at considerable cost for oneself.

---

[15] See Sunstein, Kahneman and Schkade (1998).

[16] See Jolls, Sunstein and Thaler (2000) 21-22.

In paragraph 1 I already referred to research on the influence that social norms in general have on human behavior. Although attempts have been made to reconcile rational choice theory and social norms,[17] both approaches might also be regarded as alternatives, one stepping in where the other fails.[18] If this viewpoint is taken, individuals are also regarded to follow social norms in cases in which it is not in their self-interest to do so.

Incorrect probability estimations

The classical research of Daniel Kahneman and Amos Tversky involved heuristics and biases regarding probability estimations, that is to say rules of thumb that people tend to use in assessing probabilities and the systematic errors they make in doing so.[19] The three specific heuristics Kahneman and Tversky distinguished are the *availability, representativeness,* and *anchoring and adjustment* heuristics.[20]

When people use the availability heuristic they assess the probability of the occurrence of an event on the basis of the ease with which they can remember specific instances of that event. For example, the probability of an airplane accident is usually overestimated, because people can vividly remember examples of such an accident.

The representativeness heuristic is used to judge the likelihood that a particular event belongs to a certain class on the basis of the similarity of the case with the image or stereotype of the class. In an experiment the participants were given a description of several individuals that were selected at random from a group consisting of 100 lawyers and engineers. In the first experiment the participants were told that 70 engineers and 30 lawyers made up the group, while in the second experiment it was 30 engineers and 70 lawyers. In judging the probability that a specified individual was an engineer the participants in both experiments reached similar outcomes. The in itself relevant knowledge about the initial probability of an individual being an engineer was completely outweighed by the importance attached to the degree in which a particular description was in accordance with the stereotype of an engineer.

Application of the anchoring and adjustment heuristic leads individuals to base their judgments on an initial value. They make insufficient adjustments on the basis of subsequent information.

A fourth heuristic that gained attention in behavioural law and economics is known as *hindsight bias.* Individuals tend to overstate the predictability of past events. In judging in hindsight, they consistently exaggerate what could have been anticipated in foresight. For example, judges who have to decide whether a

---

[17] For example, Posner (2000).

[18] See Elster (1989).

[19] For example Tversky and Kahneman (1974).

[20] See Thaler (1991) 152, as well as the literature cited in note 2.

defendant in a tort case could reasonably have taken precautionary measures are likely to overrate the foreseeability of the damage as it happened.

3.2   Some Implications for Contract Law

Behavioural law and economics applies the insights mentioned above to a large number of fields of law, including contract law. I will briefly mention possible consequences for the analysis of consumer protection, liquidated damages, contract default rules, and the issue of damages versus specific performance.

Consumer protection

The desirability of protection of consumers seems to follow directly from the occurrence of cognitive distortions. This is particularly the case with contractual provisions that are hard to understand or with issues of product safety.[21] Manufacturers are regarded to be in a better position than consumers in making a rational response to safety incentives given by law. Individuals often exaggerate some dangers and underestimate others. Usually they overestimate the risks of low-probability events and underestimate the risk of high-probability events. Individuals do not follow the principles of probability theory in judging the likelihood of uncertain events. They regard themselves as less vulnerable to a particular risk than others are. Consumers may overestimate the significance of their own control over products. Moreover, consumers tend to ignore information that casts doubt on their decision to buy a product.

Liquidated damages

A typical law and economics explanation for contractual provisions that liquidate damages for breach is given by Judge Posner in *Lake River Corp.* v. *Carborundum Co.*[22] Posner states that in deciding whether to include a penalty clause in their contract, parties weigh the gains against the costs and will include the clause only if the benefits exceed those costs. Focusing on the limits of cognition, Melvin Eisenberg doubts whether parties can imagine all the scenarios of breach and the consequences of an eventual liquidated damages provision.[23] For example, the availability heuristic may induce 'a contracting party to give unduly weight to his present intention to perform, which is vivid and concrete, as compared with the abstract possibility that future circumstances may compel him to breach'.[24] Because liquidated damages provisions are subject to the limits of cognition, special scrutiny of such provision is justified.

---

[21]   See generally Hanson and Kysar (1999).

[22]   769 F.2d 1284 (7th Cir. 1985).

[23]   See Eisenberg (1995) 227.

[24]   Eisenberg (1995) 228.

Contract default rules

According to Russell Korobkin, if contracting parties fall prey to the status quo bias they 'might place a higher value on a particular contract term if they perceive it to be consistent with the status quo than if they perceive it to represent a change from the status quo'.[25] Parties might therefore prefer terms that are the legal default terms to alternatives. In order to test this hypothesis Korobkin conducted a number of experiments. In one of those experiments the participants were told that they represented a shipping company that was negotiating with a company that sold gift items. They also heard that the parties had agreed on a shipping price of $ 20 per package. The client the participants were supposed to work for allegedly sought a contract term that would limit its liability to reasonably foreseeable damages. One group of participants was told that such a provision was part of an industry form-contract. These participants were asked to indicate the per-unit price at which their client would be willing to accept full liability instead. Another group of participants was told that that full-liability was the default rule. Their task was to state the per-unit price that their client was willing to pay to obtain a limitation in liability. In accordance with the endowment effect and status quo bias the seller's price considerably exceeded the buyer's price.

Specific performance versus damages

Behavioural law and economics also deviates from the law and economics theories on efficient breach. Those theories generally plead for damages over specific performance in case an optimal remedy for breach of contract has to be found.[26] A problem with awarding damages, however, is that it is hard for a judge to take the endowment-effect into account. If specific performance is ordered the good still may end up with a third party, but only if his willingness to pay is higher than the willingness to accept of the creditor in the original contract. As noted above, the acquisition of a right to a good is likely to lead to a higher valuation of that good. Bargaining between the debtor and the first creditor in case a third party comes up who tries to move the debtor to breach the initial contract, is facilitated by norms of fairness, suggesting how the gain of a breach should be divided between debtor and first creditor.

3.3   The European Context: Arguments for Uniformity

Behavioural law and economics does not provide a clear-cut case against a uniform European Contract Law. On the contrary, at first sight some of its observations seem to point into the direction of centralized lawmaking.

---

[25] See Korobkin (2000) 120.

[26] Korobkin and Ulen (2000) 1137-1138.

A general point that was noted above is that consumers are more likely to suffer from all type of cognitive distortions than producers. For example, the latter have more means to do research that allows for a correct assessment of probabilities. This pleads for consumer protection and one might argue that this protection should be uniform over Europe. If different levels of protection would be allowed, a race to the bottom would occur. Producers would offer cheap products in jurisdictions with minimal protection, making use of the limited capacity of consumers in judging about the dangers of defective products.

A related argument for central lawmaking – and therefore a uniform European Contract Law – is that it allows for economies of scale in doing the research needed for curing the behavioural distortions. If indeed individuals succumb to distortions that are to be discovered in scientific experiments, it is better to assign one lawmaker to the task of developing law that takes the findings of science into account, rather than letting 25 legislators invent the wheel. This is the same argument as was made in the context of traditional law and economics, where it was stated that centralized lawmaking allows for thorough research for the efficient rules. It is only a bit stronger since the information required is more extensive, and therefore the analysis needed to develop an efficient contract law becomes more complicated.

3.4 The European Context: Arguments for Diversity

In spite of what is stated in paragraph 3.3, arguments for a uniform European Contact Law seem to be outweighed by the arguments for diversity. To state it more precisely: insights from behavioural law and economics further the cause of bottom-up formation of law, rather than a top-down approach. Those bottom-up processes might lead to harmonization of law, but there is certainly no guarantee that they will do so.

A first point concerns the diversity of preferences among citizens. In itself the existence of a diversity of preferences is not a typical behavioural law and economics argument. The important issue is that of knowledge about those preferences. Generally it is extremely hard to obtain information about international differences in preferences at a central level. National legislators – or in apt cases local lawmakers – are in a better position to observe differences in preferences and to design laws that are in accordance with those preferences.

However, in a behavioural law and economics perspective the diversity of preferences argument becomes even stronger. Individual preferences are no longer regarded as given,[27] but as a cultural phenomenon. All types of cultural differences are recognized to shape differences in preferences.

---

[27] See Stigler and Becker (1977) as the classical treatment of the economic assumption of stable preferences.

A second argument for diversity is that the endowment effect or status quo bias in itself yields an argument against change, in particular against an imposed change. Given the existing diversity among the contract laws of the countries of the European Union, the emergence of a uniform contract law would require many legal provisions in many countries to change. If indeed individuals have a preference for the status quo, and if indeed this status quo is not uniform over legal systems, this argument pleads against change and therefore against a uniform European Contract Law.

A third point derived from law and economics is that legislators, who are equally human, suffer from cognitive distortions as well. This undermines the argument that centralized lawmaking is likely to filter out the typical heuristics and biases in human decision-making. In some respects the problems that legislators face if it comes to adjusting wrong judgments may even be more severe than those of consumers. The relevant issue is how much both categories are likely to profit from learning effects.

Generally, people may be confronted with negative consequences of particular cognitive distortions, and therefore be induced to avoid the same errors in the future. Learning effects may be even more important than is suggested in the behavioural law and economics literature. The explanation is that learning effects are more likely to occur in the real world than in a laboratory experiment.[28] It takes time to learn, and time is usually lacking in experiments under laboratory conditions. Moreover, in real life the stakes are usually higher, increasing the incentives to learn from one's mistakes. A McDonalds enthusiast who is made to believe that Big Macs will make him lose weight, will learn over time that the contrary is true. The limited effect of sources of cognitive error on a mass of people able to learn over time and able to learn from each other, could be labelled the Marley-principle: 'You can fool some people some times, but you can't fool all the people all the time'.[29]

Legislators do not have the same opportunities to engage in learning processes as (market) parties. Although laws can be adjusted or repealed, they are normally not made with the intention of being a tool in a process of trial and error. In particular, a European Civil Code is meant to persist for a long time.

A process of trial and error is more likely to occur in judge made law or in customary law. In judge made law the point is that faulty judicial decisions are more likely to be put through a new trial.[30] Merchants whose relations are governed by poor customs are relatively likely to be forced out of business.[31]

If provisions of a European Civil Code would be the result of a long evolutionary development toward an efficient rule, learning effects could play a

---

[28] See Arlen (1998) 1769.

[29] See (or rather hear) Bob Marley and The Wailers (1973).

[30] This mechanism is analyzed in Priest (1977).

[31] See Benson (1989).

beneficial role. This is, however, unlikely to be the case if such a Civil Code is imposed from above rather than the result of a codification of a spontaneously emerging law. As noted, learning processes inevitably play a role in the bottom-up lawmaking that is typical for customary law and a 'client-driven' judge made law. Due to learning effects it is unlikely that competition among legal systems will result in a race to the bottom of consumer protection.[32] Consumers who are fooled are likely to find out and to opt for better protection in the future.

A fourth point pleading for diversity is that norms of fairness, and social norms in general, are not universal, not even over Europe. If the importance of those norms is stressed, as behavioural law and economics does in downplaying the importance of rational choice, the arguments against uniformity are strengthened.

An illuminating example concerning norms of fairness is the *laesio enormis*. This figure has developed in Roman Catholic, but not in protestant countries.[33] The requirement of a fair relationship between performance and counterperformance is limiting the freedom of contract. Thomas Aquinas was among the fathers of the Christian doctrine that a just price (*iustum pretium*) should be paid in exchange for what one would get. Although the voidableness of a contract on the basis of *laesio enormis* found its way to the civil codes through natural lawyers, it is no coincidence that it was picked up by the French and the Austrian Civil Codes.

A fifth point is that the susceptibility to cognitive distortions is not as universal as is claimed in some of the literature. Differences may exist over people, and differences may exist over countries. Actually, this is a finding that inevitably follows from many empirical studies. Whenever an experiment is conducted, it turns out to be the case that a certain percentage of the participants succumb to a cognitive error, but also that a certain percentage does not. A consequence is that some individuals need more protection than others, so that diversity is more likely to result in an optimal satisfaction of preferences than uniformity.

In particular, the evaluation of risk is heavily biased by culture. Of old, risks in society were not regarded as the results of random processes but rather as a manifestation of a divine will.[34] A lasting consequence is that members of particular religious groups – for example orthodox-protestants in some areas in the Netherlands – are reluctant to enter into insurance contracts. Again, this observation pleads for diversity.

The conclusion of this paragraph can be clear. Behavioural law and economics yields more arguments for diversity than for uniformity. This does not completely undermine the argument from traditional law and economics that

---

[32] A corresponding but more elaborate analysis of the race to the bottom argument can be found in Smits (2002) 64-66.

[33] Zweigert and Kötz (1998) 329.

[34] See Bernstein (1996).

for a particular legal issue a particular efficient legal rule might be determined. It is, however, unlikely that this rule will be enacted as the result of a centralized process of lawmaking. If a uniform and efficient legal rule will emerge, this will happen through a spontaneous process of learning.

4 How Facts might Support the Logic

As I stated in paragraph 1, traditional and behavioural law and economics may well be able to support each other. More specifically, behavioural law and economics may be useful in adding empirical flesh to the bones of traditional law and economics' models. On the other hand, the simplicity of the traditional models makes them useful as a starting point for analysis. They yield clear ideas, which logic can be proven. In this paragraph I will investigate whether indeed law and economics can gain from its behavioural counterpart.

4.1 Better Prediction?

For several reasons adding elements derived from empirical studies data might make sense. Among those reasons, Cass Sunstein's argument that behavioural law and economics allows for better prediction seems to be the least convincing. Although Friedman's point that assumptions must be unrealistic in order to have sufficient generality was taking his argument to the extreme, it is true that a lower degree of generalization might lead to less predictive determinacy. The more elements are added to the assumptions of a theory, the less it is a tool for prediction and the more it becomes a description. Of course, this statement could be rebutted by proof that the predictions of behavioural law and economics also hold outside the laboratory and at the level of hypotheses tested in the world of experience. However, behavioural law and economics research of this type seems to be very limited.

4.2 Better Understanding?

The arguments for a behavioural law and economics are, however, not depleted if doubt is cast on its predictive power. In criticizing Milton Friedman's positive methodology, Ronald Coase argued that even if predictions on the basis of unrealistic assumptions are correct, a theory based upon them might fail in providing insight in the working of the legal system.[35] This is not so much of a problem if one is only interested in prediction and the use of unrealistic assumptions indeed is not an obstacle – or even useful – for forecasting the effects of legal rules. If, however, the goal is explanation, an approach based

---

[35] See Coase (1994a).

on unrealistic assumptions is not really helpful in providing insight in what really moves a person and in how legal rules really have effects.

In another essay, Coase referred to Adam Smith, who is best known for his *The Wealth of Nations*, but whose earlier work the *Theory of Moral Sentiments* might be regarded as behavioural law and economics *avant la lettre*.[36] If the complicated theory on human motivation as developed in *Theory of Moral Sentiments* is used as the starting point of an economic analysis the conclusions of *The Wealth of Nations* still hold, but are made more plausible. The same is likely to hold for modern behavioural law and economics. A result that is derived from an understandable picture of real man, or of course woman,[37] is more likely to be understood than the outcome of an analysis in which the otherworldly economic man was the input.

4.3   More Acceptability?

Plausibility of a theory might well contribute to its acceptability and in this respect it is likely that adding the behavioural to law and economics eases some of the annoyances that traditional law and economics provokes in many lawyers. These annoyances typically exist as to the simplicity of economics' behavioural assumptions, the imperialism of economics, and economics' lack of recognition of cultural differences. The first issue has already been treated above, and I will now discuss the other two points in turn.

The uneasy feeling of economic imperialism is likely to diminish if insights from other sciences are incorporated, as behavioural law and economics does. By adding elements from psychology and sociology, economics becomes less remote from the lawyers' intuition about the social sciences being relevant for the understanding of society.

Next, I will say a few words on the allegation that traditional law and economics does not recognize the importance of cultural differences. Indeed it is true that traditional law and economics neglects the cultural differences that shape differences in preferences and social norms. One should, however, be aware that the most important differences as to the understanding of the law of different countries are not those in psychological or sociological aspects, but those that relate to differences in legal institutions. Admittedly, law and economics scholars overlooked foreign alternatives in attempting to rationalize Common Law peculiarities like consideration,[38] or when downplaying the importance of good faith. Remarkably, the issue seems to be that traditional law and economics scholars often showed an unconscious stickiness to their

---

[36]   See Coase (1994b).

[37]   Compare West (1988).

[38]   See Cooter and Ulen (1997) 163.

own legal culture, attempting to find economic justifications of idiosyncrasies instead of making an objective analysis. There is definitely no reason why the framework of traditional law and economics could not be applied to Civil Law.[39] Acceptability seems to be furthered most by an objective analysis of legal institutions as they are.

4.4   Two Sides of a Coin?

I started this paper with opposing behavioural law and economics to the mathematical model-based approach that is common in law and economics. However, there is more to traditional law and economics than math and models. It holds as a general rule that the more an author is striving for a policy-relevant law and economics, the less likely he is to stick to mathematics, and the more likely he is to enrich his theory with empirical findings. Seen in this light the development of behavioural law and economics is not so much a revolution, but rather a next step in a separation that already had emerged in law and economics.

On the one hand, there is law and economics for economists. This field is increasingly focused on mathematical models and less on their meaning for concrete legal issues. The European Association of Law and Economics (EALE) clearly has chosen this direction, witness the papers presented at their conferences in recent years.

On the other hand, there is law and economics for lawyers. Rather than aiming for mathematical sophistication its practitioners look for elements that contribute to the ongoing debates in legal circles. In debating the desirability of a uniform European private law, traditional law and economics scholars have indeed taken a non-mathematical approach, indeed recognizing differences in preferences and national situations. In line with the statements made in paragraph 3.4, this approach resulted in a number of arguments against a forced harmonization of European private law. [40]

Obviously, behavioural law and economics is more in line with this law and economics for lawyers, than with law and economics for economists. An important point is that transaction costs and information costs have found their way into economic analysis of law. A problem in traditional law and economics is that the concept of transaction costs is still left somewhat open. A specific problem for the mathematical approach is that transaction costs are hard to put into a tractable mathematical model. In this respect behavioural law and economics of course cannot do much, but it is quite helpful in specifying those transaction costs in the context of a non-mathematical theory.

---

[39] Compare Schäfer and Ott (2003).

[40] See Van den Bergh (1998) 132.

5 Conclusions

I started with opposing traditional law and economics and behavioural law and economics. The first is based on a kind of universal mathematical approach and provides for central-lawmaking and thus for a uniform European Contract Law. The latter stresses limits to the universality of rational behavior, inevitably focuses on differences and thereby brings in arguments for diversity and against a forced harmonization of European Contract Law.

The distinction made is not razor-sharp, but it is real and in one aspect gaining in importance. Law and economics has been picked up by economists, who seem to be more and more interested in a mathematical approach, regardless of its effects on the applicability of the economic analysis to the real problems of contract law. On the other hand, law and economics also has become a part of the lawyer's toolkit. If, as lawyers are inclined to do, empirical flesh is added to the bones of the models in order to make law and economics relevant for policy issues, the distance between this law and economics for lawyers and behavioural law and economics seems to disappear. The desirability of a uniform European Contract Law is such a policy issue. Traditional law and economics provides a framework that gives an excellent starting point for analysis, while behavioural law and economics is able to specify issues of transaction costs, such as cognitive distortions.

The arguments against forced harmonization of European Contract Law that result from a behavioural law and economics approach are that diversity of preferences of citizens pleads for decentralized lawmaking, that the endowment effect is a bias against change of the present situation that is a variety of contract laws, that cognitive distortions of legislators make other sources of law more attractive, that differences in social norms and in norms of fairness exist and that susceptibility to cognitive distortions is not universal and therefore does not require a universal approach.

The case against forced unification is not necessarily one against spontaneous harmonization. In case norms of contracts law exist that are efficient everywhere, bottom-up processes of lawmaking might yield those norms. If parties have the opportunity to litigate they are more likely to do so in the case of inefficient norms. Efficient customs are more likely to survive than inefficient alternatives. Where spontaneous evolution fails, for example due to high information costs, inefficient precedents that only can be changed gradually, or important institutional differences, a legal formants approach can help. Traditional law and economics can provide ideas about those formants, that is to say legal propositions that affect the solution of a legal problem.[41] The logic of traditional law and economics might be helpful, in particular in an international context in which the traditional appeal to – national – authorities is often not

---

[41] See Mattei (1997).

convincing. But the understandability and acceptability of law and economics will gain from a behavioural approach. It provides the facts that turn economic man into a real human being.

REFERENCES

ARLEN (1998)
J. Arlen, "Comment: The Future of Behavioral Economic Analysis of Law", 51 *Vanderbilt Law Review* (1998) 1765-1788

BENSON (1989)
B.L. Benson, "The Spontaneous Evolution of Commercial Law", 55 *Southern Economic Journal* (1989) 644-661

VAN DEN BERGH (1998)
R.J. Van den Bergh, "Subsidiarity as an Economic Demarcation Principle and the Emergence of European Private Law", 5 *Maastricht Journal of European and Comparative Law* (1998) 129-152

BERNSTEIN (1996)
P.L. Bernstein, *Against the Gods. The Remarkable Story of Risk* (New York: John Wiley 1996)

COASE (1994A)
R.H. Coase, "How Should Economists Choose?", in: *Essays on Economics and Economists* (Chicago and London: University of Chicago Press 1994) 15-33

COASE (1994B)
R.H. Coase, "Adam Smith's View of Man", in: *Essays on Economics and Economists* (Chicago and London: University of Chicago Press 1994) 95-116

CONFERENCE PROCEEDINGS (1998)
Conference Proceedings, "Social Norms, Social Meaning, and the Economic Analysis of Law", 27 *Journal of Legal Studies* (1998) 2

COOTER AND ULEN (1997)
R. Cooter and T. Ulen, *Law and Economics*, 2nd ed. (Reading Mass.: Addison Wesley 1997)

CURRAN (2000)
C. Curran, "The Endowment Effect", in: B. Bouckaert and G. De Geest (eds.), *Encyclopedia of Law and Economics. Volume I: The History and Methodology of Law and Economics* (Cheltenham and Northampton (Mass.): Edward Elgar 2000) 819-835

EISENBERG (1995)
M.A. Eisenberg, "The Limits of Cognition and the Limits of Contract", 47 *Stanford Law Review* (1995) 211-259

ELLICKSON (1991)
R.C. Ellickson, *Order without Law: How Neighbors Settle Disputes* (Cambridge (Mass.) and London: Harvard University Press 1991)

ELSTER (1989)
J. Elster, *Nuts and Bolts for the Social Sciences* (Cambridge: Cambridge University Press 1989)

FRIEDMAN (1953)

M. Friedman, "The Methodology of Positive Economics", in: *Essays in Positive Economics* (Chicago and London: Chicago University Press 1953) 3-43

HANSON AND KYSAR (1999)

J.D. Hanson and D.A. Kysar, "Taking Behavioralism Seriously: The Problem of Market Manipulation", 74 *New York University Law Review* (1999) 630-749

HOFFMAN, McCABE AND SMITH (1998)

E. Hoffman, K. McCabe and V.L. Smith, "Experimental Law and Economics", in: P. Newman (ed.), *The New Palgrave Dictionary of Economics and the Law*, Volume 2 (London and Basingstoke: Macmillan 1998) 116-123

HOLZHAUER AND TEIJL (1995)

R.W. Holzhauer and R. Teijl, *Inleiding rechtseconomie*, 2nd ed. (Arnhem: Gouda Quint 1995)

JOLLS, SUNSTEIN AND THALER (2000)

C. Jolls, C. Sunstein and R. Thaler, "A Behavioral Approach to Law and Economics", in: C. Sunstein (ed.), *Behavioral Law and Economics* (Cambridge: Cambridge University Press 2000) 116-143

KAHNEMANN AND TVERSKY (1972)

D. Kahneman and A. Tversky, "Subjective probability: A Judgment of Representativeness", 3 *Cognitive Psychology* (1972) 430-454

KAHNEMANN AND TVERSKY (1973)

D. Kahneman and A. Tversky, "On the Psychology of Prediction", 80 *Psychological Review* (1973) 237-251

KOROBKIN (2000)

R. Korobkin, "Behavioral Economics, Contract Formation, and Contract Law", in: C. Sunstein (ed.), *Behavioral Law and Economics* (Cambridge: Cambridge University Press 2000) 116-143

KOROBKIN AND ULEN (2000)

R.B. Korobkin and T.S. Ulen, "Law and Behavioral Science: Removing the rationality assumption from law and economics", 88 *California Law Review* (2000) 1051-1144

BOB MARLEY AND THE WAILERS (1973)

Bob Marley and The Wailers, *Get up, Stand up* (London: Island Records 1973)

MATTEI (1997)

U. Mattei, *Comparative law and Economics* (Ann Arbor: University of Michigan Press 1997)

POSNER (2000)

E.A. Posner, *Law and Social Norms* (Cambridge (Mass.) and London: Harvard University Press 2000)

POSNER (2003)

E.A. Posner, "Economic Analysis of Contract Law After Three Decades: Success or Failure?", 112 *Yale Law Journal* (2003) 829-880

POSNER (1998)

R.A. Posner, *Economic Analysis of Law*, 5th ed. (New York: Aspen 1998)

PRIEST (1977)

G.L. Priest, "The Common Law Process and the Selection of Efficient Rules", 6 *Journal of Legal Studies* (1977) 65-82

SCHÄFER AND OTT (2003)

H.-B. Schäfer and C. Ott, *Economic Analysis of Civil Law* (Cheltenham and Northampton (Mass.): Edward Elgar 2003)

SHAVELL (1980)

S. Shavell, "Damage Measures for Breach of Contract", 11 *Bell Journal of Economics* (1980) 466-490

SHAVELL (1987)

S. Shavell, "Economic Analysis of Accident Law" (Cambridge (Mass.) and London: Harvard University Press 1987)

SHAVELL (2003)

S. Shavell, *Economic Analysis of Contract Law* (Harvard John M. Olin Discussion Paper Series No. 403, 02/2003)

SMITS (2002)

J.M. Smits, "How to predict the differences in uniformity between different areas of a future European private law? An evolutionary approach", in: A. Marciano en J.-M. Josselin (eds.), *The Economics of Harmonizing European Law* (Cheltenham and Northampton (Mass.): Edward Elgar 2002) 50-70

STIGLER AND BECKER (1977)

G.J. Stigler and G.S. Becker, "De Gustibus Non Est Disputandum", 67 *American Economic Review* (1977) 76-90

SUNSTEIN, KAHNEMAN AND SCHKADE (1998)

C. Sunstein, D. Kahneman and D. Schkade, "Assessing Punitive Damages (With Notes on Cognition and Valuation in Law)", 107 *Yale Law Journal* (1998) 2071-2153

SUNSTEIN (2000)

C. Sunstein (ed.), *Behavioral Law and Economics* (Cambridge: Cambridge University Press 2000)

THALER (1991)

R.H. Thaler, *Quasi Rational Economics* (New York: Russell Sage Foundation 1991)

TVERSKY AND KAHNEMAN (1973)

A. Tversky and D. Kahneman, "Availability: A Heuristic for Judging Frequency and Probability", 5 *Cognitive Psychology* (1973) 207-232

TVERSKY AND KAHNEMAN (1974)

A. Tversky and D. Kahneman, "Judgment Under Uncertainty: Heuristics and Biases", 185 *Science* (1974) 1124-1131

WEST (1988)

R. West, "Economic Man and Literary Woman: One Contrast", 39 *Mercer Law Review* (1988) 867-878

ZWEIGERT AND KÖTZ (1998)

K. Zweigert and H. Kötz, *An Introduction to Comparative Law*, 3rd ed. Translated by Tony Weir (Oxford: Oxford University Press 1998)

CHAPTER 5

The Psychology of Conflict of Laws

Jeffrey J. Rachlinski

By all accounts, the United States and Europe now face the potential for a massive trade war over genetically modified organisms ('GMOs').[1] Europe seems committed to maintaining a ban on foods manufactured or grown with GMOs while the United States seems intent on producing foods made with GMOs. This conflict might reflect different values or a different commitment to technological approaches to agricultural production, but more probably, it reflects a difference in beliefs about the dangers such products might pose to human health or the environment. If so, then one of the two approaches must be correct; either GMOs represent a danger to public health that merits strict regulation, or any danger GMOs pose little threat and should fall into widespread use. Although the looming trade war will likely be costly and pressure already strained trans-Atlantic relations, it has a hidden upside. The resolution of a trade dispute will provide a novel forum in which to addresses the substantive issue of the danger – or lack thereof – of GMOs. This is the hidden upside whenever legal regimes clash. The process of resolving conflicts between laws inspires the re-examination of substantive rules.

Substantive variations in law presents a nagging problem for sovereign entities. In the United States, if state A adopts a rule of liability for manufacturing defects in mass-produced goods and state B adopts a different rule, the two must also embrace some mechanism for determining which rule applies in any dispute. Suppose a good is manufactured in state A, but sold in State B where it causes some harm to a citizen of State B; which state's law should determine liability? In the United States, each state has developed its own conflict of laws rules to resolve these issues. The states have essentially adopted rules that weigh the relative interests each state might have in implementing its own law.[2] State B's courts might express an interest in protecting their citizens from defectively manufactured products, but it must weigh this against State A's interest in creating a particular kind of liability regime for its manufacturers.

Litigation governing choice of laws can seem particularly wasteful. After all, such litigation does little to resolve the dispute, but merely addresses what substantive rules will govern its resolution. Disputes between countries concerning their choice of law rules are no less burdensome. The international versions of conflicts of laws can be dramatically more intractable than conflicts within a single sovereign nation. Resolution of international conflict of laws can require international treaties that invoke complex and expensive dispute-resolution mechanisms. Determining which law applies can be just as expensive as applying the law once it is identified.

With every problem, however, comes an opportunity. Even though resolving differing substantive laws is expensive, the process of doing so creates the opportunity for a new forum in which to address the important business of law.

---

[1]   Wiener and Rogers (2002).

[2]   Simson (1997).

Indeed, the fora in which conflicts of laws are resolved might present a superior perspective to that of the individual sovereigns themselves. Sovereign democratic nations often have difficulty remedying irrationality and inefficiency in their own lawmaking processes. Within a single sovereign, most countries have some check on cognitive failures and inefficiency in the democratic process, but such checks have limitations.[3] In the United States, the judicial branch refuses to overturn legislation as irrational unless it interferes with some central constitutional protection.[4] Administrative bodies likewise attempt to carry out the will of the legislature, rather than try to restore rationality to irrational statutes. These entities, of necessity perhaps, consider respect for the will of the legislature to be so central to the constitutional framework of a democracy that they resist trampling on the results of the legislative process, even when the results are transparently misguided. Remedying the irrational product of the democratic process might well require a novel perspective. A court attempting to apply conflict of laws rules or a global body attempting to reconcile inconsistent substantive laws might well provide that needed perspective.

This paper assesses the claim that mechanisms to resolve conflict of laws inherently present the opportunity for reducing irrationality in legal regimes. The paper begins with an assessment of the causes of irrational laws and then ends with an assessment of how the conflict of laws paradigm might avoid irrationality.

I Cognitive Limitations in the Democratic Process

By its nature, human judgment and decision making produces flawed choices. People rely on simple mental processes, or heuristics, to make decisions.[5] Heuristics are useful, but can lead people to make erroneous choices. Reliance on heuristics influences the creation and development of law in two ways: first, widespread reliance on misleading heuristics by the general public can direct the public's attention towards particular problems, thereby influencing the demand for law; and second, legislators, judges, and bureaucrats might misunderstand social problems and choices because of a reliance on misleading heuristics.[6]

---

[3] Rachlinski and Farina (2002).

[4] Ely (1980).

[5] Tversky and Kahneman (1974).

[6] Rachlinski (2004).

A Demand for Law and Regulation

In a democratic system, it should not be surprising that the demand for legislative action reflects how people think about social problems. The cognitive processes that guide how people think produces the public-policy preferences that shape the political process. Because many social problems are vastly complicated and most citizens have limited time and interest in their resolution, people's political preferences are apt to be heavily influenced by simple heuristics.[7] Simple heuristics might influence choice in the voting booth, decisions on campaign contributions, and lobbying efforts, all of which puts pressure on legislatures. Although people doubtless adopt a variety of mental shortcuts when evaluating social and political issues, legal scholars have clearly identified the role of three potentially misleading cognitive processes in the democratic process: availability, the representativeness heuristic, and framing effects.

1 Availability and Public Policy

'Availability' refers to the tendency for individuals to assess the frequency of events by the ease with which they can recall exemplars.[8] For example, many people express the belief that the English language contains more words that begin with the letter 'k' than have the letter 'k' in the third position. This belief is false – by quite a bit, in fact; there are nine times as many words with 'k' in the third position. But words that begin with 'k' are easier to call to mind than words with 'k' in the third position. Hence, people are relying on ease of recall as a cue to frequency. In general, this cue is a sensible one. The easier it is to recall an example of an event, the more common that event is apt to be. At the same time, application of the heuristic can produce errors in judgment.

The availability heuristic arguably plays a central role in modern political life.[9] Vivid, salient issues that make memorable impressions will seem like more significant problems to most people. Consequently, they will tend to command greater public attention and have a disproportionate impact on public opinion than more pallid concerns.

Public perception that a crisis exists commonly drives legislative and regulatory responses, even when evidence of a crisis is uncertain and even when the responses are of questionable benefits.[10] For example, the perception that jury verdicts are out of control in the Unites States arises largely from widespread

---

[7] Sunstein (2000).

[8] Tversky and Kahneman (1974).

[9] Kuran and Sunstein (1999).

[10] Kuran and Sunstein (1999).

reports of exorbitant jury awards. The case in which an elderly woman won a $4 million award for a burn she sustained after spilling hot McDonalds' coffee on herself has achieved almost legendary status for proponents of tort reform.[11] Doctors and legislators also frequently cite exorbitant awards as causing increases in insurance premiums. Public opinion on this issue, however, seems unaffected by the underlying facts and statistics. Studies of the tort system in general show that extremely high awards are rare exceptions from the sobering mass of sane and sensible jury verdicts.[12] Studies of medical malpractice litigation rates show no trends or increases that explain spikes in insurance rates; rather.[13] Even the facts in the McDonalds case are misleading–the plaintiff ultimately settled for a mere $40,000.[14] The vivid, cognitively available stories, however, create a misleading impression.

The impact of the availability heuristic on public policy might have a particularly troublesome impact on the regulation of health and safety. In many cases, the public's concerns fail to reflect hard evidence of an underlying problem and instead track vivid news accounts.[15] For example, in environmental policy, experts commonly decry the public's fleeting concern with 'the chemical of the month.'[16] News stories can create a widespread perception that a toxin or chemical is dangerous, even when such stories are later disproved.[17] Anecdotal accounts of supposedly dangerous chemicals can create a 'phantom risk' that then guides both public opinion and, in turn, legislative and regulatory policies designed to curb these ostensible risks.[18] Cognitive availability is also fleeting. Even in instances in which the salience of a health or safety risk reflects a serious underlying hazard, the public's attention might drift off the topic long before social institutions can craft and adopt a coherent regulatory response.

To be sure, cognitive availability can play a constructive role by directing public attention to otherwise underappreciated problems. The availability heuristic can also create legislative pressures that overcome the power of entrenched interest groups and a stubbornly slow legislative process. For example, although the United States Congress had considered adopting legislation to address the problem of abandoned hazardous-waste dumps for many years, it took the publicity of the events at Love Canal, New York, before Congress finally acted.[19] At Love Canal, a school and a residential neighborhood had been

---

[11] Eisenberg (2001).

[12] Eisenberg (2001).

[13] Saks (1986).

[14] Eisenberg (2001).

[15] Slovic, Fischhoff and Lichtenstein (1982).

[16] Shapiro and McGarity (1989).

[17] Kuran and Sunstein (1999).

[18] Foster, Bernstein and Huber (1993).

[19] Kuran and Sunstein (1999).

constructed on an abandoned waste-disposal site containing a huge volume of hazardous chemicals. Dramatic media coverage of the events, including an 'evacuation' of pregnant women and children, and photographs of rusted barrels surfacing in a school playground, finally made a legislative response to the problem irresistible.

Widespread reliance on the availability heuristic, however, means that public opinion is subject to easy manipulation. Interest groups might act as 'availability entrepreneurs', working to make certain anecdotes salient.[20] Availability entrepreneurs try to make news events salient so as to mobilize public opinion in favor of legislation that furthers their own ends. Also, the public pressure that availability creates can get coopted by well-heeled lobbyists serving special interests, rather than the general public. For example, public concern over the great stock market crash of October 1929 ultimately produced legislative reforms of the securities markets that had nothing to do with the underlying causes of the crash.[21] The financial industry used the public's demand for reform to facilitate the passage of legislation that served their own interests. Cognitive availability is thus a troublesome influence on the legislative process in a democratic society.

2   Representativeness and Statistical Fallacies Affecting Public Opinion

Representativeness refers to the tendency to judge the likelihood that an event is a member of a broad category based on the similarity between that event and a canonical member of that category.[22] In effect, the heuristic reflects the tendency to believe that if something looks like a duck, walks like a duck, and quacks like a duck, then it's a duck. The heuristic is obviously useful, but it can mask other factors that might influence the likelihood that the exemplar is actually a member of the broader category. Widespread reliance on the representativeness heuristic to evaluate environmental hazards can misdirect legislative and regulatory efforts. For many people, an activity is risky if it sounds risky, regardless of the likelihood with which the activity might occur, which is reliance on the representativeness heuristic.[23] Although this heuristic probably works well to identify many actual problems, it can lead people to demand far stricter regulation of some activities than the actual degree of threat warrants.

For example, excessive opposition to novel technologies might arise from the tendency for new technologies to sound intimidating and dangerous. The

---

[20] Kuran and Sunstein (1999).

[21] Macey (2002).

[22] Kahneman and Tversky (1972).

[23] Slovic, Fischhoff and Lichtenstein (1982).

regulation of nuclear power plants in the United States provides one example of this phenomenon.[24] Nuclear power plants in the United States have caused far fewer environmental problems than their principle alternative – coal-fired power plants. Most people find the risks that nuclear power poses, however, to be far more frightening than the air pollution that coal creates. Consequently, the regulatory environment for nuclear power is such that no new plants have been constructed in the United States for 25 years, even as scores of new coal-fired plants have been constructed.

To be sure, the cognitive account of American demand for heavy regulation of nuclear power fails to explain why Western Europe and Japan have embraced nuclear power. Although the answer to this puzzle is unclear, Europe is not without cognitively motivated aversions to new technologies. Currently, most European countries ban the sale of foods made from GMOs. Like nuclear power in the United States, this regulatory regime occurs despite an absence of hard evidence of adverse effects and despite a comparative lack of regulation of more dangerous substitutes. In this case, the production of some kinds of GMOs have allowed farms to reduce the use of pesticides that are known carcinogens.[25] Although the product is different, the reasoning process is similar. Novel technologies that sound dangerous lead people to neglect the potential benefit and demand a rigid regulatory structure that effectively bans the product.

Like the availability heuristic, the representativeness heuristic directs attention to particular social problems, as well as leading people to support particular regulatory solutions. Activities that sound more dangerous produce a 'zero-risk' mentality.[26] People view the reduction of the likelihood that certain adverse events will occur from 10% to 0% as more significant than a reduction in risk from 50% to 40%.[27] This reaction produces demand for laws that completely eliminate risk, and disfavors demand for laws that produce a measured response.[28] Several examples of such laws haunt the system of environmental regulation:

- the Federal 'Superfund' program requires polluters to removes substantially all hazardous substances from leaking abandoned hazardous waste disposal facilities, regardless of the degree of risk these chemicals might pose.[29] Similarly, laws governing the management of hazardous waste disposal facilities mandate that no amount of any waste deemed hazardous migrate from the facility – regardless of the amount or likelihood that anyone will ever come into contact with the waste.
- the Delaney Clause of the Food, Drug and Cosmetics Act forbids food

---

[24] Slovic, Flynn and Layman (2000).

[25] Sunstein (2003).

[26] Breyer (1993).

[27] Tversky and Fox (1995).

[28] Sunstein (2002).

producers to add any amount of any substance that has been shown to
cause cancer in humans or animals. Before it was repealed in 1995, this
statute forced food manufacturers to avoid risks that were as small as the
equivalent of a lifetime of eating 'one peanut . . . once every 250 days.'
Public Citizen v. *Young*, 831 F.2d 1108 (D.C. Cir. 1987).
- the Federal Clean Air Act mandates the implementation of regulations
  designed to ensure that air pollution has no 'adverse effect on human
  health', regardless of the cost of achieving this goal. Similarly, the Federal
  Water Pollution Control Act completely bans the addition of any pollutant
  to the waterways of the United States. Although in both cases, exceptions
  and implementing regulations soften the effects of these absolutist statutes, on their face, they demand zero risk.[30]

The representativeness heuristic cannot take full credit for these 'zero tolerance'
regulations. Other cognitive processes play a role as well.[31] Reliance on the representativeness heuristics lies at the heart of the problems in the context of public
debate, however. The hazards that people find most frightening, and insist upon
eliminating, all seem to share similar properties. They involve unfamiliar, novel
technology, involuntary risk, and harm on a potentially catastrophic scale. The
public apparently tolerates inflation and unemployment rates greater than zero,
but insists upon zero risk from toxins that sound life-threatening. Representativeness focuses public attention and, hence, legislative action on eliminating
risks at all cost. This might explain why environmental law seems particularly
plagued by zero-risk statutes.

3   Framing and Public Policy

The character of public choices as involving gains or losses
also influences legislative choice. Psychologists have noted that people treat
decisions characterized as involving an improvement, or gain, from the status
quo differently from decisions involving a deterioration, or loss, from the status
quo.[32] People treat any departure form the status quo as more significant than a
risk-neutral calculation would suggest. Additionally, people treat losses as if they
are more significant than gains of comparable magnitude. Individuals or corporations affected by legislative decisions treat would thus treat lost opportunities
as less costly than incurred losses. Consequently, they can be expected to fight
harder against legislation that imposes losses on them than in favor of legislation that would provide benefits.

---

[29] Salzman and Thompson (2003).

[30] Salzman and Thompson (2003).

[31] Sunstein (2000).

[32] Kahneman and Tversky (1979).

Perhaps no other aspect of public decision making illustrates the role of framing in legislation more than revenue policies.[33] The remarkable sensitivity of taxpayers to gains and losses can be seen most clearly in data on taxpayer compliance. Each year, as individual taxpayers file their returns, they confront an opportunity to cheat by understating their revenue or exaggeration their allowable deductions or tax credits. Some taxpayers who have overpaid during the year incur gains if they cheat, while taxpayers who have underpaid during the year avoid losses if they cheat. Although cheating has the same effect on the amount of annual taxes one pays, most individuals who cheat are doing so to reduce the losses they incur upon filing.[34]

The same bias favoring the status quo also influences voters' assessment of tax policy.[35] The bias can make it difficult for the government to increase its revenue stream to accommodate new projects and new mandates. Often, the only way that the government can increase revenue is through a refusal to update the tax code to reflect inflation. In an inflationary economy, unless the government raises the tax bracket cutoffs to match increases in wages and prices, the actual tax rate will rise. Caps and phase-outs on deductions for wealthier taxpayers designed to create a progressive rate structure will also impose hidden tax increases if not adjusted for inflation. Although this result might seem like a happy compromise, it can hardly be said to constitute an ordered debate over public finance. Changes in public revenue end up determined more by the interaction of inflation with quirks in the tax code than by informed legislative discussion over the appropriate size of government programs.

Numerous laws outside of the tax code evidence an unwillingness to impose new costs on existing individuals and corporations. In the 1970's, as Congress began passing tough environmental regulations requiring compliance with strict new pollution permits, it simultaneously exempted existing polluters from such regimes.[36] For example, those who would build new electric-generating facilities must incorporate the most stringent pollution-control technologies available, while little is required of existing plants. Similarly, even as new pesticide regulations simultaneously imposed careful restrictions on the sale of new forms of pesticides, the same regulations made it nearly impossible for regulators to ban the sale of pesticides already in use. The aversion to losses among polluters might have made such compromises an essential part of modern environmental law, but these compromises have had the effect of 'freezing' technology in place and placing new pollution-saving innovations at an extreme competitive disadvantage against existing technologies.[37]

---

[33] McCaffery (1991)

[34] Robbenn et al. (1990).

[35] McCaffery (1994).

[36] Salzman and Thompson (2003).

[37] Salzman and Thompson (2003).

B   Biases among Public Officials

Erroneous judgment is not exclusive to the general public. Legislators and bureaucrats might also rely on misleading heuristics, which might also produce undesirable legal rules.

1   Biases among Legislators

Legislators face a cognitively difficult job that almost certainly forces them to rely on mental shortcuts. Legislators must determine positions on hundreds of pieces of legislation each year, each of which might address issues of staggering complexity. The annual federal budget in the United States alone requires thirteen separate appropriations requests, each thousands of pages long. At the same time, legislators must balance the desires of a bewildering diversity of demands from their constituents, voters, and contributors.

Although little evidence on the decision making processes of legislators exists, the demands on their time ensure that they will adopt some kinds of shortcuts that might lead them astray. Availability might play a particularly significant role in legislators' decision making. Legislators become painfully aware of mistakes that cost their predecessors their jobs. In Chicago, for example, an ill-timed, pre-election snowstorm in 1978 cost the mayor his position, because impatient voters felt the city took too long to clear the streets.[38] To this day, Chicago's elected leaders spend the City's limited resources disproportionately on snow-removal equipment.[39] Similarly, as they approached the 2004 election, leading Republicans were haunted by fears that a military action will cause the public to believe that the President lacked interest in the American economy, just as occurred in 1992. This perception encouraged Republicans to proceed with large tax cuts to convey the impression that they were addressing economic sluggishness.

Legislators might also misconstrue or overstate biases among the general public. It might be that legislators possess exaggerated concern for the public's attachment to the status quo or its demand for regulation of the chemical of the month.[40] Lawmakers might assume that voters are more simplistic than is the case and simply avoid addressing so-called 'third rail' issues such as entitlement programs. Legislators might rely on polls or focus groups to identify the public's beliefs and concerns. These can be inaccurate barometers of public opinion, however. Focus groups produce results based on extremely small samples, and polls produce results that can be extremely sensitive to the form of the question or to recent events. In a kind of 'base-rate neglect,' legislators might fail to

---

[38]   Byrne (1979).

[39]   McGraw and Montemurri (1999).

[40]   Rachlinski (2003).

appreciate that they should discount the results of surveys and focus groups as somewhat unreliable. This process thereby magnifies the impact of transient or erroneous attitudes among the public on legislative policy.

2 Biases among Bureaucrats

Bureaucrats working in administrative agencies have an easier cognitive mission than legislators. They can focus their attention on a single aspect of the law and tend to be experts in their field. Delegating public decisions to expert bureaucratic bodies, however, will not avoid erroneous judgment. Experts sometimes rely on the same kinds of cognitive processes that produce errors in lay persons.[41] At the same time, they often develop ways of avoiding the common pitfalls that plague novices. Little research has been done on the decision-making processes of regulatory experts in government, and so conclusions about the quality of such decisions are somewhat speculative. Given the available data on expert decision making, however, a few good guesses about the likely errors bureaucrats make can be identified.

First, experts tend to be overconfident in their judgment.[42] Experts in government might, therefore, be expected to underestimate the likelihood that their predictions are wrong. This could, in turn, lead them to fail to incorporate adequate margins of safety into their predictions. Many health, safety, and environmental statutes require experts to build caution into their predictions; overconfidence might undermine this process. For example, the Clean Air Act directs the Environmental Protection Agency ('EPA') to protect the public health with an 'adequate margin of safety.'[43] To fulfill this mandate, the EPA must estimate the harms that ambient levels of air pollutants might cause as well as identify the functional equivalent of a confidence interval around this estimate, so as to ensure that most people are not adversely affected by air pollution. The literature on overconfidence predicts that the EPA's point estimate will be reasonably unbiased, but that its confidence interval will be too narrow.[44] In other contexts, agencies must estimate a likely outcome over time and then assess their confidence in this estimate so as to facilitate planning. For example, several agencies that provide estimates of the likely solvency of governmental benefits programs typically provide estimates of how long current conditions will persist. These estimates depend heavily on confidence in the outcome, and hence might be unreliable.

Second, expertise can create myopia.[45] All disciplines adopt their own goals that focuses attention on some aspects of a problem at the expense of others.

---

[41] Camerer and Johnson (1991).

[42] Griffin and Tversky (1992).

[43] Salzman and Thompson (2003).

[44] Koehler, Brenner and Griffin (2002).

[45] Camerer and Johnson (1991).

For example, doctors rarely worry about a patient's financial condition, and accountants spend little energy determining their client's health. Government bureaucrats are thought to suffer from similar problems. Developing an expertise sometimes can dictate the types of solutions that bureaucrats adopt, limiting the kinds of solutions federal agencies might pursue.[46] The Army Corps of Engineers, which consists largely of civil engineers, might support solutions to problems such as flooding that rely on civil engineering rather than better zoning or flood insurance programs. The Department of Defense might emphasize military solutions to complex problems like terrorism, that might be better served with intelligence and foreign aid. Engineers in the EPA might support technological fixes to pollution when better economic incentives might reduce pollution more effectively. Similarly, the State Department worries about 'clientism', which refers to the tendency of career employees assigned to particular countries to believe that their assigned country should lie more closely at the center of American foreign policy than it does.[47]

Recent scholarship has also documented another manifestation of regulatory myopia. Just as individual juries fail to see the case before them in a broader context, so too might regulators.[48] Agencies that set civil and criminal penalties for violations of the regulations that they enforce might create penalty schedules that fail to match the violations well. For example, the Fish and Wildlife Service probably views a deliberate, illegal killing of a grizzly bear as a more serious crime than might the public at large. For the Fish and Wildlife Service, such an act would be among the most serious crimes within its jurisdiction. While most people would likely view the act as less serious than a minor violation of food-safety regulations that leads to severe illness among a few consumers, the Food and Drug Administration might view the food-safety violation as among the less serious crimes it reviews. Consequently, the deliberate killing of the bear might be penalized more heavily than the food-safety violation. In a preliminary assessment of this issue, Sunstein and his coauthors have found some indication that inter-agency myopia creates exactly these kinds of inconsistencies.[49]

3   Biases among Judges

Even though they are somewhat insulated from the political process, judges are capable of producing rules that are the products of cognitive error as well. Research on judicial decision making demonstrates that when making decisions, judges rely on many of the same kinds of mental shortcuts that lead ordinary people astray.[50] Furthermore, although the sources of legal

---

[46] Rachlinski and Farina (2002).

[47] Starr (1998).

[48] Sunstein, Schkade, Kahneman and Ritov (2002).

[49] Sunstein, Schkade, Kahneman and Ritov (2002).

[50] Guthrie, Rachlinski and Wistrich (2001).

rules are hard to track, in at least one instance, reliance on cognitive errors appears to have led directly to the production of legal rules by the courts.

The instance involves the incorporation of the 'inverse fallacy' into a legal rule. The inverse fallacy refers to the tendency to treat the probability of a hypothesis given the evidence (for example, the probability that a defendant was negligent given that a plaintiff was injured) as the same as, or close to, the probability of the evidence given the hypothesis (for example, the probability that the plaintiff would be injured if the defendant were negligent). In one demonstration of this phenomenon, medical doctors were asked to estimate the likelihood that a patient who had tested positive for a certain rare disease actually had that disease.[51] The doctors were told that the test was 90% reliable and that the prevalence of the disease in patients such as the one in the example was one in one thousand. Although the actual likelihood is quite small (less than 1%), 80% of the doctors indicated that it was more likely than not that the patient had the illness. The doctors found the 90% reliability statistic compelling, but discounted the importance of the prevalence of the disease.

To test whether judges would commit the inverse fallacy, one study[52] asked judges to assess problem based loosely on the classic English case, *Byrne* v. *Boadle*:

The plaintiff was passing by a warehouse owned by the defendant when he was struck by a barrel, resulting in severe injuries. At the time, the barrel was in the final stages of being hoisted from the ground and loaded into the warehouse. The defendant's employees are not sure how the barrel broke loose and fell, but they agree that either the barrel was negligently secured or the rope was faulty. Government safety inspectors conducted an investigation of the warehouse and determined that in this warehouse: (1) when barrels are negligently secured, there is a 90% chance that they will break loose; (2) when barrels are safely secured, they break loose only 1% of the time; (3) workers negligently secure barrels only 1 in 1,000 times.

The materials then asked the judges to assess 'how likely is it that the barrel that hit the plaintiff fell due to the negligence of one of the workers?' Judges selection from one of four probability ranges: 0-25%, 26-50%, 51-75%, or 76-100%. When presented with a problem like this one, most people commit the inverse fallacy and assume the likelihood that the defendant was negligent is 90%, or at least quite high. In fact, however, the actual probability that the defendant was negligent is only 8.3%. Relative to other groups, judges did relatively well on this inverse fallacy problem: 40.9% selected the right answer by choosing 0-25%; 8.8% indicated 26-50%; 10.1% indicated 51-75%; and 40.3% indicated 76-100%. Although more than 40% of the judges analyzed this problem correctly, a comparable percentage chose the 76-100% range, suggesting that many of the judges committed the inverse fallacy.

---

[51] Cascalls et al (1978).

[52] Guthrie et al (2001).

The case for this study was not selected at random. In Anglo-American jurisprudence, *Byrne* v. *Boadle* is the foundational case for a doctrine known as 'res ipsa loquitur.' According to the doctrine, an injured plaintiff can recover damages from a defendant without proving that the defendant's conduct was negligent if the defendant possessed exclusive control over the source of the plaintiff's injury and the injury was of the type that did not normally occur when the defendant undertakes reasonable precautions. Although the rule seems reasonable, at a superficial level, it actually incorporates the inverse fallacy. In order to assess whether the plaintiff's injuries were likely to have been the product of the defendant's negligence, the fact finder would have to know not only the rate of injury given reasonable precautions, but the rate of injury given negligent precautions, and the rate of negligence itself. Thus, the doctrine is founded upon an erroneous inference process. The doctrine of res ipsa loquitur instructs judges to take no account of the base-rate of negligence, thereby cementing the inverse fallacy into important legal precedent.[53] Recently, reform efforts from the American Law Institute (a group of distinguished academics, judges, and practitioners) have led to a correction of the doctrine's formulation.[54] Before this effort, however, courts in both the United States and England maintained and applied this fallacious formulation of res ipsa loquitur for well over a century.

C Conclusion

Cognitive errors thus have the potential to influence the law making process in several ways. Erroneous beliefs can affect the demand for law, thereby sending a bad signal to the legislature. Bureaucrats, legislators, and judges might themselves rely on misleading heuristics, thereby creating undesirable law. Although many legal systems include design features that might reduce the likelihood that its laws will be the product of mistaken beliefs[55], misguided law is probably an inevitability. Democratic systems in particular cannot easily withstand widespread demand for regulatory intervention. If lawmakers themselves suffer from cognitive errors, then the ability of institutional design features of a government to correct for erroneous lawmaking is also going to be limited.

Furthermore, any legal system will have difficulty identifying its own errors. Lawmakers are certainly members of the same society that embraces erroneous beliefs and hence might well fail to identify mistaken beliefs for what they are. Fealty to democratic ideals cautions against a bureaucrat or judge overriding democratically expressed preferences, even if they are thought to be the product

---

[53] Kaye (1979).

[54] ALI (2001).

[55] Rachlinski and Farina (2002).

of cognitive errors. If bureaucrats or judges are the source of the error, then correction is similarly unlikely, since the institution that produced the error must observe the mistake in its own processes. Identifying cognitive errors in oneself is notoriously difficult,[56] the same might be true of identifying errors within one's society.

II The Debiasing Effect of Mediating Institutions

The process of resolving conflicts between legal systems creates an opportunity for correcting laws that are the product of cognitive error. To the extent that erroneous laws are the product of erroneous beliefs, a different legal system is unlikely to duplicate the same error. So long as the mediating institution can identify cognitive errors in an effort to resolve conflicting legal regimes, then that institution has the opportunity to identify and correct the rule that is the product of erroneous beliefs. Indeed, the perspective of an outside body can facilitate the avoidance of several common cognitive errors in judgment. In turn, this correction might lead the society that adopted the erroneous belief to reconsider its laws. Identifying the legal regime that has adopted a law based on an erroneous belief, as opposed to a sensible cultural or economic difference between the two nations, will be challenging. Incorporating some simple principles, however, can facilitate resolution of conflict of laws in a way that identifies cognitive error.

A   Path Dependence and Cognitive Errors

Erroneous legislation might said to be 'path dependent.' That is, minor variations between country's histories or cultures can lead to huge differences in laws. The reason for this lies in the context-dependent nature of cognitive errors. Cognitive sources of errors such as availability, framing, and representativeness all arise from highly particularized aspects of a decision-making problem. Furthermore, the error correction mechanisms inherent in legislative processes vary between countries such that some countries will be cementing errors into a misguided regulatory response while others avoid such regulatory mistakes. Even as individuals in different countries rely on similar cognitive mechanisms, they are apt to embrace different specific cognitive errors and produce different erroneous legislation.

Consider, for example, the path dependence of errors arising from availability. The availability cascades that produce erroneous legislation require attention and interest. Different social problems are apt to be cognitively 'available' in different places. Interest in disasters tends to be localized. In my own

---

[56] Kahneman and Lovallo (1995).

small town of Ithaca New York, my colleagues fondly recall the headline in a local paper after the 1989 Loma Prieta Earthquake near San Francisco, California ('Ithaca man unharmed in California Earthquake') . Because interest in disasters tends to be localized in nature, availability cascades will be somewhat erratic. The local nature of availability cascades could hardly be more apparent than by noting that the incident at the Three Mile Island nuclear reactor in Harrisburg, Pennsylvania did more harm to the nuclear industry in the United States than the vastly more serious incident at Chernobyl. So long as destructive events are somewhat random, the localized nature of interest in them will ensure that availability cascades will be also random. Different areas will suffer from different sets of disasters and hence the public will direct their regulatory focus in different directions.

Framing effects will also vary by local circumstances because the status quo that creates framing effects will vary from place to place. A country that has to decide affirmatively to allow the sales of GMOs is apt to treat the decision differently from a country that experienced a sudden influx of such products before regulatory agencies act. The perspective of the country that is considering allowing the sale of GMOs is that of potential gains, thereby making its citizens somewhat risk averse about such products. For the country that already allows the sale of GMOs, any effort to remove them from commerce will involve the potential loss of products, thereby making its citizens somewhat risk seeking about such products. Furthermore, industry groups already selling the product will also see its regulation as a loss. To the extent that people treat losses as more significant than foregone gains, as prospect theory predicts, then these groups will expend more resources lobbying to continue selling GMOs than they will spend to try to open up new markets. Similarly, other groups who have a stake in prohibiting the sale of GMOs (organic farmers, existing purveyors of seed and fertilizer) will face potential losses in countries that are considering opening up their markets to GMOs and foregone gains in countries that are already selling GMOs. This perspective will also influence the lobbying efforts of interest groups, thereby further embedding the framing effects into domestic politics.

To be sure, the situation involving GMOs might be somewhat unique. GMOs came to have a heavy presence in the American market without regulation somewhat by accident. Such products fell into regulatory cracks in the United States between the Food and Drug Administration, the Environmental Protection Agency and the Department of Agriculture. These products entered the market quickly and with little notice, thereby creating the different frame than in Europe. Although this situation might be unusual in the public health setting, variations are less unusual in the commercial setting. Business practices seem heavily path dependent.[57] Although firms in different countries are often trying to solve the same underlying economics problems, they often do so

---

[57] Kahan and Klausner (1997).

in very different ways. Consider for example, the dominance of equity financing of major business in the United States as contrast with debt financing in Germany.[58] These radically different business models invariably will produce different underlying legal regimes. Even within one country, commercial laws can vary dramatically, as evidenced by the variations in corporation law among the different states in the United States. Framing effects make shifting from one to another difficult, even if doing so would produce a more efficient legal regime.[59]

Representativeness is also quite context dependent. Activities that seem dangerous to one person might not be noticed by others. A society condition to embrace a bewildering mix of food products brought by immigrants from different countries might well be less apt to see new food products as unwholesome or risky as compared to a country that does not have a long experience with immigration. In a society in which food products are not thought to entail much danger, ordinary citizens might well be satisfied relying on experts to ensure food safety. By contrast, countries with stable cultures and food consumption patterns might be more prone to seeing novel foods as risky. American farmers, for example, have long faced difficulties with consumer acceptance of American agricultural products in Japan, in part because of safety concerns that dwarf those in the United States. For Americans, food is not commonly thought to be a source of danger, although chemical additives and pesticides are. Because foods do not sound dangerous, the zero-risk mentality representativeness often inspires does not seem to occur.

Different legal systems are also apt to incorporate different error correction devices, thereby both making them vulnerable and resistant to different errors. The common-law process, for example, with its emphasis on precedent and analogical reasoning is apt to produce very different content than civil-law traditions, with their greater attention to the abstract purity of rules. Similarly, a parliamentary system might be both more and less vulnerable to shifting tides of public opinion than the American system that separates legislative and executive branches of government. These variations might weed out the influence of some misleading cognitive processes and allow others to influence lawmaking.[60]

In the United States for example, adopting a regulatory program at the federal level can be quite cumbersome. If new legislation is required, then approval from both halves of a two-chambered legislation is required, plus the approval of the President (or an override by a supermajority of both houses of Congress). This multi-stage process is intended to slow legislation, and has the effect of ensuring that members of government with different perspectives must all approve legislation before it is enacted. Additionally, for many health and

---

[58] Enriques and Macey (2001).

[59] Korobkin (1998).

[60] Rachlinski and Farina (2002).

safety issues, legislation would likely require further regulations, which would be conducted through the executive branch and supervised by judicial review. Any one of these steps can prevent the adoption of misguided legislation. Not only does this process ensure that different political perspective influence regulation, it also ensures that the different cognitive perspective of each part of the government influence it as well. A governmental system with a different process might well facilitate or impede the implementation of misguided legislation.

The differences in legal rules that different countries adopt might certainly be the product of different cultural norms. But to the extent that cognitive error can produce misguided laws, then different legal rules might also be the product of differential vulnerability to cognitive errors. Mistakes in judgment about risk, in particular, are so sensitive to context that minor variations in a nation's history or lawmaking process creates differential sensitivity to cognitive errors. Thus, a conflict in legal rules might reflect the influence of cognitive errors in one of the countries.

B   How Mediating Bodies Can Avoid Cognitive Error

By its nature, the necessity that different legal sovereigns compare and contrast their substantive provisions of law demands that they consider the potential irrationality of their own laws. Any mechanism for resolving conflicting legal rules must make something of the fact that different legal regimes answer identical questions differently. Such differences might arise from different cultural values or variations in the political influence of interest groups, but they might also be the product of differential filtering of erroneous beliefs among lawmakers and the general public.

Any mediating body that must decide which of two conflicting legal rules to apply has the potential to avoid adopting a rule that was the product of cognitive error. When one of two conflicting legal rules was the product of cognitive error, then merely flipping a coin would give the body at least a fifty percent chance of accepting the correct rule. Bodies that mediate conflicting legal rules, however, are likely to do better. The nature of the processes used to resolve conflicting legal rules comports well with many of the kinds of de-biasing procedures that psychologists recommend using to avoid erroneous judgment.

Many debiasing techniques arise from altering the decision maker's perspective. For example, treating a decision as one of a category or type of decision can avoid common cognitive errors.[61] Several noted errors in judgment attributable to heuristics do not occur when the underlying problem is restated using frequencies (e.g., 3 in 10) rather than subjective probabilities (e.g., 30%). Studies of over-confidence show that even though people make poorly calibrated assess-

---

[61] Gigerenzer (1991).

ments of the accuracy of their predictions in subjective probability formats, they are reasonably accurate when expressing the same judgments in frequentist formats. For example, people evaluating their answers to trivia questions who say they are 99% confident in their answers often get about 80% correct, but at the same time they (correctly) report that they would get about 8 out of 10 such questions correct. Similarly, difficulties with the inverse fallacy can be largely remedied by expressing the probabilities in frequentist format.[62]

Resolution of conflicting legal regimes almost invariably triggers a frequentist perspective of at least one sort. Mediating institutions often look to similar jurisdictions to see if they have adopted similar laws. In effect, the effort to identify a dominant rule embraces a kind of a frequentist perspective. Furthermore, if misguided legal rules are most commonly the product of random events (as is perhaps the case with availability cascades) then these events, and the legal rules they produce, should be infrequent. Hence, the majority rule in similar jurisdictions might well be the sensible rule. Attention to counting similar regimes rather than the circumstances of an individual country, is itself a frequentist perspective on evaluating law.

Similarly, for health and safety decisions, the heavy reliance on scientific information by bodies like the WTO also facilitate a perspective that can reduce the influence of cognitive error. Although reliance on science as a basic for resolving conflicting legal rules can raise troublesome questions,[63] it at least has the potential to weed out cognitive errors. Availability cascades produce laws that often cannot be justified in terms of the risks they avoid at the costs they impose.[64] Likewise, decision frame matters little when one is simply assessing scientifically justified costs and benefits. In many of the experiments that demonstrate framing effects, such effects could be avoided by simply multiplying out the probabilities of various outcomes by the value of these outcomes.[65] Furthermore, most problems involve base-rate neglect or representativeness are solved easily with a straightforward application of Bayes Rule.[66] The tendency for bodies like the WTO to insist upon scientific evidence to justify a restrictive legal rule thus creates a perspective that will immunize that body from many decision making problems.

The resolution of conflicting legal regimes also invariably creates a useful 'outside' perspective on the lawmaking process. Many errors in judgment are best resolved by adopting the perspective of an outsider reviewing a decision being made by someone else rather than an insider making the decision oneself.[67] Consider a problem called the planning fallacy. This fallacy refers

---

[62] Gigerenzer (2003).

[63] Jasanoff (1997).

[64] Kuran and Sunstein (1999).

[65] Rachlinski and Guthrie (2004).

[66] Koehler (1996).

[67] Kahneman and Lovallo (1993).

to the tendency to underestimate the amount of time needed to complete a complex task (such as writing an academic paper!). The fallacy can be avoided by asking oneself how often one has completed such a task within the estimate given. Often, the answer is 'never', thereby giving one some indication that the time estimate is too low. In effect, the question about how commonly the task can be completed essentially moves the decision maker from the perspective of an outside observer. The resolution of a conflict of laws necessitates taking the outsider perspective. It requires a tribunal to ask itself to adopt the perspective of a third party (even when the tribunal consists of a court from one of the two competing sovereigns). Resolving conflicts requires asking 'outsider' question such as identifying the factors that explains the split in laws. As noted above in the discussion of the inverse fallacy and res ipsa loquitur, an outside body – the American Law Institute – intervened to correct the misperception that the courts had adopted. Deciding cases one at a time, the courts had incorporated the error, and only when an outside body viewed from the problem as a whole did the error get corrected.

The resolution of conflicting legal regimes also has the potential to undo the status quo bias status that framing can create. Different legal regimes might have different default positions. This would inherently reveal to the decision maker the arbitrariness of the status quo. The research on framing suggests that one way of combating its effects is to consider the problem from the opposite frame. The tribunal charged with resolving conflicting laws would necessarily see that any conflict arising from a difference in status quo is arbitrary.

It is thus clear that one of the principal lessons of the cognitive psychology of judgment and choice is that different representational structures produce different ways of thinking about problems. This finding in psychology suggests one of the possible mechanisms for how different, but similar, sovereign nations would adopt such different legal rules. It also suggests that by its nature, the resolution of these disputes creates an the opportunity to gain yet another perspective on the underlying rationality (or lack thereof) of a law. In effect, conflict resolution between nations might ameliorate errors of judgment.

Mediating bodies can also be useful in one other way. Not only would they likely resolve the dispute before them by rely on legal rules that are less likely to be the products of cognitive error, the resolution of these disputes might inspire the sovereign entity that had codified a cognitive error into its law to reconsider. Admittedly, this is not the most common reaction to the outcome of a dispute resolution panel. Countries that lose in front of WTO panels often react negatively to the WTO, and worry about intrusions on their sovereignty rather than question the sensibility of their own laws. Nevertheless, losing in front of a neutral panel at least raises the possibility that a nation's laws might well be misguided in some fashion.

C Identifying Erroneous Legislation: Basic Cognitive Principles

At the same time that a mediating body charged with resolving conflicting legal regimes has the potential to identify legal rules that arise from cognitive error, it has to be careful to avoid mistakenly declaring a rule to be irrational. Apart from cognitive error, variations in legal regimes can result from variations in cultural values or because an organized coalition in one country has a greater ability to influence politics than its analogue in another country. A mediating body thus might explain a variation in legal rules as a product of either: differential cognitive error, differential political power, or meaningful cultural variations.

Of these three possibilities, the latter merits the most respect from a mediating body. For example, an Islamic country should clearly be able to enforce prohibitions against the import and sale of alcohol, even though most countries do not do so. Public-choice considerations do not stack up as well. Although a victory by a concentrated interest group in front of a legislature is not to be taken lightly, such victories often constitute inefficient protectionism. A mediating body seeking to reconcile conflicting laws that result when one country's legislature has been politically captured faces a relatively easy choice. One nation's decision to favor one or more interest group is a product of its own political process, and should not be exported to affect others. Finally, a mediating body can sensibly override legislation that is the product of cognitive error on the part of one country.

Classifying a conflict between legal regimes into one of these three categories is obviously not easy. Lawmakers rarely identify the political power of an organized group as the primary reason for supporting legislation and even less frequently cite cognitive error by themselves or their constituents. Legislative history, however, can provide some clues. Lawmakers sometimes cite the economic benefits for a discrete group as a motivating actor behind their legislative efforts, although they couch such discussions in terms of merit or long-term interest of the entire economy. Legislative discussion concerning the preservation of a particular industry or economic region might provide a clue that the legislation arises from interest-group pressure, rather than the interest of the public as a whole. Some cognitive errors might be identifiable as well. Disaster followed by a deluge of media coverage followed by a rapid and extreme legislative response might well be a sign that an availability cascade is in progress.

Apart from tell-tale signs of interest group pressure or cognitive error many cases will elude easy categorization. In such instances the approach of the mediating body will likely dictate the outcome. Two general approaches to resolving conflict of laws exist – the approach in the United States for resolving conflicts among competing state law and the approach by international bodies like the WTO or European Union. In the United States, rules for resolving conflicts between different states are well-developed, and quite detailed. Despite their detail, these rules can be said to rely on the basic principle that the interests of the two sovereigns should be balanced.[68] That is to say, the weightiest governmental interest is supposed to prevail. Over time, the courts recognize that in certain circumstances, some interests are generally more prevalent. For example in tort cases, United States courts apply the law of the place where the injury occurs because that state likely has the most significant interest in preventing the injury.

By contrast the international trade regimes incorporate much more of a scientific approach. For example, the Sanitary and Phytosanitary agreement from the Uruguay round of the World Trade Organization allows signatories to restrict product sales only to the extent necessary to protect health and safety and only to the extent that the protection is justified by scientific evidence or international protocols. Rather than attempt to measure or assess the strength of interest of the signatories in adopting their rules, these agreements emphasize scientific justification. Thus, the approach is different from the United States' regime, which is indifferent to the rationale of the rule, and attends only to the intensity of the interest.

To be sure, the principal reason that these two regimes differ is that they have different purposes. The domestic conflict of laws regime is simply an effort to resolve individual disputes between private parties. In fact, the analog to the WTO in the United States is probably not best thought of as the conflict of laws rules but as the rules prohibiting states from adopting restraints on interstate commerce. The WTO, in contrast, is an effort to harmonize global trade. Nevertheless, the two approaches also would address laws arising from cognitive error very differently. The United States' approach does little to identify the source of the conflict. It hardly matters whether a state has adopted a particular tort rule out of an affirmation of some public value, political opportunism by an interest group, or cognitive error; if the injury occurred in the state, that state's law will be applied. To the extent that the system does any sorting, it will undermine laws adopted out of interest-group politics. The general interest of a state in laws that serve only a small segment of its population is almost necessarily less weighty than the interests of a state that has a law designed to benefit the population at large. And certainty the United States' conflict of law system takes no stock of cognitive error as a source of lawmaking. Indeed, a rapidly passed law in response to a sudden perception of an emergency might well be though of as evidence of a critical state interest.

In contrast, the WTO's focus on a scientific basis and international protocols for resolving conflicts is much more amenable to weeding out cognitive error than the United States' system. As noted above, the scientific perspective

---

[68] Simson (1997).

is apt to be insensitive to availability cascades, frame, and errors in judgment of probability. The emphasis on international protocols also creates a frequentist perspective that is conducive to avoiding cognitive errors in judgment. The emphasis on science might also be away of combating interest-group politics, because laws that favor one political group are often hard to justify, but this much is well understood already by scholars and commentators. After all protectionist regulations often arise from political capture. Less noticed is the ability of mediating institutions like the WTO to bring a fresh perspective on a problem that can avoid cognitive error.

III Conclusion

Efforts to resolve conflicting legal rules are invariably costly and raise concerns about national sovereignty and cultural sensitivity. At the same time, efforts to resolve conflicting legal rules creates the opportunity for a novel tribunal with a novel perspective to assess the wisdom of a legal regime. Many legal scholars are coming to accept the possibility that cognitive errors in the polity and the lawmakers might codify erroneous beliefs into law.[69] Most reforms that this problem suggest involve adjustments to the lawmaking process that are internal to a nation's lawmaking process. Such reforms include greater deference to scientific and bureaucratic expertise or the addition of cost-benefit analysis to the lawmaking process. Heretofore unrecognized is the power of an international body to identify cognitive errors. Such bodies can bring fresh perspective to a legal rule that avoids errors in judgment that might have produced it, particular if the system is not deferential to the governmental interests that produced the law.

---

[69] Korobkin and Ulen (2000).

REFERENCES

ALI (2001)
American Law Institute, *Restatement (Third) of Torts* (Council Draft
No. 1, Sept. 25, 1998) § 15

BREYER (1993)
S. Breyer, *Breaking the Vicious Circle: Toward Effective Risk Regulation*
(Cambridge: Harvard University Press 1993)

BYRNE (1979)
J.M. Byrne, "Snow Brings an Avalanche of Change", *Chicago Sun-
Times*, December 10, 1999

CAMERER AND JOHNSON (1991)
C.F. Camerer and E.J. Johnson, "The process-performance paradox
in expert judgment: How can experts know so much and predict so
badly?", in: K.A. Ericsson and J. Smith (eds)., *Toward a general theory of
expertise: Prospects and limits* (New York: Cambridge University Press
1991) 195-217

CASCALLS ET AL (1978)
W. Cascalls, A. Schoenberger and T. Greyboys, "Interpretations by
physicians of clinical laboratory results", 299 *New England Journal of
Medicine* (1978) 999-1000.

EISENBERG (2001)
T. Eisenberg, "Damage Awards in Perspective: Behind the Headline-
Grabbing Awards in *Exxon Valdez* and *Engle*", 36 *Wake Forest Law
Review* (2001) 1129-1155

ELY (1980)
John Hart Ely, *Democracy and Distrust* (Cambridge: Harvard
University Press 1980)

ENRIQUES AND MACEY (2001)
L. Enriques and J.R. Macey, "Creditors versus capital formation: The
Case against the European legal capital rules", 86 *Cornell Law Review*
(2001) 1165-1204

FOSTER, BERNSTEIN AND HUBER (1993)
K.R. Foster, D.E. Bernstein and P.W. Huber, *Phantom Risk: Scientific
Inference and the Law* (Cambridge: The MIT Press 1993)

GIGERENZER (1991)
Gigerenzer, G., "How to make cognitive illusion disappear: Beyond
'heuristics and biases'", 2 *European Review of Social Psychology* (1991)
83-115

GIGERENZER (2003)
G. Gigerenzer, *Calculated Risks: How to know when numbers deceive you*
(New York: Simon and Schuster 2003)

GRIFFIN AND TVERSKY (1992)
> D. Griffin, D. and A. Tversky, "The Weighing of evidence and the determinants of confidence", 24 *Cognitive Psychology* (1992) 411-435

GUTHRIE, RACHLINSKI AND WISTRICH (2001)
> C. Guthrie, J.J. Rachlinski and A.J. Wistrich, "Inside the judicial mind", 86 *Cornell Law Review* (2001) 777-830

JASANOFF (1997)
> S. Jasanoff, *Science at the Bar: Law, Science, and Technology in America* (Cambridge: Harvard University Press 1997)

KAHAN AND KLAUSNER (1997)
> M. Kahan, and M. Klausner, "Standardization and innovation in corporate contracting (or 'the economics of boilerplate')", 83 *Virginia Law Review* (1997) 713-770

KAHNEMANN AND LOVALLO (1993)
> D. Kahneman and D. Lovallo, "Timid choices and bold forecasts: A Cognitive perspective on risk taking", 39 *Management Science* (1993) 17-31

KAHNEMANN AND TVERSKY (1972)
> D. Kahneman and A. Tversky, "Subjective probability: A Judgment of Representativeness", 3 *Cognitive Psychology* (1972) 430-454

KAHNEMANN AND TVERSKY (1979)
> D. Kahneman and A. Tversky, "Prospect theory: An Analysis of decision under risk", 47 *Econometrica* (1979) 263-291

KOEHLER, BRENNER AND GRIFFIN (2002)
> D.J. Koehler, L. Brenner and D. Griffin, "The Calibration of expert judgment: Heuristics and biases beyond the laboratory", in: T. Gilovich, D. Griffin and D. Kahneman (eds.), *Heuristics and Biases: The Psychology of Intuitive Judgment* (Cambridge: Cambridge University Press) 686-715

KAYE (1979)
> D. Kaye, "Probability theory meets res ipsa loquitur", 77 *Michigan Law Review* (1979) 1456-1484

KOEHLER (1996)
> J.J. Koehler, "The base rate fallacy reconsidered: Normative, descriptive and methodological challenges", 19 *Behavioral and Brain Sciences* (1996) 1-53

KOROBKIN (1998)
> R.B. Korobkin, "Inertia and preference in contract negotiation: the psychological power of default rules and form terms", 51 *Vanderbilt Law Review* (1998) 1583-1651

KOROBKIN AND ULEN (2000)
> R.B. Korobkin and T.S. Ulen, "Law and Behavioral Science: Removing the rationality assumption from law and economics", 88 *California Law Review* (2000) 1051-1144

KURAN AND SUNSTEIN (1999)

T. Kuran and C.R. Sunstein, "Availability cascades and risk
regulation", 51 *Stanford Law Review* (1999) 683-768

MACEY (2002)

J.R. Macey, "Cynicism and trust in politics and constitutional theory",
87 *Cornell Law Review* (2002) 280-308

McCAFFERY (1991)

E.J. McCaffery, "Cognitive theory and tax", 41 *UCLA Law Review*
(1991) 1861-1947

McGRAW AND P. MONTEMURRI

B. McGraw and P. Montemurri, "Other Cities Plow All Streets – But
Detroit Lets it Snow", *Detroit Free Press*, Jan. 6, 1999

RACHLINSKI (2003)

J.J. Rachlinski, "The Uncertain psychological case for paternalism", 97
Northwestern University Law Review (2003) 1165-1225

RACHLINSKI (2004)

J.J. Rachlinski, "Heuristics, biases, and governance", in: D.J. Koehler
and N. Harvey (eds.), *Blackwell Handbook of Judgment and Decision
Making* (Malden MA: Blackwell Publishing 2004) 567-584

RACHLINSKI AND FARINA (2002)

J.J. Rachlinski and C.R. Farina, "Cognitive psychology and optimal
governmental design", 87 *Cornell Law Review* (2002) 549-615

RACHLINSKI AND GUTHRIE (2004)

J.J. Rachlinski and C. Guthrie, "Heuristics, Biases, and Expert
Negotiators" (Unpublished manuscript)

ROBBENN ET AL. (1990)

H.S.J. Robbenn et al., "Decision frame and opportunity as
determinants of tax cheating: An International experimental study", 11
Journal of Economic Psychology (1990) 341-363

SAKS (1986)

M.J. Saks, "If there be a crisis, how shall we know it?", 46 *Maryland
Law Review* (1986) 63-72

SALZMAN AND THOMPSON (2003)

J. Salzman and B.H. Thompson, *Environmental Law and Policy* (New
York: Foundation Press)

SIMSON (1997)

G. Simson, *Issues and Perspectives in Conflict of Laws: Cases and
Materials*, 3rd ed. (Durham: Carolina Press 1997)

SHAPIRO AND McGARITY (1989)

S.A. Shapiro and T.O. McGarity, "Reorienting OSHA: Regulatory
alternatives and legislative reform", 6 *Yale Journal on Regulation* (1989)
1-63

SLOVIC, FISCHHOFF AND LICHTENSTEIN (1982)
> P. Slovic, B. Fischhoff and S. Lichtenstein, "Facts versus fears: Understanding perceived risks", in: D. Kahneman, P. Slovic, and A. Tversky (eds.), *Judgment Under Uncertainty: Heuristics and Biases* (Cambridge: Cambridge University Press 1982) 464-489

SLOVIC, FLYNN AND LAYMAN (2000)
> P. Slovic, J. Flynn and M. Layman, "Perceived risk, trust and the politics of nuclear waste", in: P. Slovic (ed.), *The Perception of Risk* (London: Earthscan Publications 2000) 275-284

STARR (1998)
> A. Starr, "At Home Abroad: Why It's Time to Reform the Foreign Service", *Washington Monthly,* 30 (on-line).

SUNSTEIN (2000)
> C.R. Sunstein, "Cognition and cost-benefit analysis", 29 *Journal of Legal Studies* (2000) 1059-1096

SUNSTEIN (2002)
> C.R. Sunstein, "Probability neglect: Emotions, worst cases, and law", 112 *Yale Law Journal* (2002) 61-107

SUNSTEIN (2003)
> C.R. Sunstein, "Beyond the precautionary principle", 151 *University of Pennsylvania Law Review* (2003) 1003-1058

SUNSTEIN, SCHKADE, KAHNEMAN AND RITOV (2002)
> C.R. Sunstein, D. Kahneman, D. Schkade and I. Ritov, "Predictably incoherent judgments", 54 *Stanford Law Review* (2002) 1153-1214

TVERSKY AND FOX (1995)
> A. Tversky and C.R. Fox, "Weighing risk and uncertainty", 102 *Psychological Review* (1995) 269-283

TVERSKY AND KAHNEMANN (1974)
> A. Tversky and D. Kahneman, "Judgment under Uncertainty: Heuristics and Biases" 185 *Science* (1974) 1124-1131

WIENER AND ROGERS (2002)
> J.B. Wiener and M.D. Rogers, "Comparing precaution in the United States and Europe" 5 *Journal of Risk Research* (2002) 317-349

The Ethical Pluralism of Late Modern Europe and Codification of European Contract Law

Thomas Wilhelmsson

1 Introduction

The ongoing debate on a European unification/harmonisation/
codification of private law/contract law, which already has become so volumi-
nous that it seems impossible to follow in all its details, appears as surprisingly intra-juridical. Lawyers discuss the pros and cons of harmonisation and
codification measures with other lawyers and views on society and its present
condition are only occasionally reflected into the debate. The Commission, in its
much-debated Action Plan for a more coherent European contract law,[1] follows
this line as well. The only societal question of importance for the Commission
– and this is understandable, bearing in mind the role of the Commission – is
the internal market question: Does the existence of different contract laws in the
member states form an obstacle to cross-border trade within the Union and does
it increase the transaction costs of those engaged in such trade?

To be fair, I should underline the general nature of this picture. Of course
many and various interesting attempts to formulate a more societal vision of the
development of a uniform contract law can be found,[2] but these easily drown in
the more specifically legal debate.

In the debate concerning a possible European civil code lawyers often draw
parallels with the situation when the great European codes, the French *Code
Civil* and the German *Bürgerliches Gesetzbuch*, were adopted and with the clashes
between the Savignys and the Thibauts of that time.[3] The societal function of
the codes, as symbols of the French revolution and the unification of Germany,
is often mentioned. Much less attention is devoted, however, to the question of
the societal basis of these codes and possible changes in this basis. Is European
society today sufficiently similar to that of 19th Century France and Germany
to make the codification idea feasible, albeit with a partially different content, or
is society different in such a way that a general codification would appear less
appealing today? Or is the question of codification only a question of form which
is largely independent of the societal conditions and the normative content
prevailing at any point in time?

One approach, out of several possible approaches, to this issue focuses on
the ethical and epistemic coherence of society – or rather within those groups
having influence and power in society – and its relationship to the coherence of
the legal system. The *BGB* was made for a bourgeois society and for a original
market capitalism and in that sense could reflect a fairly homogeneous world
outlook. Its strong foundations in a market-liberalist vision of society made it
possible to erect it as a relatively coherent edifice.[4] Those parts that did not fit

---

[1]   COM (2003) 68 final.

[2]   Much debated ones are *e.g.* Joerges (2003), Teubner (1998). See also the recently published 'Manifesto'
      of the so called Study Group on Social Justice (2004).

[3]   E.g. Lando (2000a) and Lando (2000b).

[4]   Wieacker (1974), especially 9 *et seq.*

into this structure were already at that time left out to be treated in special legis-lation – a *Sonderprivatrecht* – and societal visions that conflicted with the basic credo were neglected.[5] The mechanisms of market society were also probably understood and interpreted in a relatively simple manner at that time.

It should be noted that I here refer to the homogeneity of (the dominating perceptions) of society, not to the coherence of the state structure and the law related to it. The unification of Germany and the introduction of the BGB was, on this level, accomplished in an environment that was much more fragmented than the present situation. However, this is another matter than the ethical and epistemic coherence of society. The fragmentation thesis of this paper claims that the experience of coherence on this societal level is more limited than in the time of the great codifications.

In this paper I will defend a claim that such an ethically homogeneous approach, combined with an epistemically simple understanding of society, is not convincing and that this claim has implications for the usefulness of grand European codifications of private law. The complex structure and chaotic causal-ity chains of the globalised late modern society require an experimental and learning law, and the ethical pluralism of this society requires a law that leaves space for contextually determined pragmatic moral reasoning. Neither of these requirements seems to be well at ease with projects of general codifications of the traditional type.

Sectoral codifications, *e.g.* of contract law, may be easier to accept, but also within such projects the societal changes since the 19th century are of course highly relevant. I will in the concrete sections of the paper focus the general arguments especially on the issue concerning harmonisation of European contract law.

The Europeanisation of private law, which I fully support as such, should rather have the form of a *free movement of legal ideas and doctrines*, a concept that I have presented before on various occasions,[6] and that I partially share with Jan Smits.[7] However, Smits speaks about a free movement of legal 'rules' instead of 'ideas and doctrines'. By speaking about 'ideas', I have noted that it is not the rules as such but the arguments upholding the rules that are moving and by including 'doctrines' I have wanted to stress the role of systematic legal doctrine as one of the important players in the game. I do not think, however, that Jan Smits necessarily is of a different opinion than I am in these respects.

I will in the following mainly focus on the ethical pluralism of late modern society and the difficulties related to reconciling the European codification projects with such a pluralist understanding of the ethics of contemporary

---

[5] Well known is the contemporary criticism by Menger (1904).

[6] See Wilhelmsson (2002a) 353, as well as Wilhelmsson (2002b). I have also presented the idea of a free movement of legal ideas and doctrines earlier in Swedish in Wilhelmsson (2001).

[7] Smits (2002) 63.

European society. It is one way of formulating the argument that Jan Smits has
summarised under the heading 'The Idea of a Binding Codification seems to
be Contrary to the Spirit of the Times'.[8] However, as the ethical uncertainty is
connected with, and cannot be clearly distinguished from the epistemic uncertainty of our society, I will start by presenting a few notes concerning the latter
issue, containing parts of an analysis that I have presented earlier and published
elsewhere.

The analysis of both kinds of uncertainty starts by presenting some prominent diagnoses of contemporary society within the social sciences that have
offered important insights when I have constructed my own view of reality.
I want to stress, however, that diagnoses of this kind do not offer knowledge
which can be empirically tested in any strict sense. These diagnoses are contributions by social science to the debates on society rather than verifiable scientific 'truths' that can be taken for granted by legal science when building its
own models. However, the fact that various analyses within social science have
emphasised certain features of contemporary society may be taken as an indication of those features being, so to speak, 'in the air', although not scientifically
proven to be important in any strict sense.

In many inspiring diagnoses of contemporary society the specific temporal
setting and the features usually attributed to this setting are referred to by using
the term 'post-modern'. However, I have here preferred to use the term 'late
modern' instead of 'post-modern'. I speak of 'post-modern' and 'post-modernity' only when referring directly to writings in which these terms are used. As
the term 'post-modern' seems to be loaded with a lot of emotions both among
protagonists as well as opponents it may provoke discussions which are not
productive in relation to the theses I want to bring forward. In addition, the use
of the term 'post-modern' might give an impression of a more dramatic break
with the past than I believe in. Some may think that one could legitimately
speak about a 'post-modern law' only if one could show that not only legal
culture but also the common deep-structure of modern Western law would
have undergone important changes.[9] Although such a requirement for allowing
the terminology is not necessarily well-founded – as post-modernity in post-
modernist writing indeed has been characterised for example as 'fully developed
modernity', as 'modernity conscious of its true nature'[10] – also these doubts can
be avoided by using the term 'late modernity' instead.

---

[8]   Smits (2002) 29.

[9]   Tuori (1999) 39, bases his criticism against the idea of a 'post-modern' law on this prerequisite. As the
      deep-structure of law has not changed one should not speak about a new post-modern law, but rather a
      coming of age, a final maturation of modern law.

[10] Bauman (1992) 187.

2 The Uncertainty of the Risk Society and the Necessary Fragmentation of Law[11]

The concepts 'choice' and 'risk' – and especially the latter – have been prominent in social theory ever since Ulrich Beck presented his well known analysis of the 'risk society' in 1986.[12] Various interpretations of the concept of risk society have been advanced in the discourse. At first, the discussion often focused on catastrophe scenarios.[13] Many have brought not only catastrophic risks, but also risks of less magnitude, even those facing individual persons, into the debate. This has led to a more general emphasis on the fact that the growing complexity of technology is continuously creating new risks. In addition, the concept of risk has been broadened to cover not only technological risks, but also various kinds of institutional risks well,[14] connected for example with the functioning of the stock exchange and the globalised financial markets. The risk discourse does not, however, necessarily reflect an actual increase of risks in today's society. Some claim that the focus on risks does not arise as much from actual changes in reality as from how we look at reality. What is typical of our times is perhaps not so much the proliferation of real risks, but rather the growing awareness of risks.[15] These two views are not necessarily in contradiction with each other. It is possible to claim that risks are a part of the reflexive modernity, where they exist in technology, in society and in our minds.[16] For the present purposes, it is sufficient to note that in today's culture many consider risks to be a key problem.

The concept of risk is as such very vague, and it has been used with rather different meanings in different disciplines.[17] The interesting feature of the risk society discourse is not, however, the precise meaning of risk in this discourse, but rather the use of the concept of risk to identify profound changes in society that have been caused by the growing risks and/or the growing perception of risk. In the culture of the risk society there is a new kind of emphasis on decision-making. This emphasis generates what I call the paradox of the risk society.

One side of this paradox is the growing *demand for decisions*, an increasing interest in decision-making and decision-makers. It is, of course, self-evident that many of the new and problematic risks of the high technology society are

---

[11] This section contains a much shortened version of parts of my paper "The Paradox of the Risk Society and the Fragmentation of Consumer Law", forthcoming in the proceedings of the Ninth International Conference on Consumer Law in Athens April 2003.

[12] Beck (1986).

[13] Beck (1986) 254.

[14] See especially Giddens (1990).

[15] Luhmann (1991).

[16] So Nielsen (1996) 77.

[17] See *e.g.* Baldwin (1997) 1 and Bechmann (1991) 214.

caused by human action. The connection between risks and decision-making,
however, is more far-reaching than this. In the risk society, traditional dangers
are also interpreted as risks that call for decisions. Almost nothing is seen as
caused only by nature or fortune; Instead, everything that threatens us is at least
partially a consequence of human decisions.[18] Most dangers can, at least in principle, be averted if they are foreseen, they are felt to be unacceptable and capable
of elimination by taking appropriate measures. Lack of appropriate action, for
whatever reason, is also understood as a form of decision-making.

The other side of the paradox lies in the growing *uncertainty* prevailing in
the late modern risk society. At the same time as the importance of decision-
making is emphasized, there is a widespread feeling that more and more decisions are made under conditions of obvious uncertainty. Chaos and ambivalence
are seen as characteristic features of society.[19] This means that 'the risk issues
necessitate, or, more cautiously, appeal for, the "recognition of ambivalence"'[20].

Recognising that decision-making takes place under a cloud of uncertainty
changes the perception of the role of expertise in the processes of decision-
making. The lack of experience in dealing with many new risks means that the
so-called experts cannot claim a monopoly on knowledge. Science and expert
knowledge are no longer trusted as the only bases for decisions: The introduction of nuclear power and the ecological awakening are important turning
points in this development.[21] Other factors than the probability of damage can be
decisive for the decision, for example the distribution of the risk within a given
population.[22] Ultimately it is a question of which risks one can or cannot accept
within a given culture.[23]

This conclusion is not altered by the fact that some risks in concrete situations may be calculated quite accurately. The different perspectives and interests
of decision-makers and of those who are affected by the decisions reinforces
the skepticism even in such situations. What from the perspective of a decision-maker and an expert looks like a calculated risk, may seem an uncontrolled
danger in the eyes of those affected by it. The efforts of a decision-maker to
minimise the risk with the help of risk calculations and risk strategies are
experienced as failures by those who fear the remaining risk.[24] Every risk that
materialises and causes damage increases the distrust of the expertise.

Because of the distrust of expertise, risk communication is being forced to
be more openly moral. The basic uncertainty of decision-making in the risk soci-

---

[18] Bechmann (1991) 217.

[19] Bauman (1991).

[20] Beck (1994) 10.

[21] So for the USA Shapiro (1997) 325.

[22] Ogus (1997) 144, analyses this very interestingly.

[23] Beck (1994) 9.

[24] Bechmann (1991) 227.

ety and the recognition of the fact that decisions cannot be made solely on the basis of scientific expertise, again emphasises the political and moral character of many decisions that previously could be regarded as primarily apolitical and technical. This underlines the paradox of the risk society, as the return to morality does not add any certainty to the decision-making processes. I will discuss this issue in the later parts of this paper.

The paradox of the risk society in other words lies in the ever-growing demand for decisions concerning risks combined with the simultaneously increasing realisation that they have to be made under conditions of great uncertainty with regard to their factual consequences and their moral implications. This paradox obviously has some implications for law and legal decision-making both generally and – perhaps most significantly – in branches of law predominantly dealing with risks, like environmental law and consumer law.

An obvious consequence of the paradox of the risk society is a growing cleavage between the expectations we have of decision-making and the results it produces. Decisions are required, but their outcomes do not meet our expectations. The legitimacy of the decisions is decreasing together with the legitimacy of expertise. In the legal sphere the paradox means that the cleavage between regulatory expectations in society and the performance of actual regulation is increasing. The situation is confusing. On the one hand there is a constant demand for new regulatory measures as new risks are perceived. On the other hand the trust in such measures is diminishing, as the results of the regulation are not convincing and may even lead to demands for the removal of regulatory mechanisms. Such demands are likely to be fuelled by ideologically grounded deregulatory tendencies connected with the privatisation and marketisation of society.[25] In other words, the paradox of the risk society produces conflicting demands on regulation. It is expressed in more or less simultaneous demands for regulation, deregulation, reregulation, more regulation, less regulation, regulation with a new approach etc., etc. The time-frames are short, and the need for rapid responses and actions increases the uncertainty of the outcomes.

As it is inevitable under these circumstances that law will make mistakes – whatever that means in this context – it has to be able to learn from these mistakes. The risk society needs a law that can adapt quickly to new experiences – a learning law. In contract law the need for quick reactions to problematic situations, as well as for continuous learning processes under conditions of uncertainty, are probably most obvious within the area of consumer law in many jurisdictions.

The partial – real or at least perceived – failure of regulatory measures and the demand for a law that can learn have various consequences. Firstly, there is a stronger call for private law mechanisms to deal with risks. Court activism is

---

[25] This issue has been scrutinized in detail elsewhere. Many interesting contributions may be found in the volume Wilhelmsson and Hurri (1999).

offered as one answer to the problem. Although the American model of putting
private liability proceedings in the centre of regulatory activity has few adherents
elsewhere and its drawbacks are obvious,[26] the advisability of increasing the use
of such mechanisms is currently under debate in Europe as well.[27] For example,
tort law is said to offer at least some answers to the challenges faced by the risk
society in coping with uncertainty.[28] Case law can be seen as one of the learning-
by-doing mechanisms that are necessary to manage complex regulatory risks. It
is a question of what some in German consumer law doctrine already decades
ago termed 'Entdeckungsverfahren Praxis'.[29]

As risks in the risk society are increasingly transnational, this learning may
also reach across national borders. Efficient learning processes require a sufficient amount of legal practice. Answers to new risk issues found in one country
can be taken into account when a court in another country is faced with similar
questions. Private law in the risk society is forced to become internationalised.
Law can (and should) learn from experiences in other countries as well as in its
own.

However, private law can function as a generator of new norms based on
accumulated experience only if it is sufficiently flexible. Anthony Ogus has
presented his view of court-based risk management under the heading 'Judicial
Interpretation of General Standards'.[30] Other scholars, analysing the effects
on private law of the uncertainty of contemporary risk patterns, have likewise
underlined the need for 'large elements of flexibility'[31] and emphasised that
a highly differentiated society is incompatible with a generalised and formalised liability law.[32] Adequate learning concerning new risks and their optimal
management cannot be gathered within a very rigid and abstract normative
structure. In the risk society, private law must be geared more towards concrete
situations and risks than towards general abstract categories. Its flexibility is
situation-oriented.

To be sure, the private law solutions, however, do not quiet the demands for
more administrative/public law regulation. On the contrary, every private law
case may be seen as a failure of regulation that may lead to debate in the media
and to demands for new regulation. Put in the language of a learning law: by
subjecting new forms of risk behaviour to legal sanctions, private law 'discovers'
possible targets of administrative action.[33] Therefore, what we find in a risk soci-

---

[26] See the comparison between European and American approaches in: Howells and Wilhelmsson (1997)
207.

[27] See for example the interesting paper of Steele (1999) 479.

[28] Brüggemeier (1997) 63.

[29] Joerges (1983) 64.

[30] Ogus (1997) 140.

[31] Steele (1999) 486.

[32] Brüggemeier (1999) 24.

[33] Brüggemeier (1999) 23.

ety struggling to find quick answers to growing uncertainty is an increasingly pluralist set of normative steering mechanisms with private law and public law having different functions in this mix. This underlines the fact that flexibility, even in the relationship between the branches of law, is a cardinal characteristic of law in contemporary risk society.

The flexibility and rapid changes that are typical of law in the risk society bring to mind another feature which is less accepted: the fragmentation of law.[34] Not only is law flexible, and has to be so, it is also to some extent fragmented, and has to be so. The focus on situations rather than on general (legal) categories tends to mitigate the effects of any effort to develop a coherent system of rules and principles. Learning that originates in other jurisdictions has the same effect when it impinges on national systematic edifices.[35] As the risk society tries to cope with its risks, at least to some extent, through experimental learning-by-doing, these mechanisms cannot, and should not, be tightly bound to an established system that reflects only already existing experience. Both courts and legislatures – and especially the latter – should have room for realistic and adequate responses to new situations.

There is, however, an obvious objection to this analysis. The focus on risk in present society is not only accompanied by uncertainty and the need for experimentation. On the contrary, new methods for collecting experience and calculating risks have fostered new rational ways of managing risks which in some ways even may have changed our world outlook. François Ewald's theory concerning the insurance society[36] offers a useful perspective on this. This notion not only implies that such institutions as private and public insurance developed as a result of our needs for security, but it goes much deeper. It claims that a certain way of thinking, a certain rationality permeates society as a whole. Insurance is a practice which follows from a type of rationality that has been formalised in probability calculus; insurance is collective, as risks can be calculated only within a population.[37] The rationality of the insurance society rests on these two

---

[34] In this context I understand fragmentation of law as something contradicting the character of law as a coherent system of concepts, principles and values. The more fragmented the law is, the more difficult it is to present it as a system based on coherent reasons. A coherent body of law, on the contrary, appears to have relatively uniform basic principles and can thus more naturally be described as a system. Fragmentation of law is not the same thing as flexibility, but these features are interconnected, as flexibility usually increases the possibility of fragmentation, and as fragmentation, because of the internal value contradictions it produces within the legal material, often increases the range of options of the legal decision-maker.

[35] Berger (2001) 890 notes very appropriately: 'The realisation that foreign legal systems are able to cope with certain factual problems without a highly sophisticated dogmatic legal framework may lead the judge to realize that the systemisation of the law in his own country is not so much done in a concern for the functioning of the legal system but merely "out of a tendency to suffer theoretical controversies"'.

[36] Ewald (1986) and, in German, Ewald (1989).

[37] Ewald (1989) 390.

elements, calculability and collectivity. This rationality sheds a different light on the demands for a flexible private law commensurate to the needs of the risk society. The demand for calculability in the insurance rationality requires clear rules instead of flexible *ad hoc* solutions. In addition, the focus on collectives is not compatible with an approach based on individualised and unique legal assessments. When dealing with mass transactions, such as consumer transactions and standard form contracting more generally, efficiency alone requires rules that are sufficiently clear to be followed without undue need to resort to litigation.

However, the existence of, indeed the need for more precise rules does not contradict the fragmentation thesis. It rather confirms it. Contemporary clear-cut rules are often not expressions of a general coherent system of norms, but only detailed normative interventions in special areas with more or less limited spheres of application. They are additional ingredients in the complex risk management mix of the risk society. The oscillation between the risk society's need for flexibility and the insurance society's need for precise rules only underlines the fragmentation of law.

Legal fragmentation is not only an unavoidable, if deplorable, necessity, but also an adequate answer to the needs of society, an answer that opens up new possibilities. Fragmentation, situation-orientation and the diminishing influence of general normative edifices offer opportunities for learning from experience, both nationally and across the borders. This insight adds a new dimension to the ongoing debate on codification of European private law. A general code could at worst seriously damage the development of a good and adequate private law, as it would disregard the need for continuous experimentation and learning from new experiences in law. The present situation, with the possibilities of accumulating legal knowledge both through national experiments and through European learning processes, seems to be better suited to meet the needs of contemporary society. National boundaries should be lowered, not through a common static code, but through the *free movement of legal ideas and doctrines*. Such a flow of ideas should take place both directly between the member states and via Brussels, where the European Commission can function as a centre for collecting, cultivating and using legal experience. The European fragmentation not only creates confusion and difficulties, it can also be a source of opportunities.

3 The Ethical Uncertainty of Late Modern Society and the Need for Legal Contextualism

The uncertainty of late modern society is not only connected with our limited possibilities to acquire sufficient knowledge to take charge of a complex technology in a complex society. The uncertainty is not only epistemic, but also ethical. There is also an ambivalence concerning value issues that makes the decision-making processes in late modern society still more problematic. Also this ambivalence creates new social demands on law. Having above described the need for an experimental and learning law related to the impossibility of having sufficient knowledge of the complex causalities of modern technology and society, I will here turn to a similar need for a law that is able to 'learn' contextual moral assessments. First I will give a short description of late modern ethical uncertainty as it is understood in some well-known societal diagnoses of late modernity.

The characterisation of late modern society as a fragmented society is related to the dissolution of traditional structures of understanding under the pressure of globalised information and economy. The bulk of shared national and local beliefs is replaced by a marketplace of understandings. The claim has been made that even history is dead: "modernist history' is the first casualty and mysterious absence of the postmodernism period'.[38] Historical experience is not accepted as legitimation for normative claims. Not even a creation like the European Union can base its legitimacy on history.[39]

The decreasing contact with the past pushes tradition to the background. Late modernity is said to destroy traditions.[40] Globalisation puts local and national traditions in competition with other ways of thinking and acting.[41] Traditions therefore survive only as long as they can be discursively defended, as long as they seem justified in comparison with alternative patterns of behaviour.[42] Traditions no longer necessarily offer a solid ground for choices of actions. Even those who still emphasise the important role of tradition admit that 'there is a gradual decline in the traditional grounding of action and in the role of traditional authority – that is, in the normative and the legitimation aspects of tradition'.[43]

Tradition is closely connected with authority. The late modern non-traditional culture diminishes the role of homogenising basic sources of authority like religion, philosophy and ideology – even though varying groups in society may be very strongly committed. to e.g. religious beliefs and patterns of action justified by reference to religion. In the secularised and ideologically cynical European society, grand ideological narratives have anyway lost much of their integrating force. Even class consciousness and other group-specific sources of

---

[38] Jameson (1991) xi.

[39] See e.g. Wadenström (1998), who speaks about many small contradictory narratives that allow for many constructions of Europe. See also the interesting analysis of the project-based identity of the EU by Castells (1999) 330-355.

[40] Giddens (1994) 91 et seq describes how already 'modernity destroys tradition', but how modernity in earlier phases at the same time needed tradition as a partner.

[41] Giddens (1994) 95 et seq.

[42] Giddens (1994) 105.

[43] Thompson (1996) 93.

meaning are breaking up.[44] There is a kind of ideological chaos, an unregulated market for ideologies and philosophies of life.

Therefore, present society is said to exist in an age without ethics.[45] There is no longer, even on the national level, any generally accepted code for how one should behave. Ethical behaviour can no longer be described as behaviour in accordance with norms based on tradition and be explained by ethical and ideological expertise. There is little belief in an ethics that could be rationally justified with reference to some common basic principles and ethical expertise is not regarded as highly important. There is no agreement – not even on a national level, not to speak about the global – on who would deserve the status of such an expert.

The decline of the belief in universal ethical systems and in the ethical expertise which claims to know how to interprete these systems does not, however, necessarily imply that we have stepped into an age characterised by a lack of morality. The fact that there are no absolute universal values does not imply that values would lack importance altogether. The perspective on moral behaviour must, however, be different when the common understandings of the value structures of society is diminishing.

Although the loss of common ethical systems is frightening, it need not be seen as a completely negative development. Some in fact assess the 'liberation' from the ethical systems in a rather optimistic light. One of the leading contemporary advocates of a new kind of moral responsibility, Zygmunt Bauman, sees here at least an opportunity for a deeper morality. The crisis of ethics does not necessarily imply a crisis of morality, on the contrary the end of the 'ethical era' may be seen as a gate to the 'era of morality'.[46] The decline of authoritative ethical guidance that would remove the responsibility for moral decisions from the subjects themselves returns to people the opportunity of moral choice and moral responsibility. For Bauman, this is the ethical paradox of postmodernity: at the same time that people are constantly reminded of the relativity of all ethical codes they receive full moral choice and responsibility.[47] People are forced to encounter moral issues 'point blank, in all their naked truth', when the ethical clouds which have obscured personal responsibility have vanished.[48]

There is of course no automatism between the decline of ethics and the emphasis on moral responsibility. However, as the distrust of universally accepted ethical authority, at least at this moment in time, seems inevitable, the only possible way forward seems to be to insist on a growing personal responsibility for everyone concerning individual moral choices. The alternative, neither ethics nor morality, is too frightening to be contemplated.

---

[44] Beck (1994) 7.

[45] Very much discussed are the analyses of Zygmunt Bauman, see: Bauman (1993) as well as Bauman (1995).

[46] Bauman (1995) 42.

[47] Bauman (1992) xxii.

[48] Bauman (1995) 43.

Our freedom from universal ethical authority forces us in a higher degree than before to make personal choices: 'In post-traditional contexts, we have no choice but to choose how to be and how to act.'[49] The individual is forced to an increasing extent to make her own decisions both regarding her way of life as well as regarding her actions within this framework. The increasing importance of continuous decision-making, without pre-established models and firm knowledge, that in the previous section of the paper was tied to the epistemic uncertainty of the risk society, is most certainly fuelled by society's ethical uncertainty as well.

The freedom to make decisions untied by tradition and authority implies a new moral responsibility for those decisions. The new 'era of morality' that is hoped for is an era during which everybody accepts to be responsible for his own responsibility.[50] At best the freedom from the ethical systems generates a new form of ethics, focusing on the individual responsibility for moral behaviour.

Such a model cannot be a substantive system of accepted ethical norms, behind which the individual could hide her personal choices and decisions. Rather it has to be a pragmatic morality that ties moral decisions to the persons and the context of the actual decision-making situation. Decisions cannot be made only on the basis of abstract norms, but has to be justified also with reference to the actual context in which the decision is made. Moral decisions have to be made on practical grounds, without philosophical assurances.[51] Moral roads are not made with the help of any pre-existing map, but we make the roads by walking them.[52]

The map metaphor illustrates well the fact that an individual and pragmatic morality is not the same as total value relativism. As the roads are made by walking them common paths and roads emerge as we need them. Also old roads, tradition, endure, as long as somebody is walking them. Morality is, and has to be, something societal, something we share with others.

In a late modern individual morality this community in moral questions grows from below, from experience on the grass root level rather than from above, through systematic ethical, religious or ideological authority. The collective moral is created through a continuing contextual learning process without definite answers. The moral issues continuously have to be reassessed and renegotiated in the light of new experience.[53] Traditions can survive only as long as they are felt to be justified.

---

[49] Giddens (1994) 75.

[50] Zygmunt Bauman, in an interview in the journal *Niin & Näin*: Bauman (1997) 46.

[51] Bauman (1992) xxxiii.

[52] Bauman (1995) 17.

[53] Statements like this are very common in late modern literature. See *e.g.* Hutchinson (1997) 35: 'citizenship under radical democracy is not committed to one common good, but to an engaged practice of civility in which the common good is always up for consideration and conversion.'

A model like this presupposes a continuing exchange of experiences concerning moral issues. In addition to the individual moral responsibility and the pragmatic-contextual approach, moral communication is a third important element of the model. The morality of today is to be found 'in the processes of moral communication rather than in specifically moral institutions'.[54] When our society does not have a universal ethics, social interaction and communication become the source for moral assessments: 'Similarity of views on morally relevant issues in social interaction needs to be cautiously negotiated in specific communicative processes between the parties to a social encounter'.[55]

To some extent, and more than before, decision-making in late modern society has to be based on a pragmatic and contextual moral reasoning. The ethical uncertainty of late modernity supports the emphasis on contextualism and pragmatism that in the previous section of this paper was linked to the epistemic uncertainty surrounding this society. Continuing moral learning processes – making new paths by walking them – are as required as learning processes related to the impossibility of mastering the complex causality chains of late modern society.

The legal process offers one such medium for communication through which the contextual and pragmatic moral communication and encounter may take place. Sometimes even the moral communication in various relationships – between the parties, between the parties and the judge, in relation to other interested parties, in relation to the media as well as in relation to the population as a whole – may be a more important function of a case than the actual solution of the problem.[56] It has been claimed that law can offer a context in which one within the present fragmented multicultural society can discursively approach at least some moral issues: 'Legal communication and legal identity may be interpreted as constructions to *make possible* a dialogue between different views of life, different conceptions of the good life, different language games and, perhaps, different expert cultures.'[57]

This communicative function of the law is relevant not only nationally, but also in a European and globalised context. It may become important for the moral discourse across the borders that is needed in the era of globalisation. The role of law as a forum for an internationalised moral discourse in an extreme form has become visible for example in the establishment of international war crimes tribunals and similar institutions. However, this function of the law can be seen also in mundane contexts that are of more interest in this paper. For example, the development of an international *lex mercatoria* can be understood in this way. Its rules for international business transactions reflects a pragmatic

---

[54] Luckmann (1996) 76.

[55] Luckmann (1996) 81.

[56] Raes (1996) 25 emphasises the communicative side of the legal procedure.

[57] Raes (1996) 38.

morality, based on the expectations those engaged in such transactions have of each other and it has grown out of a discursive confrontation of various views on what one regards as acceptable behaviour in such activity.

Offering a medium for moral communication law becomes a part of the continuing and infinite learning process that is typical of moral building in late modern society. This requires a law that is sufficiently open towards moral assessments and does not close its eyes to the inevitable moral judgments that have to be made. At the same time the law has to recognise the individual moral responsibility of those using and applying the law.

The pragmatic moral learning processes require a sufficiently flexible law. It should be a law with a contextual focus, allowing space for pragmatic moral decisions to be made in their context. It is a law that formulates its arguments in categories of real life rather than in abstract legal categories.

4 Implications for a Contract Code

Societal diagnoses of the above kind indeed seem to have implications for the idea of general codifications of private law. Present society needs another form of law than the German and French societies did when the great European codifications were created. Law should today be much more open than before to processes of constant learning and reassessments of both epistemic and ethical questions and its approach should be pragmatic and contextual.

These requirements seem difficult to fulfil in an optimal manner within the reign of a general civil code, at least if the concept of a code is understood in the traditional way, referring to a collection of norms which should not only fulfil strong demands for systematic coherence, but also be relatively stable and immune to quick changes. Contextual morality is difficult to connect with a general civil code with a strong systematic structure. A code does not allow to a sufficient degree the learning processes within law that are required today. It does not offer room for creating the roads by walking them, neither for the courts nor – and this is still more important – for the legislature. A systematic codification seems incompatible with the pragmatic morality of late modernity. The more abstract the envisaged codification is, obviously the more acute the tension becomes.[58]

The system represents tradition in law and tradition is loosing force here, as elsewhere, due to the general decline of systematic normative authority in late modern society.[59] The grand narrative of law as a system is as unconvincing

---

[58] See examples in my paper Wilhelmsson (2002a) 365 *et seq.*

[59] On the concrete legal level national legal systematisations of course lose force also due to the pressure from pragmatic and pointillist European and international new legal materials that the national systems are constantly confronted with. It is a fact that Europeanisation has removed much of the importance from civil law's traditional 'programmatic desire to fit new cases and legislation into the national

as other systematical normative authority based on tradition. Legal tradition,
and legal systematisations, can only survive as far as they can be constantly
and pragmatically justified in the face of contextual solutions that do not fit the
system.

In this light, the codification ideal of the 19th century no longer seems very
well-founded. However, abstract societal analysis and empirical facts do not
necessarily fit seamlessly together. There is an obvious empirical counterclaim
to the claim that large scale codifications are an outmoded form of regulation:
there has relatively recently been a 'successful enactment of new civil codes' in
the Netherlands and in a variety of post-socialist countries.[60] A closer look at this
counter-argument, however, reveals it to be less convincing. The Dutch and the
post-socialist enactments either were prepared over a very long period of time
or were the result of thorough societal upheavals, but the contextual morality
and need for continuing learning processes, relating both to the dynamic of
commercial life and to varying welfarist demands, generate needs for changes
also in a shorter time-perspective and within more stable general social structures.[61]

The criticism of codification seems most forceful when speaking about a
general civil code, especially if the code contains a fairly abstract systematic
structure, crowned by a 'general part'. The criticism does not seem equally
convincing when speaking about more limited parts of the private law edifice.
The lack of belief in a grand, all-compassing narrative on late modern society of
course does not as such rule out the possibility and even desirability of systematical part-structures. Within the legal sphere, does contract law not represent
a part which could form a useful system of its own? Are the above arguments
against a total codification of European private law relevant with regard to a
systematical European Contract Code?

Most certainly a contract code is less problematic than a general civil code
in this respect, but I still think that the arguments sketched here have some
force in this context as well. Within the sphere of contract law, however, there
is an obvious counter-argument against the thesis that the general systematic
structure of a code does not function well under the ethical uncertainty of late
modernity. This counter-argument relates to the perceived technical nature of
contract law: Is contract law not so legal-technical that ethics plays a minor role
in this context?

The obvious and easy answer to this counter-argument is a reference to one
of the basic themes of the contract law discourse during many decades, namely

system', Smits (2004) 237. This fact as such cannot, however, be used as an argument against proposals
for new European systematisations, as it rather is one of the main arguments for a European codification of those who still believe in the usefulness of a general code in present society.

[60] Basedow (2001) 40 et seq.

[61] The Dutch code in fact reflects this by being very flexible, as it has been said to 'provide the courts with
so much freedom that they essentially determine what the law is', Smits (2002) 30.

the confrontation of 'traditional' or 'liberalist' contract law with something that could be described as the '"Social" Side of Contract Law'.[62] The vision of contract law as mainly a collection of default rules that facilitate the functioning of the 'free market' is confronted with new phenomena that have been described with the help of concepts like 'social contract law'[63], 'welfarism in contract law'[64] and 'contractual solidarity'[65]. It is of course impossible to denounce the ethical relevance of discussions of this kind.

However, the situation is in fact much more complicated than the relatively obvious dichotomies of the above kind suggest. Within the 'social' or 'welfarist' paradigm new ethical cleavages appear. One has to recognise that from this perspective of contract law several basic issues of value are constantly at play, issues that relate to other dichotomies like those between commutative and distributive justice, between market-rational and market-rectifying regulation, between internal and external perspectives of contract, between ability-orientation and need-orientation as well as between the protection of the parties to the contract and the protection of other values. I have analysed these dichotomies elsewhere and suggested that six main varieties of welfarism in contract law can be distinguished:[66]

1. Market-rational welfarism	Regulation aimed at improving party autonomy and the function of the market mechanism (*e.g.* information rules)
2. Market-correcting welfarism	Regulation aimed at rectifying outcomes of the market mechanism in order to promote acceptable contractual behaviour (*e.g.* substantive fairness rules)
3. Internally redistributive welfarism	Regulation aimed at redistributing benefits in favour of a group of weaker parties in a contractual relationship (*e.g.* rules affecting main subject matter of contract)
4. Externally redistributive welfarism	Regulation aimed at redistributing benefits in favour of the disadvantaged within a group of contract parties in similar situations (*e.g.* equality rules)
5. Need-rational welfarism	Regulation aimed at giving benefits to parties with special needs in comparison with other parties in similar situations (*e.g.* rules on *social force majeure*)
6. Public values welfarism	Regulation aimed at giving contract law protection to interests and values not related to the parties (*e.g.* protection of environmental values and human rights)

---

[62] Lurger (2004). Many examples can be found in the collection of essays Wilhelmsson (ed.) (1993).

[63] See *e.g.* my book *Social Contract Law and European Integration*: Wilhelmsson (1995), in which I tried to bring the issue of social justice on the then rather premature harmonisation agenda.

[64] Brownsword, Howells and Wilhelmsson (1994).

[65] Lurger (1998).

[66] Wilhelmsson (2004).

All these kinds of welfarism are represented in various combinations in national contract laws in Europe and most of them in the *Acquis* as well. Obviously there is no coherent system of values behind the contract laws of the EC and the member states and I believe that it is not even possible to combine the existing varieties in any coherent system. One has to take a stand on various questions on a issue by issue and case by case basis. The variety of possibilities in other words implies that the solutions are necessarily too political, too decisionistic to be carved in stone once and for all. Also in contract law there should be a sufficient scope for pragmatic and contextual solutions, based on open moral reasoning, both for the legislatures and the courts.

As my examples indicate, juridically incoherent and rapidly changing contextual solutions are obviously relatively common when dealing with issues like consumer protection and the protection of other weaker party interests within contract law. Therefore it is not surprising that for example the Principles of European Contract Law refrains from making special provision for consumer contracts, as they 'raise policy issues more appropriately determined by Community law and national legislation'.[67] However, the PECL has not drawn the most obvious conclusion from this statement, that is to limit the application of the Principles only to commercial contracts like the corresponding UNIDROIT Principles do, but has chosen the 'worst' solution, that is to formally adopt a general sphere of application but then largely ignore the consumer issues. This solution represents precisely – in this respect[68] – such an abstract approach that is hard to accept in view of the need for constant contextual and morally transparent assessments of good regulation in late modern society.

However, the need for contextualism does not relate to the 'social side' of contract law alone. Also within the commercial sphere proper one finds various 'sub-cultures' within which the understandings of morally right behaviour differ. Of course national commercial cultures are different, ranging *e.g.* from the more cooperative Scandinavian, and – to a lesser degree – German commercial cultures to the more competitive British one,[69] and these variations produce different expectations of good moral behaviour[70] in these cultures which can be reproduced in various Europeanised and internationalised commercial settings. It is for example felt to be completely natural that contracting in the maritime area is strongly affected by British views, whilst the regulation of some other contracts – such as commercial agency – may acquire for example a more

---

[67] Lando and Beale (eds.) (2000) xxv.

[68] In other respects the PECL have striven towards a commendable realistic and less abstract language. The authors of the Principles of European Contract Law at least 'tried to avoid legal concepts and used a factual language, which is easier to translate', Lando (2001) 5.

[69] Teubner (1998) 11 relates his analysis to this difference.

[70] Cf. *e.g.* the various attitudes towards pre-contractual information duties in these countries, see *e.g.* Brownsword, Hird and Howells (eds.) (1999).

German flavour. Special branches of business – like the IT sector – may also produce their own standards of good behaviour that affect the contextual assessments of what a good law should contain. New types of contracts are constantly produced by the market actors to respond to new needs in the marketplace and the various roots of such contract types may make different contextual judgments desirable.

So, despite the fact that codification of contract law is less problematic than the adoption of a complete civil code, it seems that also in this sphere there are good reasons for restraint. Also here one could well justify a more fragmented European approach, containing perhaps one or a few general (re)statements like the PECL, a codification of some important contract types, like the CISG, and contextual regulation of problems that have been considered especially acute from an internal market perspective or from a social justice point of view, like many of the rules to be found in the present *Acquis*. Such a pluralist approach would also in this area leave sufficient room for the free movement of legal ideas and doctrines.

If the codification road is embarked upon, obviously a minimum code[71] that would accept local assessments above the minimum set by the code would be easier to accept than a completely harmonised instrument. If successful, it would retain the learning capacity of the law and the possibility of free movement of legal ideas and doctrines, but guarantee some minimum level of protection to all persons under EU jurisdiction. There is, however, on the other hand always a risk that the minimum in practice will be considered the rule towards which national legislation and practice will converge, and the necessary flexibility and possibilities of development will be lost.

Much of the discussion today seems to point in the direction of adopting an optional European code, to be chosen by the parties. This solution would obviously be less destructive than a code that would directly replace existing national laws. However, also here the risk of the option becoming the general norm is self-evident, and for at least some participants in the discourse this is the ultimate goal. Therefore I would be rather cautious, also with respect to this alternative and stick to the idea of a continuously renewable, perhaps semi-official (re)statement of European contract law rather than having an optional code that might be quite difficult to improve and amend in the light of new commercial and social realities.

---

[71] Cf. Mattei (2002) 215.

5   A Grand Legal Narrative after all: Fundamental Rights?

The above analysis proceeds on the assumption that tradition, authority and ethics in late modernity have collapsed into a fragmented mess of contextual morality that makes it difficult to uphold the (Continental) idea of a systematic and coherent law. Is this assumption, reflected in diagnoses of contemporary society offered by many respected social scientists, credible or do we believe in some common societal grand narrative that would offer the basis for a coherent codification of contract law after all? Two possible candidates for such a story are easy to name: the Free Market and Fundamental (Human) Rights.

One may indeed claim that the belief in the free market today represents the generally accepted grand narrative, that through the collapse of common local values we are rather experiencing a return to a pure market-liberalist ethos on a more global scale. This diagnosis certainly reflects much of the development going on in the world, and it is also closely connected with basic features of the European Union.[72] If accepted, the narrative would repudiate much of the argument that the societal situation of today requires a different stand on the issue of codification than 19th century market-liberalist society. Personally I doubt, however, that the free market narrative would be so generally credible that it could convince others than those that are already saved. I rather assume that the economists have lost their position as unquestionable authority together with other experts.

This is not necessarily, however, the relevant angle for the contract law issue. Even without accepting the free market as the only grand societal narrative, one could claim that it has such a position that contract law at least should be coherently constructed based on free market ideals.[73] However, contemporary legal experience in Europe does not support an approach in which the free market is seen as the only key to ethical coherence even within the limited sphere of contract law. The story of the Europeanisation of contract law on the contrary has been focused on mandatory regulation, at least partially with a market-recti-

---

[72]   In the context of EC regulation one may perhaps also refer to a more specific narrative concerning the
       creation of an Internal Market. However, this narrative has a relatively restricted substance as such,
       especially when discussing the content of European rules. As it balances between dismantling national
       mandatory rules that can constitute barriers of trade and harmonising such mandatory rules in the
       interest also of consumers (and other affected parties) it just produces what Norbert Reich originally
       quite adequately called the Janus-face of European consumer law, see Reich (1993) 45. The internal
       market agenda is therefore not a substantive tool that could remove the need for contextualism. On the
       contrary, it is a new and complicating element in the contextual decisions that have to be made.

[73]   In this context I pass over the fact that in the legal sphere the market narrative in addition suffers from
       an unavoidable circularity: as the market is constituted by its ground (legal) rules – there is no market
       without such rules – the ground rules cannot, at least in their entirety, be deduced from the idea of the
       very market they are constituting.

fying rather than only a market-rational flavour.[74] As mentioned above, the varieties of welfarism in European contract law are multifarious. Only if one strives to dismantle the mandatory regulation in this area – which indeed seems to be the agenda of some of the proponents of a European code[75] – can the free market agenda be offered as a key for a coherent contract code.[76] This is, however, a strongly moral-political decision that seems very much at odds with actual legal experience in the European Union and its member states, and it is probably also in conflict with the fundamental rights narrative which I consider a more promising candidate for the role of a convincing new grand narrative. The fact that the Principles of European Contract Law mostly contain default rules is due to the unofficial nature of the collection as principles that only can be offered to be chosen by the parties and does not reflect any attitude according to which there is no need for mandatory regulation.

The free market narrative cannot explain many of the substantive mandatory rules in contemporary contract law and it cannot offer much guidance either as to when such rules should be used. In the final assessment the free market narrative needs to be balanced with other views in each context. Even when leaning more in the direction of market rationality than I personally would find necessary, one cannot escape the need for pragmatic contextual assessments.

Having said this I do not want to denounce the possible special 'constitutional' position of both free market and internal market arguments in the European Union. If one uses such constitutional arguments in this context,[77] however, one rather brings the issue under the heading of the other possible candidate for a grand narrative of today, the fundamental rights narrative. Then the 'fundamental right of the free market' would have to be confronted with other fundamental rights rather than form *the* key for building the system. I will now take a closer look at the fundamental rights narrative that, as I mentioned before, I see as a more challenging candidate to become a convincing grand ethical narrative for present society than the free market narrative.

---

[74] See *e.g.* the discussions on justifications of limits to party autonomy in many of the contributions in Grundmann, Kerber and Weatherill (eds.) (2001).

[75] To mention just one example: Tilmann (1993) 278, has expressly supported a European codification with the argument that he sees in it a way of restoring the balance between the rules for standard cases honouring private autonomy and exceptional rules for unbalanced situations which have been emphasised in Community law.

[76] Even in this case the key would have to be refined, however. Also default rules may have various ethical backgrounds. One such ethical issue related also to commercial contract law is the tension between rules furthering co-operation and rules rewarding self-interest.

[77] In Finland Juha Pöyhönen, *Uusi varallisuusoikeus (New property law)* (Pöyhönen (2000)) 82 has argued that the idea of a functioning market can be understood as an unwritten fundamental right in line with other fundamental rights.

Despite the decline of the authority of ethical systems and ethical expertise
on local and national levels, there have been continuous attempts to create new
even global ethical systems often dressed in the language of human rights.
The doctrine on human rights (fundamental rights) today clearly aspires to a
central place in an ethical world order. To be fair, globally there is probably still
a relatively weak basis for any real consensus, as the acceptance of human rights
in many places seems more rhetorical – amounting just to a formal acceptance
of international and national legal instruments – than real. However, within the
European Union far-reaching agreement concerning many issues has emerged,
first based on the European Convention on Human Rights. These fundamental
rights have been included in the EU *acquis* by the European Court of Justice.[78]
In 2000, in connection with the Treaty of Nice, the Charter of Fundamental
Rights of the European Union was adopted. Although formally only soft law, it is
increasingly cited as argument in legal reasoning. The fundamental rights will
be a part of the European Constitutional Treaty, if it eventually will be accepted.

Is this growing emphasis on fundamental rights becoming the grand narrative that could offer a basis for a coherent codification of European contract law?
Even though the intuitive answer of lawyers, who distinguish horizontal private
law relations from vertical public law relations and place fundamental rights
issues in the latter box, would be negative, more recent legal experience shows
that a closer look at the issue is worthwhile.

It is in fact fairly easy to find examples that show fundamental rights to have
relevance in contract law. Traditionally in many countries the constitutional
protection of ownership has been used to counteract retroactive or too severe
limitations of the principle of freedom of contract. In such cases the fundamental rights arguments are used in their traditional role, as devices to protect
citizens against state measures that are perceived as wrongful, and which
only indirectly affect the regulation of the horizontal relationship between the
parties. However, to a growing extent fundamental rights principles are applied
directly to this relationship. The variety of fundamental rights principles that
has been considered relevant is surprisingly large. I will mention just a few
startling examples.

The German guarantee case has to be mentioned in this context, as it is
very well known and often cited in comparative discussions. The decision of
the German Constitutional court concerned the validity of a personal guarantee given by an uneducated and unemployed daughter for her father's (business) debt. As the Supreme Court in Germany had upheld the bank's claim
against the guarantor she appealed successfully to the Constitutional Court. It
held that the courts had a constitutional obligation to intervene, on the basis of
the general clauses of the *BGB*, in contracts which are exceptionally onerous
because of a structural imbalance of bargaining power. This result was based on

---

[78] See already the ERT case, Case C-260/89 [1989] ECR I-2925.

the fundamental right protection of not only private autonomy, but also of the social state (the so called *Sozialstaatsklausel*[79]).[80]

The connection between the social justice agenda inherent in the *Sozialstaatsklausel* and contract law is fairly obvious. As far as economic and social rights are protected as fundamental rights, their possible impact on contract law is easy to imagine, as rights that counterbalance the freedom rights of private autonomy and property. However, other fundamental rights as well may – perhaps more surprisingly – occasionally be used horizontally to determine the outcome of contract cases. In an Italian case freedom of association was used to legitimate a decision according to which it was contrary to good faith for the insurer to uphold a life insurance contract, when the owner of the insurance company (Mr. Berlusconi) founded his own political party with the help of the acquisition network of the insurance company: the insured could not be forced to contribute to the founding of a political party he did not like.[81] And in a German case freedom of speech – that included the freedom to receive information – gave a Turkish tenant the right to install a satellite dish to receive Turkish TV programmes despite the landlord's refusal to grant permission.[82]

In fact, in private law doctrine and practice in many European countries[83] there seems to be a tendency to increasingly use fundamental rights arguments in private law reasoning. This turn towards fundamental rights is both understandable and commendable against the background of the needs of late modern society, as analysed in this paper.

The increasing emphasis on fundamental rights reasoning in private law opens the private law system to more transparent moral reasoning. Fundamental rights often seem to be used as tools to achieve morally acceptable solutions in cases where the established private law norms are seen to produce unjust results. The German personal guarantee case is a very good example of this. Fundamental rights reasoning in contract cases also usually has to be closely connected with the context of the particular case. The fundamental rights agenda, in other words, provides new tools for reaching acceptable contextual judgments. In short, late modern society's need for more contextual moral assessment seems well reflected in the increasing weight given to fundamental rights arguments in horizontal relationships.

In addition, in a European context the fundamental rights agenda is able to some extent to serve and develop the connection between the local (national)

---

[79] The German *Grundgesetz* art. 20 and 28.

[80] BVerfGE 89, 214, *NJW* 1994, 36.

[81] Trib. Milano, 30-3-1994, *Foro it.*, 1994, I, 1572, cit. per Hesselink (2003) 4.

[82] BVerfGE 90, 27.

[83] See *e.g.* Friedmann and Barak-Erez (eds.) (2001), Canaris (1999), Debet (2002) and Hesselink (2003). In Finland the debate has been intense: *e.g.* Pöyhönen (2000) and Länsineva, *Perusoikeudet ja varallisuussuhteet (Summary: System of Basic Rights and Property)* (Länsineva (2002)).

and European levels of law.[84] As fundamental rights belong to the common
European deep structure of legal thinking,[85] they are parts of a common
substantive legal language in Europe. The free movement of legal ideas and
doctrines is facilitated by such a language.

Of course these advantages of fundamental rights reasoning can only be
realised if the arguments are indeed used contextually and in a morally transparent way. If the fundamental rights reasoning develops into strongly special-
ised forms of legal-technical discourse mastered only by constitutional lawyers
and human rights lawyers, much of these gains are lost. The moral transparency
just becomes more blurred in yet another confusing playground for the legal
expertise. Even though one certainly could mention examples of human rights
law becoming too legal-technical, both nationally and in the European setting, I
think (hope) such a tendency can be avoided.

The fact that the turn towards fundamental rights in private law can be
assessed in a positive light does not, however, solve the codification issue. I
cannot see fundamental rights providing the hoped for basis for a coherent
contract law system.

Fundamental rights reasoning obviously could fulfill such a task only if
the fundamental rights themselves could be understood as a coherent system.
However, this does not seem to be the case. The three generations of fundamental rights, that is traditional freedom rights, economic and social rights
and collective rights, have their roots in different ethical environments that at
least partially may contradict each other. These aspects are reflected in various
ways in the European Charter of Fundamental Rights – containing chapters on
dignity, freedoms, equality, solidarity, citizen's rights and justice – with obvious
internal tensions as a result. In fundamental rights doctrine even those who
believe in the systematic nature of the rights have to admit tensions, for example
between formal and real equality, that is between freedom rights and economic
and social rights; the only solution offered is then a coherent balancing (whatever that can be) of the various fundamental rights principles against each other
in individual cases.[86] In other words, moral contextualism cannot be avoided
with the help of fundamental rights, but is rather reinforced by this mode of

---

[84] Therefore it is strange that the relationship between fundamental rights and contract law is not analysed
in the Communication and the Action Plan on European contract law (Communication from the
Commission to the Council and the European Parliament on European Contract Law, COM (2001) 398
final and Communication from the Commission to the European Parliament and the Council. A More
Coherent Contract Law. An Action Plan, COM (2003) 68 final). It is striking that the Commission in its
contract law agenda ignores such elements, despite the fact that the preparation of the Constitutional
Treaty, including the fundamental rights of the Europeans, has been going on at the same time.

[85] This is one of the recurring themes in Tuori (2002).

[86] Länsineva (2002) 116–132.

legal thinking. Fundamental rights do not offer a homogeneous basis on which to build a coherent system of contract law.

In addition, even if it were possible to construe a coherent system of fundamental rights, the relationship between many, even important contract law issues and the fundamental rights seems so distant that a fundamental rights based understanding of these issues feels very artificial. How does one, for example, connect the perhaps most important contract law issue, that is the question concerning the proper basic liability rule – strict liability, control liability or negligence – in a convincing way[87] to the system of fundamental rights? Can fundamental rights offer any real guidance when discussing important practical issues like for example the definition of non-conformity or the obligation to give notice concerning lack of conformity? Although important choices connected with values are reflected in these questions they are politico-moral choices that are to be made within the sphere of alternatives that the fundamental rights leave open to the decision-makers rather than to be determined by these rights.

Fundamental rights reasoning does not solve the problem of fragmentation. It tends to open up the law to more transparent moral assessment and contextual judgment, and it is in this sense in line with the needs of late modernity, but it cannot offer any systematic key for creating a general and coherent European Contract Code.

---

[87] The thought of a liability for the party's own sphere of control, like the liability rule adopted in CISG, may in very general terms be connected with the value of freedom and the responsibility connected with freedom. But the same kind of connection may be made also for the other possible liability rules.

REFERENCES

BALDWIN (1997)
R. Baldwin, "Introduction – Risk: The Legal Contribution", in: R.
Baldwin (ed.), *Law and Uncertainty; Risks and Legal Processes*, (London
etc.: Kluwer 1997)

BASEDOW (2001)
J. Basedow, "Codification of Private Law in the European Union: the
making of a Hybrid", 9 *European Review of Private Law* (2001) 35-50

BAUMAN (1991)
Z. Bauman, *Modernity and Ambivalence* (Oxford etc.: Polity Press 1991)

BAUMAN (1992)
Z. Bauman, *Intimations of Postmodernity* (London: Routledge 1992)

BAUMAN (1993)
Z. Bauman, *Postmodern Ethics* (Oxford etc.: Blackwell 1993)

BAUMAN (1995)
Z. Bauman, *Life in Fragments. Essays in Postmodern Morality* (Oxford
etc.: Blackwell 1995)

BAUMAN (1997)
Z. Bauman, interview in: 3 *Niin & Näin* (1997)

BECHMANN (1991)
G. Bechmann, "Risiko als Schlüsselkategorie der
Gesellschaftstheorie", 74 *Kritische Vierteljahresschrift für Gesetzgebung
und Rechtswissenschaft* (1991) 212-240

BECK (1986)
U. Beck, *Risikogesellschaft, Auf dem Weg in eine andere Moderne*
(Frankfurt am Main: Suhrkamp 1986)

BECK (1994)
U. Beck, "The Reinvention of Politics: Towards a Theory of Reflexive
Modernization", in: U. Beck, A. Giddens and S. Lash (eds.), *Reflexive
Modernization* (Cambridge: Polity Press, 1994) 1-55

BERGER (2001)
K. P. Berger, "Harmonisation of European Contract Law: The
Influence of Comparative Law", 50 *International and Comparative Law
Quarterly* (2001) 877-900

BROWNSWORD, HIRD AND HOWELLS (EDS.) (1999)
R. Brownsword, N. J. Hird and G. Howells (eds.), *Good faith in
Contract. Concept and Context* (Aldershot: Ashgate 1999)

BROWNSWORD, HOWELLS AND WILHELMSSON (EDS.) (1994)
R. Brownsword, G. Howells and T. Wilhelmsson (eds.), *Welfarism in
Contract Law* (Aldershot: Dartmouth 1994)

BRÜGGEMEIER (1997)

G. Brüggemeier, "The Control of Corporate Conduct and Reduction of Uncertainty by Tort Law", in: R. Baldwin (ed.), *Law and Uncertainty; Risks and Legal Processes* (London etc.: Kluwer 1997) 57-74

BRÜGGEMEIER (1999)

G. Brüggemeier, *Prinzipien des Haftungsrechts* (Baden-Baden: Nomos 1999)

CANARIS (1999)

C. W. Canaris, *Grundrechte und Privatrecht* (Berlin etc.: Walter de Gruyter 1999)

CASTELLS (1999)

M. Castells, *The Information Age: Economy, Society and Culture*, Vol. III End of the Millennium, revised edition (Oxford etc.: Blackwell Publishers 1999)

DEBET (2002)

A. Debet, *L'influence de la Convention européenne des droits de l'homme sur le droit civil* (Paris: Dalloz 2002)

EUROPEAN COMMISSION (2001)

European Commission, *Communication from the Commission to the Council and the European Parliament on European Contract Law*, COM (2001) 398 final

EUROPEAN COMMISSION (2003)

European Commission, *Communication from the Commission to the European Parliament and the Council. A More Coherent Contract Law – An Action Plan*, COM (2003) 68 final

EWALD (1986)

F. Ewald, *L'état providence* (Paris: Grasset 1986)

EWALD (1989)

F. Ewald, "Die Versicherungsgesellschaft", 22 *Kritische Justiz* (1989) 385-393

FRIEDMANN AND BARAK-EREZ (EDS.) (2001)

D. Friedmann and D. Barak-Erez (eds.), *Human Rights in Private Law* (Oxford: Hart Publishing 2001)

GIDDENS (1990)

A. Giddens, *The Consequences of Modernity* (Cambridge: Polity Press 1990)

GIDDENS (1994)

A. Giddens, "Living in a Post-Traditional Society", in: U. Beck, A. Giddens and S. Lash (eds.), *Reflexive Modernization* (Cambridge: Polity Press 1994) 56-109

GRUNDMANN, KERBER AND WEATHERILL (EDS.) (2001)

S. Grundmann, W. Kerber and S. Weatherill (eds.), *Party Autonomy and the Role of Information in the Internal Market* (Berlin: Walter de Gruyter 2001)

HESSELINK (2003)

M. W. Hesselink, "The Horizontal Effect of Social Rights in European
Contract Law", *Europa e Diritto Privato*, Fasc. 1 (2003) 1-18

HOWELLS AND WILHELMSSON (1998)

G. Howells and T. Wilhelmsson, "EC and US Approaches to Consumer
Protection – Should the Gap Be Bridged?", 17 *Yearbook of European Law*
1997 (Oxford: Clarendon Press 1998) 207-268

HUTCHINSON (1997)

A. Hutchinson, "Life After Shopping: From Consumers to Citizens",
in: I. Ramsay (ed.), *Consumer Law in the Global Economy* (Aldershot:
Ashgate 1997) 25-46

JAMESON (1991)

F. Jameson, *Postmodernism or, the cultural logic of late capitalism*
(London etc.: Verso 1991)

JOERGES (1983)

C. Joerges, "Der Schutz des Verbrauchers und die Einheit des
Zivilrechts", 28 *Die Aktiengesellschaft* (1983) 57-67

JOERGES (2003)

C. Joerges, "Zur Legitimität der Europäisierung des Privatrechts:
Überlegungen zu einem Recht-Fertigungs-Recht für das
Mehrebenensystem der EU", in: C. Joerges and G. Teubner (eds.),
*Rechtsverfassungsrecht; Recht-Fertigung zwischen Privatrechtsdogmatik
und Gesellschaftstheorie* (Baden-Baden: Nomos 2003) 183-212

LANDO (2000A)

O. Lando, "Optional or Mandatory Europeanisation of Contract Law", 8
European Review of Private Law (2000) 59-69

LANDO (2000B)

O. Lando, "Some Features of the Law of Contract in the Third
Millennium", in: *Scandinavian Studies in Law* Vol. 40 (Stockholm:
Stockholm Institute for Scandinavian Law 2000) 343-402

LANDO (2001)

O. Lando, "The Structure and the Salient Features of the Principles of
European Contract Law", 6 *Juridica International* (2001) 4-15

LANDO AND BEALE (EDS.) (2000)

O. Lando and H. Beale (eds.), *Principles of European Contract Law, Parts
I and II* (The Hague: Kluwer 2000)

LÄNSINEVA (2002)

P. Länsineva, *Perusoikeudet ja varallisuussuhteet* (Helsinki:
Suomalainen lakimiesyhdistys 2002)

LUCKMANN (1996)

T. Luckmann, "The Privatization of Religion and Morality", in: P.
Heelas, S. Lash and P. Morris (eds.), *Detraditionalization. Critical
Reflections on Authority and Identity* (Oxford: Blackwell 1996) 72-86

LUHMANN (1991)

N. Luhmann, *Soziologie des Risikos* (Berlin: Walter de Gruyter 1991)

LURGER (1998)

B. Lurger, *Vertragliche Solidarität* (Baden-Baden: Nomos 1998)

LURGER (2004)

B. Lurger, "The 'Social' Side of Contract Law and the New Principle of Regard and Fairness", in: *Towards a European Civil Code*, 3rd ed, edited by A. Hartkamp *et al* (The Hague: Kluwer Law International 2004) 273-295

MATTEI (2002)

U. Mattei, "Hard Minimal Code Now! – a Critique of 'Softness' and a Plea for Responsibility in the European Debate over Codification", in: S. Grundmann and J. Stuyck (eds.), *An Academic Green Paper on European Contract Law* (The Hague: Kluwer Law International 2002) 215-233

MENGER (1904)

A. Menger, *Das Bürgerliche Recht und die besitzlosen Volksklassen*, 3rd ed. (Tübingen: Laupp 1904)

NIELSEN (1996)

T. H. Nielsen, "Risici – i teknologien, i samfundet og i hovederne", 73 *Retfærd* (1996) 61-77

OGUS (1997)

A. Ogus, "Risk Management and 'Rational' Social Regulation", in: R. Baldwin (ed.), *Law and Uncertainty. Risks and Legal Processes* (London: Kluwer 1997) 139-153

PÖYHÖNEN (2000)

J. Pöyhönen, *Uusi varallisuusoikeus* (Helsinki: Kauppakaari 2000)

RAES (1996)

K. Raes, "Communicating Legal Identity: A Note on the Inevitable Counterfactuality of Legal Communication", in: D. Nelken (ed.), *Law as Communication* (Aldershot: Dartmouth 1996) 25-44

REICH (1993)

N. Reich, *Europäisches Verbraucherschutzrecht* (Baden-Baden: Nomos 1993)

SHAPIRO (1997)

M. Shapiro, "The Frontiers of Science Doctrine: American Experiences with the Judicial Control of Science-Based Decision-Making", in: C. Joerges, K.-H. Ladeur and E. Vos (eds.), *Integrating Scientific Expertise into Regulatory Decision-Making* (Baden-Baden: Nomos 1997) 325-342

SMITS (2002)

J. Smits, *The Making of European Private Law* (Antwerp etc.: Intersentia 2002)

SMITS (2004)

J. Smits, "The Europeanisation of National Legal Systems: Some
Consequences for Legal Thinking in Civil Law Countries", in: M.
Van Hoecke (ed.) *Epistemology and Methodology of Comparative Law*
(Oxford: Hart Publishing 2004) 229-245

STEELE (1999)

J. Steele, "Damage, Uncertainty, and Risk: Trends in Environmental
Liability", in: T. Wilhelmsson and S. Hurri (eds.), *From Dissonance
to Sense; Welfare State Expectations, Privatisation and Private Law*
(Aldershot: Ashgate 1999) 474-502

STUDY GROUP ON SOCIAL JUSTICE IN EUROPEAN PRIVATE LAW
(2004)

Study Group on Social Justice in European Private Law, "Social Justice
in European Contract Law: a Manifesto", 10 *European Law Journal*
(2004) 653-674

TEUBNER (1998)

G. Teubner, "Legal Irritants: Good Faith in British Law or How
Unifying Law Ends Up in New Divergences", 61 *Modern Law Review*
(1998) 11-32

TILMANN (1993)

W. Tilmann, "Das gewerbliche Rechtsschutz vor den Konturen
eines europäischen Privatrechts", 42 *Gewerblicher Rechtsschutz und
Urheberrecht Internationaler Teil* (1993) 275-278

THOMPSON (1996)

J. B. Thompson, "Tradition and Self in a Mediated World", in: P.
Heelas, S. Lash and P. Morris (eds.), *Detraditionalization; Critical
Reflections on Authority and Identity*, (Cambridge Mass. etc.: Blackwell
Publishers 1996) 89-108

TUORI (1999)

K. Tuori, "Post-Modern Law?", in: T. Wilhelmsson and S. Hurri (eds.)
*From Dissonance to Sense; Welfare State Expectations, Privatisation and
Private Law* (Aldershot: Ashgate 1999)

TUORI (2002)

K. Tuori, *Critical Legal Positivism* (Aldershot: Ashgate 2002)

WADENSTRÖM (1998)

R. Wadenström, *Stora och små europeiska historier; en avhandling om
vårt postmoderna Europa* (Helsinki: Helsingin yliopiston filosofian
laitoksen julkaisuja 1998)

WIEACKER (1974)

F. Wieacker, *Industriegesellschaft und Privatrechtsordnung* (Frankfurt
am Main: Fischer 1974)

WILHELMSSON (ED.) (1993)

T. Wilhelmsson (ed.), *Perspectives of Critical Contract Law* (Aldershot:
Dartmouth 1993)

WILHELMSSON (1995)

T. Wilhelmsson, *Social Contract Law and European Integration*
(Aldershot: Dartmouth 1995)

WILHELMSSON (2001)

T. Wilhelmsson, "Europeiseringen av privaträtten: för ett fragmenterat
utbyte av idéer", 114 *Tidsskrift for Rettsvitenskap* (2001) 1-32

WILHELMSSON (2002A)

T. Wilhelmsson, "The Design of an Optional (Re)statement of
European Contract Law – Real Life Instead of Dead Concepts", in:
S. Grundmann and J. Stuyck (eds.), *An Academic Green Paper on
European Contract Law* (The Hague: Kluwer Law International 2002)
353-372

WILHELMSSON (2002B)

T. Wilhelmsson, "Private Law in the EU: Harmonised or Fragmented
Europeanisation", 10 *European Review of Private Law* (2002) 77-94

WILHELMSSON (2003)

T. Wilhelmsson, "The Paradox of the Risk Society and the
Fragmentation of Consumer Law", forthcoming in the proceedings of
the Ninth International Conference on Consumer Law in Athens April
2003.

WILHELMSSON (2004)

T. Wilhelmsson, "Varieties of Welfarism in European Contract Law",
10 *European Law Journal* (2004) 712-733

WILHELMSSON AND HURRI (EDS.) (1999)

T. Wilhelmsson and S. Hurri (eds.), *From Dissonance to Sense. Welfare
State Expectations, Privatisation and Private Law* (Aldershot: Ashgate
1999)

CHAPTER 7

Diversity of Contract Law and the European Internal Market

Jan M. Smits*

1 Introduction: Aim of this Contribution

Does diversity of (contract) law stand in the way of the proper functioning of the European economy? Do diverging legal rules form a barrier for international trade? Is a consumer inclined to buy less abroad because he does not know about the other country's legal system? All these questions deal with the relationship between diversity of (contract) law and decisions made by businesses and consumers. This contribution intends to discuss these questions against the background of the debate on harmonisation of contract law in Europe. This implies that insights from various disciplines are drawn together. It is after all not only (comparative) law, but also economics and psychology that may have something to say about the relationship between legal diversity and the enhancement of interstate trade. The main aim of this contribution is to try to link insights from these various disciplines as they become apparent from the various contributions to this book. In doing so, it is hoped that more insight can be gained into the question to what extent diversity of law is actually a barrier to the proper functioning of the European economy.

There are at least two reasons why this question is of paramount importance. First, there is a rather practical reason. In recent years, an extensive debate has evolved on the need for harmonisation of contract law in Europe. In this debate, it is often asserted that diversity of contract law is burdensome for the European internal market. This is typically 'evidenced' by saying that an Italian businessman may be deterred from contracting in for example Belgium because he does not know about Belgian law.[1] This argument was one of the main reasons for the European Union to start a debate on the most proper way of harmonising contract law in Europe.[2] It is however still an open question to what extent legal diversity in the field of contracts is really a barrier to international trade. This question cannot be answered on basis of knowledge about the law alone. It needs an interdisciplinary approach. As long as there is no evidence for an affirmative answer to the question, it will be difficult for the European Commission to come to a true harmonisation of contract law (see section 2.3).

Second, there is an important scholarly aspect to the relationship between legal diversity and the enhancement of the European economy. In recent years, behavioural models are being incorporated more and more into traditional legal scholarship: it has become increasingly important to integrate realistic insights of what people or businesses actually do into legal and economic questions.[3] The question whether legal diversity influences decisions of companies and consumers fits in very well.

---

* The author wishes to thank Renske van Dijken for valuable research assistance.

[1] See for example Lando (1993) 157 and Lando (2000) 61.

[2] See below, section 3.

[3] For the United States, I point at the work of Cass Sunstein (*e.g.* Sunstein (2000)), Christine Jolls (*e.g.* Jolls (2004)) and Steven Levitt (*e.g.* Levitt (2001)). Also see the contribution of Heico Kerkmeester to this book.

This paper is divided into several sections. The next section describes the present situation in European contract law. This situation can be characterised as *diverse*: several contract law regimes exist next to each other. It is often assumed that this diversity is problematic. This is elaborated in the sections 3 and 4. Section 3 is devoted to the diversity created by the community *acquis* and section 4 to diversity among national legal systems. In this section, several arguments pro and against uniform contract law are discussed. Some conclusions are drawn in the fifth section of this contribution.

2 The Present Situation in European Contract Law: Diversity of Legal Systems

2.1 Four Contract Law Regimes

If one is to characterise contract law in Europe, one can do so by saying that it is *diverse*. Within the European Union, there are at least four types of contract law regimes. First, every member state has its own national contract law, which implies that there are now 25 of such national systems within the EU. Next to these national regimes, there is a set of rules on contract law of European origin. This set consists of a rapidly increasing amount of directives issued by the European Union. Third, there is the international regime created by the Convention on the International Sale of Goods (CISG). This regime is not specifically European, but it certainly does play an important role within the European Union. Finally, there are – within several countries – regional variations of the national model or even (like in the United Kingdom) several fully-fledged legal systems standing next to each other. These four types of regimes are explored in the underneath.

2.2 National Legal Systems

The 25 member states of the European Union all have their own contract law regime. This implies that each national legislator has its own competence in drafting contract law rules and that each country has its own national courts to deal with contract cases. There is at present no highest European authority that could provide binding contract law rules outside the (rather limited) competence of the European Union. This implies that, from all political, economic and monetary unions in the world,[4] the European Union is the most diverse as to the law. Whereas in the United States, contract law is not a matter for the federal government either, one cannot say that American contract law is

---

[4] The most important economic union outside Europe is the North American Free Trade Agreement (NAFTA) between the US, Canada and Mexico. See on regional integration Mattli (1999).

diverse. In fact, the regimes on sale of goods and commercial transactions are very comparable, not in the last place because of the example set by the Uniform Commercial Code, now taken over in almost all American states.[5]

It may be useful to make a distinction between four types of national contract law regimes within the European Union. These four types can be distinguished on basis of common history, the sources of law recognised and the predominant mode of legal thought.[6] The first type then consists of the common law systems of England and Ireland with their emphasis on judge-made law and the central authority of the English House of Lords and the Irish Supreme Court respectively. The common law system of Cyprus (that was a British colony until 1960) also belongs to this group. The second type consists of the traditional civil law countries, characterised by a central role for a national civil code,[7] but also by a highest court whose decisions are in practice often just as important as the code provisions. Among these countries, one can distinguish between those that have a code that is to a greater or lesser extent still based on the Code Napoleon (France, Belgium, Luxemburg, Spain, Portugal, Italy and Malta) and those that have a code more based on the German model (Germany, Austria,[8] Greece and the Netherlands). A third group consists of the Scandinavian member states (Denmark, Sweden and Finland). They are not only characterised by a common history, but also by the existence of several common statutes. Among these are a common statute on sale of movables and a common contract law act.[9] Finally, there is the large group of countries that have entered the European Union in 2004 and that almost all have a new or at least recently revised civil code (Poland, the Czech Republic, Slovakia, Hungary, Estonia, Lithuania, Latvia and Slovenia).[10] The way in which these new or revised codes are applied and inter-preted by the courts of these countries cannot be compared to the way in which this is done in the traditional civil law countries. Generally speaking, the mode of interpretation is much more literal.

Diversity among these 25 contract law regimes does not mean that it is impossible to draft principles all these legal systems have in common. There are now two sets of such principles available: the Principles of European Contract Law[11] and the Gandolfi Code.[12] Neither of these sets, however, repre-sents the individual national contract law regimes. One can only say that they

---

[5] On the UCC, see for example White and Summers (2000).

[6] Cf. Zweigert and Kötz (1998) 68 ff.; see on these types of distinctions Husa (2004) 11 ff.

[7] Cf. Zimmermann (1997) 259 ff.

[8] Austria has a special position as its AGB of 1811 is, as the French Code Civil, also a 'natural law code'.

[9] Cf. Zweigert and Kötz (1998) 280 ff.

[10] Cf. Reich (2004).

[11] Lando and Beale (2000) and Lando et al (2003).

[12] Gandolfi (2001). The Unidroit Principles of International Commercial Contracts (new edition 2004) are a third set, though not restricted to the European Union.

try to provide a common structure (a common denominator) to Europe's legal systems, leaving out essential details as to substance and the divergent ways of dealing with this substance by the courts.[13] Despite an often common history of most legal systems mentioned (most of them are to a greater or lesser extent based on the Roman law of the ius commune[14]), most systems have, over the last 200 years, had a separate history. To look at this as mere historical accident or as something one could get rid off easily does not do justice to the vigour of the differences or to the difficulties to overcome in changing this diversity.[15]

2.3   Contract Law of European Origin: Directives

A second type of contract law regime is the one created by the European Union. Unlike the national legal systems, the European Union can only act in so far as there is a legal basis for it in the EC Treaty.[16] The most important basis[17] is Article 2, which provides that the European community has for a task to promote, throughout the community, 'a harmonious and balanced development of economic activities'. This takes place through the creation of a common market and an economic and monetary union. Article 3 then makes clear that to reach this goal, an internal market characterised by the abolition of obstacles to the free movement of goods, persons, services and capital is to be established. In this context, the EC undertakes, inter alia, the 'approximation of the laws of member states to the extent required for the functioning of the common market'. All this implies that the competence of the EU in the field of contract law is only *indirect*: in so far as national contract law (or any other part of the law) stands in the way of the further development of the internal market, the EU is allowed to act. This means that the EU's interest in contract law is *functional*: only if the economic development of the EU is threatened to be disturbed, it can intervene.[18]

One of the problematic aspects of this functional demarcation of the EU competence is that the formulation of Article 3 'to the extent required for the functioning of the common market' is rather vague. In its *Tobacco* judgment of 2000,[19] the European Court of Justice held that Article 95 (in which Articles

---

[13]   For a critique of the European principles approach, see Smits (2002b) 239 ff.

[14]   A theme stressed by Reinhard Zimmermann. See *e.g.* Zimmermann (2004).

[15]   Cf. Smits (2002a).

[16]   Consolidated version of the Treaty establishing the European Community, *OJ EC* 2002, C 325/33.

[17]   There are other bases, such as Art. 61 sub c jo. 65 EC Treaty on the 'area of freedom, security and justice.' This basis was introduced with the Maastricht Treaty of 1992.

[18]   Also see the contribution of Helmut Wagner, par. 1.

[19]   ECJ Case C-376/98 *Germany* v. *Parliament and Council* [1998] ECR I-8419. See on this decision in the context of harmonization Weatherill (2001) and now also ECJ Case C-210/03 *The Queen* v. *Secretary of State for Health* (not yet reported).

2 and 3 are elaborated) does not give a general power to regulate the internal market:

'A measure adopted on the basis of Article 95 of the Treaty must genuinely have as its object the improvement of the conditions for the establishment and functioning of the internal market. If a mere finding of disparities between national rules and of the abstract risk of obstacles to the exercise of fundamental freedoms or of distortions of competition liable to result there from were sufficient to justify the choice of Article 95 as a legal basis, judicial review of compliance with the proper legal basis might be rendered nugatory.'

Instead, there must be actual or at least probable obstacles to the functioning of the internal market, if Article 95 is to be used as a basis and the elimination of these obstacles must be the purpose of the measure. With this judgment, the competence of the EU to act on basis of the provisions on the internal market (Articles 2, 3 and 95) is seriously restricted. It also explains the European Commission's eagerness to establish to what extent European companies really suffer from diversity of law.[20]

The above led to at least twelve different European directives in the field of contract law.[21] All these directives are based on the internal market provisions of the EC Treaty. This therefore implies that the justification for European intervention is that the subjects covered by the directives are of such importance that divergences in national legislation of the member states distort the internal market. Although most of the directives intend to protect the consumer, consumer protection was therefore not the primary goal. The goal was much more to avoid unfair competition between sellers of goods and suppliers of services within the EU: if national legislation shows differences (for example in the field of consumer sale), this implies according to the European Commission that 'the national markets for the sale of goods and services differ from each other and that distortions of competition may arise amongst the sellers and

---

[20] There is an interesting parallel with the United States, where the mere fact that goods and services cross state lines does as such not justify federal intervention under the 'commerce clause': see for example Krauss and Levy (2004).

[21] EC Directives 85/577 on (...) contracts negotiated away from business premises, *OJ EC* 1985, L 372/31; 86/653 on (...) self-employed commercial agents, *OJ EC* 1986, L 382/17; 87/102 on (...) consumer credit, *OJ EC* 1987, L 42/48; 90/314 on (...) package travel, *OJ EC* L 158/59; 93/13 on (...) unfair terms in consumer contracts, *OJ EC* 1993, L 095/29; 94/47 on (...) timeshare, *OJ EC* L 280/83; 97/7 on (...) distance contracts, *OJ EC* L 144/19; 1999/44 on (...) sale of consumer goods, *OJ EC* L 171/12; 2000/31 on (...) electronic commerce, *OJ EC* L 178/1; 2000/35 on (...) combating late payment in commercial transactions, *OJ EC* L 200/35; 2002/47 on (...) financial collateral arrangements, *OJ EC* L 168/43 and 2002/65 on (...) distance marketing of financial services, *OJ EC* L 271/16. An overview is also given in European Commission (2001).

suppliers, notably when they sell and supply in other member states.'[22] Another aim, to be found in several directives, is to encourage consumers to buy more abroad.

It is characteristic of the *acquis* in the area of contract law that directives do not cover contract law in general, but are only applicable to specific types of contracts and to specific parts of traditional contract law. If one takes the classic distinction between formation, content and performance of the contract, the following overview can be given. The formation of contracts is governed by rules on formal requirements,[23] agency,[24] the time of conclusion of the contract[25] and information to be provided before and after formation of the contract.[26] The content of the contract is usually governed by rules on interpretation,[27] unfair terms[28] and general conditions.[29] Most rules that exist are however about performance of the contract. Thus, there are rules on conformity on consumer sale,[30] the consumer's remedies in case of non-performance,[31] commercial guarantees,[32] the time of performance and the amount of interest to be paid in case of non-performance.[33]

The question should be raised to what extent this EC contract law is really a separate system. This question can arise since directives should be implemented in the national legal systems of the member states, leaving the choice of form and methods to the national authorities (Article 249 EC Treaty). Still, the EC *acquis* remains a European system: national courts are obliged to interpret the

---

[22] Preamble to Directive 93/13/EC on unfair terms in consumer contracts, *OJ EC* 1993, L 095/29.

[23] Art. 4 of Directive 87/102 on consumer credit; Art. 4 s. 2 of Directive 90/314 on package travel; Art. 4 of Directive 94/47 on timeshare; Art. 9 s. 1 of Directive 2000/31 on electronic commerce; Art. 3 of Directive 2002/47 on financial collateral arrangements.

[24] Art. 9 s. 1 of Directive 2000/31 on electronic commerce.

[25] Art. 11 of Directive 2000/31 on electronic commerce.

[26] Art. 3-4 of Directive 90/314 on package travel; Art. 3 of Directive 94/47 on timeshare; Art. 4-5 of Directive 97/7 on distance contracts; Art. 5-6 and 10 of Directive 2000/31 on electronic commerce; Art. 3-5 of Directive 2002/65 on distance marketing of financial services.

[27] Art. 5 of Directive 93/13 on unfair contract terms.

[28] See Directive 93/13 on unfair contract terms.

[29] Inter alia Art. 10 s. 3 of Directive 2000/31 on electronic commerce.

[30] Art. 2-3 and 5 of Directive 1999/44 on sale of consumer goods. Also see Art. 5 s. 2 of Directive 90/314 on package travel.

[31] Art. 5 of Directive 85/577 on contracts negotiated away from business premises, *OJ EC* 1985, L 372/31; Art. 4-5 of Directive 90/314 on package travel; Art. 5 of Directive 94/47 on timeshare; Art. 6 of Directive 97/7 on distance contracts; Art. 3 of Directive 1999/44 on consumer sale; Art. 6 of Directive 2002/65 on distance marketing of financial services.

[32] Art. 6 on Directive 1999/44 on sale of consumer goods.

[33] Art. 3 of Directive 2000/35 on combating late payment in commercial transactions.

national implementation in accordance with the aim of the directive. It is also the European Court of Justice that has the final word on the interpretation of the *acquis*.

2.4 The Vienna Convention on the International Sale of Goods (CISG)

In addition to the national and European systems of contract law, there is the international regime created by the Convention on the International Sale of Goods (CISG) of 1980.[34] Of the 25 European member states, 20 are a party to the CISG.[35] Its field of application is restricted to the international sale of moveable goods between professional parties. In such a case, the CISG applies *unless* the parties have opted out of it. This seems to suggest that the CISG is an important regime in practice, but there are several reasons why this suggestion is false.

First of all, the CISG is in fact often excluded by the parties. This is the case in many general conditions set by branch organisations such as FOSFA (Federation of Oils, Seeds and Fats) and GAFTA (Grain and Feed Trade Association).[36] A survey[37] among some large Dutch companies showed that most of them exclude the applicability of the CISG in their general conditions as well. Smaller Dutch companies often did not exclude the CISG, unless legal advice was sought by one of the companies involved. It is likely that other European countries show similar results. One of the reasons for opting out of CISG is that it contains many open-ended concepts (like reasonableness or impediment[38]) that still leave room for varying interpretations. Another reason seems to be that the content of the CISG is often unknown to the parties and that they do not find it worthwhile to put time and money into getting to know this content.[39] There is apparently no need to make use of it as national legal systems already fulfil these parties' needs.

Secondly, even if the CISG is applicable, this does not mean that the whole relationship between the parties is governed by it. On the contrary: in many respects national law (applicable in accordance with the rules of private international law) remains of importance. This is not only true for certain rules of national mandatory contract law (see for example Article 4 CISG on validity), but also for rules on securities and other topics not related to contract law as

---

[34] Vienna 1980. See on the CISG for example Schlechtriem (2004) and Honnold (1999). Databases on the CISG include http://www.unilex.info and http://www.cisg.law.pace.edu.

[35] Not a party are the United Kingdom, Ireland, Portugal, Malta and Cyprus.

[36] Bertrams (1995) 72.

[37] See Bertrams (1995) 72 ff. and Kanning (1996).

[38] Cf. Lubbe (2004).

[39] Bertrams (1995) 76-77.

such. This does not enhance the willingness of parties to make use of the CISG as they need to rely on some national system anyway.

2.5 Divergence within One Country

Finally, there is still a different type of diversity. It is the phenomenon of *institutionalised* diversity within one country.[40] This regional diversity can take very different forms. Here, I pay attention to the two most important examples of regional diversity as they exist in Spain and the United Kingdom.

The first example is Spain. In Spain, several autonomous regions have the competence to enact their own legislation in some areas of private law.[41] It is the region of Catalonia where the regional government has taken the most far going steps to enact a separate system of law. Since 1975, Catalonia enacted 30 different statutes in the field of civil law, building on the Catalan law as it existed before General Franco abolished the autonomy of Catalonia in 1938. Thus, Catalonia has, alongside the Spanish Civil Code of 1888, its own Code of Succession (1991) and its own Family Code (1998) and it is envisaged to draft a complete Catalan civil code in the near future.[42] As far as contract law is concerned, it is however debated to what extent the regions have in fact competence to draft their own rules. Article 149 of the Spanish Constitution grants the state competence to draft rules relating to 'the bases of contractual obligations'. The rather broad interpretation of this provision by the Spanish Constitutional Court (indeed leaving only limited competence for the regions in the field of contract law) is criticised in legal doctrine.[43]

The second example concerns the United Kingdom. Here, regional diversity takes a very different form. While in Spain there are, alongside a general Spanish law, separate regional systems, in the United Kingdom there is no uniform national law but separate systems standing next to each other. These three systems are English law (not only applicable in England, but also in Wales), Scots law and Northern-Irish law.[44] In the debate on the harmonisation of private law in Europe, it is in particular Scots law that attracted a lot of attention. Scots law, as a mixed legal system, is said to offer an example for the future development of private law in Europe:[45] if there is to be some uniform system, it will necessarily be a mix of civil law and common law.

---

[40] See on this MacQueen, Vaquer and Espiau Espiau (2003).

[41] This competence was re-established after the death of General Franco in 1975. See for an overview Badosa Coll (2003) 136 ff.

[42] See Gispert I Catalá (2003) 164 ff.

[43] See Espiau Espiau (2003) 180 ff.

[44] There are still other legal systems within the United Kingdom. Thus, the Channel Islands and the Isle of Man have their own law.

[45] MacQueen (2000); Smits (2001). For a critical view, see Evans-Jones (1998).

2.6 Problematic Aspects of Diversity within the European Union

Is the co-existence of the four types of contract law regimes as described in the above problematic? This is certainly not the case in so far as these systems do not interfere with each other. In the case of diversity within one country, there is no problem in so far as only one system applies to the contract. Problems only arise in case several regimes may be applicable to the same contract, thus in particular if the contracting parties are from different member states (or different regions). In such a case, parties have to rely on the rules of private international (or interregional) law. In the context of the European Union, the main source of conflict of law rules is the EC Convention on the Law Applicable to Contractual Obligations of 1980.[46] According to this convention, the primary reason for the applicability of a certain national legal system is that the parties made a choice of law (Article 3).[47] If they did not, the contract is governed by the law of the country with which it is most closely connected (Article 4).[48] However, this type of private international law is often criticised. In the absence of an explicit choice of law, the questions what legal system is applicable and what is the content of this system, are not always easy to answer.[49] In addition, national mandatory rules applicable on the basis of Articles 5 and 7 of the Rome Convention remain applicable, even if a choice of law was made.

In the context of this paper, attention needs to be paid to two aspects of diversity of legal systems that are often considered problematic. The first deals with the Community *acquis* (section 3), the second with national legal systems (section 4).

3 Diversity Through the Community Acquis

Despite the fact that directives in the area of contract law are supposed to create a harmonised set of rules in order to create a 'level playing field' for European business, this type of harmonisation still allows for diversity. This is the case for at least three different reasons. The first of these has to do with the minimum-character of directives. All directives issued in the

---

[46] Convention on the law applicable to contractual obligations. Rome 1980, consolidated version *OJ EC* 1998, C 27/34. It is envisaged to turn this treaty into an EC-regulation: see the Green Paper on the Conversion of the Rome Convention of 1980 (...) into a Community instrument and its modernization, COM (2002) 654 (01).

[47] Gerhard Wagner, in his contribution to this book (par. V.3.a), proposes to allow a choice of law also with respect to purely domestic transactions, thus allowing competition of legal systems to work even better.

[48] See on the problems caused by this *e.g.* Atrill (2004).

[49] Cf. *e.g.* Leible (1998) 286 ff.

field of contract law allow member states to create more stringent rules in the area covered by the directive.[50] In particular in the area of consumer protection, some member states tend to enact rules that are more protective than the directives prescribe. Although this does enhance consumer protection as such, the effect of it also is that business is still confronted with differences in national legislation among the member states and may consequently still be deterred from doing business abroad. Put differently: the question is whether minimum-harmonisation is the right means to reach the goal of promoting the internal market.

A second reason why the present *acquis* still allows for diversity, is that directives often contain abstract terms such as 'damage', 'compensation' or 'fraudulent use'. How these terms are to be interpreted in a 'European' way is unclear. The European Court of Justice usually interprets such terms in light of the particular directive, consequently several concepts of for example damage exist next to each other. This is because the Court denied that the definition of a term in one directive is indicative for the interpretation of the same term in another directive.[51] There is thus no interpretation of directives in view of the *acquis* as a whole. The creation of a 'common frame of reference', as envisaged by the European Commission, has the goal of improving this,[52] although it remains to be seen whether this non-binding instrument will really enhance uniformity.

The European *acquis* can still be criticised for a third reason. The *acquis* is fragmentary as it only deals with specific topics, whereas in most legal systems contract law is part of a comprehensive civil code. This fragmentation is reinforced because of the need for a national implementation of directives: the European rules are encapsulated in national legal systems. As national courts are obliged to interpret these implementing rules in accordance with the scope of the directive, it leads to new unintended divergences *within* the national legal system.[53] This phenomenon is sometimes referred to as 'multi-level governance': decision making at various levels leads to problems of coordination and democratic legitimacy and therefore, by necessity, to a new role for the national state.[54]

Apart from the fact that directives still allow for divergence, there are more reasons why the EC *acquis* can be criticised. One of these is that the *acquis* is impressionistic[55] (it is often unclear why some topics are covered and others are not) and suffers from inconsistencies (sometimes it contains conflicting

---

[50] The recent proposal for a directive on unfair business practices (18 June 2003, COM (2003) 356 final) is an exception to this.

[51] ECJ Case C-168/00 *Simone Leitner/TUI Deutschland* [2002] ECR I-2631 on which Smits and Hardy (2003).

[52] European Commission (2003) no. 59; European Commission (2004).

[53] Also see Teubner (1998) 11 ff.

[54] Bache and Flinders (2004).

[55] Also see Hesselink (2002) 36.

rules[56]). These problems have not gone unnoticed by the European Commission. Although the idea of creating a European Civil Code to deal with these problems was already put forward by the European Parliament in 1989,[57] it was not before 2001 that the European Commission issued a discussion paper on the future of contract law in Europe. This Communication on European Contract Law of 2001[58] was followed in 2003 by the European Commission's Action Plan[59] and in 2004 by a Communication on the revision of the *acquis*.[60] The European Commission intends to deal with diversity through directives by reconsidering the idea of minimum harmonisation in consumer directives and by creating a non-binding 'common frame of reference' that the European institutions could look at in drafting new legislation.[61]

On basis of the above, one can conclude that an important part of divergence in contract law rules is created by the European Union itself: it is European legislation *as such* that leads to undesired divergence. This conclusion fits in with what the interested parties remarked in their reactions to the 2001 Communication on European Contract Law.[62] Much more than divergence among national legal systems, they regarded the European intervention in contract law itself as problematic.

4   Diversity of National Legal Systems

4.1   Introduction

The second aspect often thought of as problematic is the diversity of *national* contract law regimes within the European Union. Does this diversity really deter businesses and consumers from contracting abroad? And would a unified contract law promote transfrontier transactions? These are

---

[56] Compare European Commission (2001) no. 35 and European Commission (2003) no. 16 ff.

[57] Resolution A2-157/89 *OJ EC* 1989, C 158/400. The call was repeated in 1994 (Resolution A3-00329/94, *OJ EC* 1994, C 205/518) and 2000 (Resolution B5-0228/2000, *OJ EC* 2000, C 377/323).

[58] European Commission (2001), on which *e.g.* Grundmann and Stuyck (2002). The Communication prompted a new Resolution of the European Parliament: Resolution C5-0471/2001, *OJ EC* 2002, C 140 E/538.

[59] European Commission (2003). Also see the Resolution of the European Parliament of 2 September 2003 (P5_TA (2003) 0355) and the Council Report of 22 September 2003, press note 12339/03.

[60] European Commission (2004). Further developments can be traced on the website http://europa.eu.int/ comm/consumers.

[61] European Commission (2004).

[62] The more than 200 reactions to the Communication are available through http://europa.eu.int/comm/ internal_market /contractlaw/overview_en.htm. Also see Smits and Hardy (2002) 827 and Staudenmayer (2003) 120 ff.

questions one can only answer on basis of empirical evidence or economic and psychological theory. In this section, these various perspectives are addressed. First, the traditional argument in favour of harmonisation is analysed (4.2). Then, this argument is contrasted with some empirical and economic evidence (4.3 and 4.4). In section 4.5, it is seen whether the behavioural perspective offers anything of interest, while section 4.6 pays attention to the traditional economic argument against unification of law.

4.2 The Traditional Argument in Favour of Harmonisation

The traditional argument in favour of harmonisation of contract law is that a contracting party that wants to deal with a foreign party is deterred from doing so because of the different legal system in the other party's country. And if the other party would still decide to contract, this will be more costly than if it would do so in its own country. This view is well formulated by Ole Lando:[63]

'The Union of today is an economic community. Its purpose is the free flow of goods, persons, services and capital. The idea is that the more freely and more abundantly these can move across the frontiers, the wealthier and happier we will become. All of these move by way of contracts. It should, therefore, be made easier to conclude and perform contracts and to calculate contract risks. (...) Foreign laws are often difficult for the businessmen and their local lawyers to understand. They may keep him away from foreign markets in Europe. (...) The existing variety of contract laws in Europe may be regarded as a non-tariff barrier to trade.'

Also the European Commission seems to be of this view. It states:[64]

'For consumers and SME's in particular, not knowing other contract law regimes may be a disincentive against undertaking cross-border transactions. (...) Suppliers of goods and services may even therefore regard offering their goods and services to consumers in other countries as economically unviable and refrain from doing so. (...) Moreover, disparate national law rules may lead to higher transaction costs (...). These higher transaction costs may (...) be a competitive disadvantage, for example in a situation where a foreign supplier is competing with a supplier established in the same country as the potential client.'

---

[63] Lando (2000) 61.

[64] European Commission (2001) no. 30-32; cf. European Commission (2003) no. 34; also see Staudenmayer (2002) 254.

It is useful to look at this argument in more detail, paying attention to both different types of parties and different types of transaction costs. Usually, parties deal with the problem of legal diversity by setting their contract terms themselves and by choosing an applicable law. But there are several reasons why this does not sufficiently deal with the problem.[65] First, it does not prevent the national mandatory law – applicable in accordance with the conflict of law rules – to apply. In the above, it became clear that part of these mandatory rules deals with consumer protection and is thus directly related to European directives.[66] A party will then still need to take advice on the unknown applicable law, which will be costly and will also present a commercial risk for that party. Second, it may be that a party with insufficient bargaining power is overruled by the other, economically stronger, party. It is likely that this party is then still deterred from contracting, *also* because of the fact that it is obliged to accept the other party's choice of law.

In this context, it is useful to make a distinction between different types of parties. It is often[67] asserted that in particular small and medium sized enterprises (SME's) suffer from problems through legal diversity. Large companies are usually more experienced in international trade and can benefit from their strong bargaining position. In addition, large companies that deal abroad typically engage in big transactions. Such transactions justify transaction costs. But as large companies usually make their own contract terms, regardless whether their business partners are located in another country or not, these transaction costs do not fundamentally differ between purely national and international contracts.[68] This is different for SME's. SME's usually do not set contract terms themselves and therefore have to rely on default law. If the applicable default law is foreign law, uncertainty about its contents could deter this party from contracting. Also the content of the other country's mandatory law could be uncertain.[69] Put differently: for SME's, it is often disproportionate to pay for legal advice compared to the value of the transaction.[70] Also consumers may be deterred from buying abroad as they typically have no knowledge at all of foreign law and are not able to choose for their national legal system in a relationship with a foreign commercial party: usually, it is the law of the supplier that is the

---

[65] Cf. European Commission (2003) no. 28 ff.

[66] Cf. Reactions to the Communication on European Contract Law, European Commission (2003) 31: 'Businesses are discouraged from cross-border transactions more by differences in the details of different consumer protection regimes than by diversity in the overall level of protection afforded.'

[67] Cf. European Commission (2003) no. 30; Basedow (1996); Ott and Schäfer (2002) 209 ff.

[68] Cf. Ott and Schäfer (2002) 209.

[69] Ott and Schäfer (2002) 213.

[70] Cf. also Staudenmayer (2002) 255 and, generally, Gerhard Wagner, par. VI.2 and Helmut Wagner, par. 4.

applicable law, be it based on the supplier's general conditions or on the basis of Article 4 of the Rome Convention.[71]

Another question is what type of transaction costs are involved in international contracting. Ott and Schäfer[72] define the transaction costs of transfrontier transactions as costs to obtain information about the legal system applicable to the transaction, the contents of this system and the differences between the other system and the system of the contracting party. Ribstein and Kobayashi distinguish in greater detail between, what they describe as, types of costs that are reduced by uniformity.[73] These costs are:

a. *Inconsistency costs.* These are costs that arise through inconsistent (divergent) state laws. If a company sells its products in different states, it will be confronted with these costs. It isobvious, however, that adopting a uniform law will still leave room for different applications of this law and will thus not completely reduce these inconsistency costs.

b. *Information costs.* These are the costs of determining what law applies in each state. These costs decrease in case of uniform law, provided that *all* relevant rules are unified, thus not only those in the field of contract law but also in property law, tax law, administrative law, etc. Here too, the problem of divergent application remains after 'unification'.

c. *Litigation costs.* It may happen that information about how to bring a claim against the other party has to be obtained. Uniform law will therefore make litigation less expensive.

d. *Instability costs.* If a contract is concluded, a change in the law applicable to this contract decreases the efficiency of the deal. Uniform law reduces these costs because information on future changes of the uniform law will be more readily available than information of changes in a foreign legal system.

e. *Externalities.* National law typically takes into account the national interests: the national legislator is inclined to help its constituents and not groups outside the state, such as foreign manufacturers. This means that costs are externalised, thus decreasing the efficiency of the uniform market as a whole. In case of uniform law, this may be avoided.[74]

f. *Drafting costs.* Ribstein and Kobayashi suggest that uniform lawmakers can concentrate their resources on drafting particular laws and can hire experts in particular fields. National legislators however would have little incentive to concentrate on carefully drafting legislation. This argument

---

[71] Kerkmeester, par. 3.2, makes the interesting suggestion that behavioural analysis of contract law supports the case for unification.

[72] Ott and Schäfer (2002) 207.

[73] Ribstein and Kobayashi (1996) 137 ff. In a similar vein, Helmut Wagner (par. 2.2.1) distinguishes costs caused by legal uncertainty.

[74] Critical, however, Ribstein and Kobayashi (1996) 140.

may be true for the United States, but does not seem too convincing in the European situation as in Europe national legislators also tend to engage in meticulous lawmaking.

Apart from this economic argument, there are other arguments available to support harmonisation of contract law (or private law in general). Thus, there is the *identity* argument: the European identity may be reinforced by a European code. It may also be that a European code would enhance the European values.[75] However, in his contribution to this book Thomas Wilhelmsson makes clear that these values consist primarily of fundamental human rights and these rights cannot offer any real guidance in contract law. More importantly, Wilhelmsson analyses present day Europe as a late modern fragmented and *risk* society. Such a society is not in need of a systematic codification of contract law, but requires a flexible and *learning* law. This is an important argument against codification that will not be further explored here. Instead, the economic argument will be tested against the background of empirical evidence and economic theory.

4.3   Empirical and Anecdotal Evidence

There are two types of empirical evidence on contracting that may be of use to the question raised in this contribution. The first is concerned with the importance of contract law *as such* for business relationships, the second with the importance of a *uniform* contract law for transfrontier contracting.

The best known survey of the importance of contract law for business relationships was done by Stewart Macaulay who interviewed businesspeople in the state of Wisconsin.[76] Macaulay discovered that in many cases businesspeople are not interested at all in the meticulous drafting of contracts, while in case of a dispute about the performance of the contract, a majority of businesspeople is not prepared to undertake legal action but instead tries to informally settle the dispute and takes its losses if it would not succeed in doing so. If a party has for example a right to price reduction or adaptation of the contract, this right is often not enforced, while if there is no right to it the other party often *does* agree to reduce the price. Macaulay's findings were confirmed for England by Beale and Dugdale.[77] One of the reasons for this reluctance to rely on contract law was that, according to these surveys, most of the time parties dealt with counterparts they regularly did business with. Too much of contract enforcement would put these relationships under pressure. Another reason was that elaborate plan-

---

[75] Cf. the contributions to ERA-Forum (2002).

[76] Macaulay (1963).

[77] Beale and Dugdale (1975).

ning of the contract is expensive and is not justified by the few cases in which a conflict arises.

These findings show that contract law as such is not as important for the enhancement of trade as governments or academics sometimes think. This also puts into perspective the need for a uniform law. The effect that unification of contract law can be expected to have, is probably not as important as the effect of Europeanisation (or even globalisation) of the market as such.

A good starting point for the second point (the influence of *uniform* contract law on international contracting) is the European Commission's Communication of 2001.[78] In this consultation paper, the European Commission asked businesses and consumers (and other interested parties) to indicate whether they experienced problems through diversity of (contract) law. Most reactions of business organisations and practitioners showed this was not the case.[79] In most reactions, it was remarked that the internal market may not function perfectly, but that this was not caused primarily by differences in private law, but much more by language barriers, cultural differences, distance, habits and divergence in other areas of the law such as tax law and procedural law.[80] *Orgalime*, representing the interests of 130.000 companies in the European mechanical, electrical and metalworking industries, remarked: 'it will of course always to some extent be easier to trade with companies and persons from your own country. This has, however, more to do with ease of communication, traditions and other factors, which are not dependent on contract law.'[81]

This anecdotal evidence is supported by several studies on consumer behaviour. A survey of consumer confidence shows that the confidence of consumers in being protected against a seller in case of transfrontier transactions is considerably less (31%) than in case of a purely national transaction (56%).[82] This is, however, not primarily related to differences in contract law. Research on transfrontier shopping[83] confirms that consumers also consider other barriers such as taxes, language, time and distance more important than contract law.

---

[78] European Commission (2001).

[79] Cf. Reactions to the Communication on European Contract Law, European Commission (2003) 30 ff.

[80] Cf. *e.g.* the Reaction of the UK Government, available through http://europa.eu.int/comm/consumers.

[81] Reaction of Orgalime, available through http://europa.eu.int/comm/consumers. This is confirmed by other reactions of business organisations.

[82] See the EOS Gallup Europe 'Consumers survey' of January 2002, published on http://europa.eu.int/comm/dgs/health_consumer/events/event42_en.html. In the Netherlands, 66% of the consumers consider its rights well protected if they deal with a Dutch seller, but only 23% consider this to be the case if it deals with a foreign seller.

[83] See for example the explanatory memorandum to the proposed Directive concerning unfair business-to-consumer commercial practices in the internal market, COM (2003) 356 final.

4.4 Economic Theory on Growth of the Economy and National Borders

The problem with the anecdotal and empirical evidence presented above is that it does not indicate what the influence of uniform law on contracting actually is. It is of course difficult to measure this influence because this could only be done by isolating the factor '(uniform) contract law' from a whole range of possible factors that influence decisions of businesses and consumers. The effect of the so-called 'natural' barriers like language or distance is difficult to assess separately from the 'policy-induced' barriers like regulation and taxation.[84] True, it is argued[85] that if people share a conviction about what is just and appropriate in the society they are part of, transaction costs are less. This point is taken up in the so-called New Institutional Economics.[86] According to the adherents of this approach, a distinction can be made between formal and informal incentives (or constraints) for transacting. Formal incentives for rational behaviour are organised by the government such as law and regulations, informal incentives are habits, traditions, 'networks' and other informal norms. Economic literature does not however elaborate on what type of contract law would be required to minimise transaction costs, other than that the law should be certain.[87] Uncertainty implies higher transaction costs, which is reflected in higher prices, leading to lower investment, lower consumption and lower national income.[88]

What *is* possible, however, is to measure the importance of borders on trade. It is clear that the existence of national borders has a negative effect on international contracting. American research shows that national borders between Canada and the United States reduce trade between these two countries by 44%, while this percentage would be around 30% for other industrialised countries. And, although this is debated, even within the United States (with one language and culture), a 'home market effect' (home bias) is visible within the different states.[89] These findings on the deterring effect of borders on contracting were confirmed for Germany in a statistic study by Volker Nitsch.[90] Nitsch shows that after German reunification, West-German shipments to the formerly East-

---

[84] Cf. for this distinction Commission Staff Working Paper Extended Impact Assessment on the Directive concerning unfair business-to-consumer commercial practices in the internal market, COM (2003) 356 final, 6.

[85] Cf. Van den Berg (2001) 416 and North (1987) 419 ff.

[86] Van den Berg (2001) 417; Mattli (1999) 45.

[87] Also see the contribution of Helmut Wagner, par. 2.1.

[88] For this 'causal chain', see Helmut Wagner, par. 2.2.2.

[89] See, be it critical of the data suggesting this, Millimet and Osang (2004) and Brown (2003). They both build on the pioneering work of McCallum (1995) 615 ff.

[90] Nitsch (2002), available through http://www.hwwa.de.

German part were 120% larger than deliveries to an otherwise similar foreign country like Austria or the Netherlands. Unfortunately, economic literature that tries to explain this effect is scarce.[91] In the case of Canada and the United States, it may be that differences among their contract law regimes may account for the lesser amount of trade, but it is likely that other factors are more important. This argument gains weight in the case of the United States, where there may be in principle different contract laws in every state, but where the Uniform Commercial Code provides in practice the uniform model for almost every state. [92] And in the case of Germany, it is even impossible that a difference in (contract) law accounts for the difference as, at the time of the survey, East- and West-Germany were already united.

These insights on the effect of borders on trade are also confirmed in the economic literature. It shows that there is a positive relationship between economic growth and globalisation. There is little doubt that economic growth is linked to globalisation although it is not certain what causes what: is it globalisation that causes economic growth or is it the other way around? In any event, evidence shows that there is 'a strong positive relationship'[93] between international trade and economic growth. This relationship is most probably bi-directional: trade causes growth and growth causes trade to increase.[94] It is part of economic science to study *why* there is such a relationship. Van den Berg[95] makes clear that economic growth rates are lower if a country is less open to trade: openness of the economy is strongly related to the growth performance of the country involved. The logical explanation for this is that international trade allows economies to specialise in producing goods in which they have a comparative advantage. Companies can also exploit economies of scale because they have a much bigger market than just their own country. Thus, international trade favours the economy more than restricted trade. This theoretical insight is evidenced by empirical material. With the strengthening of the European internal market, the amount of cross border transactions undoubtedly increased. Between approximately 1985 and 1995, the volume of commerce within the European Union doubled as compared to export to third states.[96] The economic effect of legal unification is further explored in the contribution of Helmut Wagner to this volume.

But how do economists look at the relationship between growth and the law? In economics,[97] law is usually looked at as one of the 'institutions' responsible

---

[91] Nitsch (2002) 2.

[92] Cf. Reimann (1996); Gray (1986).

[93] Van den Berg 2001) 324 and Mattli (1999) 31 ff. and 58.

[94] Van den Berg (2001) 324-325.

[95] Van den Berg (2001) 326 ff.

[96] See Grundmann (2001) 509 ff.

[97] The underneath is largely based on the textbook of Van den Berg (2001) 415 ff.

for economic growth. According to Van den Berg,[98] institutions are 'the laws, social norms, traditions, religious beliefs, and other established rules of behaviour that provide the incentives that rational people react to'. This implies that there is a causal link between institutions and rational behaviour of people: given the assumption that all people respond rationally to incentives, differences in economic growth can only be the result of different institutions in different societies. This makes highly relevant which institutions increase human welfare and which do not. If one assumes that human welfare is best served by economic growth, the most effective institutions are those that lead people to be innovative or productive from a long-term perspective.[99] There is common ground among economists that institutions that lower transaction costs are the most effective.[100] But, again, whether a uniform contract law is part of these institutions is not truly explored.

This is not to say that economic analysis does not say anything about what type of contract law serves the economic interests best. Mahoney[101] found evidence that common law countries experienced faster economic growth than civil law countries. His evidence is based on a statistic study of differences among 102 countries in average annual growth in capita gross domestic product. It followed from this study that common law countries grew, on average, significantly faster than civil law countries in the period 1960-1992. For an explanation, Mahoney refers to Hayek,[102] who argued that the common law tradition is superior to the civil law, not so much because of differences in legal rules but because of different assumptions about the role of the state.[103] Common law systems would be less inclined to impose government restrictions on economic (and other) liberties. Historically, this can be explained by pointing at the development of the common law as a system that would *protect* landowners and merchants against the Crown, while for example French civil law developed as an instrument of state power to *change* existing property rights.[104] This different ideology, it is argued, is still apparent in present day civil and common law. To quote Mahoney:[105]

---

[98] Van den Berg (2001) 409.

[99] Van den Berg (2001) 414; cf. Helmut Wagner, par. 2.2.3.

[100] North, cited by Van den Berg (2001) 415: 'In fact the costs of transacting are the key to the performance of economies.'

[101] Mahoney (2001) 503 ff.; also see Helmut Wagner, par. 2.3.

[102] Hayek (1973).

[103] Mahoney (2001) 504.

[104] Mahoney (2001) 505.

[105] Mahoney (2001) 511. This point is also apparent in the work of Pierre Legrand. He argues that this is the main reason why any harmonisation of private law in Europe is doomed to failure. See *e.g.* Legrand (1996).

'The common law and civil law continue to reflect their intellectual heritage and, as a consequence, legal origin is both relevant to the ideological background and the structural design of government. At an ideological or cultural level, the civil law-tradition assumes a larger role for the state, defers more to bureaucratic decisions, and elevates collective over individual rights. It casts the judiciary into an explicitly subordinate role. In the common-law tradition, by contrast, judicial independence is viewed as essential to the protection of individual liberty.'

Also in another way it is argued that the common law is more efficient than civil law systems. Rubin[106] argues that in the common law inefficient rules will be more readily adjudicated instead of settled. The decisions of litigants whether they want to sue or settle will therefore drive the law to efficiency. In addition to this, Helmut Wagner[107] cites research showing the strong relationship between high standards of governance or rule of law and economic growth. But it should be emphasised, again, that this does not say anything about the effect of *uniform* law on trade.

If one is to summarise the above, it is that it is difficult to separate uniform contract law from the many other factors that account for the behaviour of contracting parties. Apparently, traditional economic analysis does not provide a sufficient answer to the question under review. In the contribution of Jaap Hage to this volume, one can find a further survey of the limits of economic analysis of law. But as the effect of uniform law on contracting parties is also a question of *behaviour* of the parties, it may be useful to see whether behavioural insights can be integrated in the analysis. Behavioural analysis belongs traditionally to the discipline of psychology, but recently we have seen the incorporation of behavioural insights in economic science as well. It seems useful to pay some attention to this behavioural analysis.

4.5 Behavioural Analysis: From Homo Economicus to Homo Psycho-economicus[108]

Behavioural economics takes as a starting point that the rationality assumption of economic models is wrong: in real life, people do not always behave rationally. The idea of the *homo economicus*, on which most economic models are based, is simply not true in practice. While traditional economic analysis aims to evaluate and predict human behaviour on the basis of rationality ('rational choice theory'[109]), behavioural analysis is aimed at giving a more accurate account of human decision making. The unrealistic assumptions of

---

[106] Rubin (1977) 51 ff. and Rubin (2004).

[107] Par. 2.3.

[108] Cf. Rostain (2000) 976.

[109] Cf. Korobkin (2001) 4.

economic analysis are thus replaced by the more empirical evidence of cognitive psychology. Pioneering work on the behavioural analysis of law was done by Jolls, Sunstein and Thaler[110] and by Korobkin and Ulen.[111] In 2000, Sunstein edited a volume on this 'behavioural law and economics'.[112] It deals with questions that are also addressed in the field of 'economic psychology'.[113]

Does behavioural analysis tell us something about how contracting parties make their decisions? One general insight is that human beings generally do not consult a 'preference' menu from which rational selections are made at the moment of choice. Choices are made on basis of 'procedure, description, and context.'[114] On basis of Sunstein's book,[115] one can distinguish several psychological phenomena that can help to explain behaviour of contracting parties. One of these is the 'status quo bias': people tend to like the status quo and are often not willing to depart from it.[116] If a certain situation is to be evaluated, this is usually done by referring to a reference point that is known to them and gains and losses are evaluated from this point. This implies that contracting parties are more likely to choose for a legal system they know than for a new (uniform) system. This is confirmed by the experience with the CISG. Another insight from psychology is that it is often difficult to calculate the expected costs and benefits of alternatives and that therefore people simplify their decision making by reasoning from past cases, taking only small steps ahead.[117] This 'case based decision making' is important in the courts that make most of their decisions by analogy, but it may also explain why, again, contracting parties are often not prepared to choose for a system they do not know. A third rule of thumb is that people are loss averse and therefore twice as displeased with losses than that they are pleased with gains.[118] This may imply that parties would be less willing to take legal advice on how to draft their contract or to inform themselves about the applicable legal system and instead just wait until a conflict arises. This is confirmed by Macaulay's survey.[119] It is also consistent with the ideas of Gerhard Wagner and Jaap Hage in their contributions to this volume that, if it is uncertain whether uniformity is desired or not, it is best to take only small steps ahead, for example by way of an optional code.

---

[110] Jolls, Sunstein and Thaler (1998) 1471 ff. (also in Sunstein (2000) 13-58; Sunstein (2000).

[111] Korobkin and Ulen (2000) 1051 ff.

[112] Sunstein (2000); cf. the review by Engel (2003).

[113] Antonides (1996) 1; Webley et al (2001) 2; also see the contribution of Kerkmeester.

[114] Sunstein (2000) 1.

[115] See the overview in Sunstein (2000) 3 ff.; cf. Kerkmeester, par. 3.1.

[116] Also see the contributions of Kerkmeester (par. 3.1) and Rachlinski (par. I.A.3) to this volume.

[117] Sunstein (2000) 5.

[118] Sunstein (2000) 5.

[119] See above, section 4.3. Also Macaulay's finding that parties are often willing to cooperate instead of pursuing their own interests is mirrored in behavioural analysis. Cf. Sunstein (2000) 8.

There is one interesting insight that needs further attention here. Korobkin applies the status quo bias to default contract terms.[120] This means that the preference of the parties for certain contract terms is dependent on the status quo. Unlike the assertions in economic analysis of contract law, parties often do not choose for wealth-maximizing contract terms but for the status quo (consisting of default rules). In other words: parties often prefer inaction to action and sacrifice wealth in order to be inert.[121] This is not optimal from the efficiency viewpoint. Korobkin argues that it would therefore be more efficient for lawmakers to have initially created an alternative status quo. Next to term 'A', a term 'B' could be created as the default rule, thus allowing the parties to have both the wealth-maximizing term and the status quo term.[122] Put otherwise: if the legislator chooses a different default rule (and status quo), this influences the parties to choose the more efficient rule. If parties simply will not contract around inefficient default terms because of the status quo bias, the legislator should make default rules that the fewest number of parties have to contract around to achieve efficient agreements.[123] These are certainly not 'untailored' default rules that apply to all parties regardless their status or their circumstances.[124] Korobkin says:[125]

'The lawmaker charged with determining a tailored default term must ask not what term *most* contracting parties would have agreed to had they made provisions for a contingency – a question that does not require an inquiry into the specifics of any one transaction – but what term two *particular* parties would have agreed to had they provided for the contingency.'

This is an important argument in favour of an optional default contract regime for transfrontier contracts. In its Communication of 2004,[126] the European Commission indicates it wants to pursue a discussion on an optional contract code that could contain provisions for commercial parties that engage in international transactions. Parties opting in to such a code could thus indeed profit from both the status quo *and* an efficient international contract regime.

In his contribution to this volume, Rachlinski describes another interesting bias.[127] This 'availability heuristic' refers to the tendency to assess the frequency of events by the ease with which one can recall exemplars. Vivid salient issues

---

[120] Korobkin (2000) 137 ff.

[121] Korobkin (2000) 138.

[122] Korobkin (2000) 138; cf. Kerkmeester, par. 3.2.

[123] Korobkin (2000) 139.

[124] Korobkin (2000) 140.

[125] Korobkin (2000) 140.

[126] European Commission (2004).

[127] Rachlinski's contribution to this volume, par. I.A.1; also see Kerkmeester, par. 3.1.

that make memorable impressions seem more significant than others. Rachlinski applies this bias to the lawmaking process: the legislator is likely to address issues that attract greater attention, leaving aside more important issues. It could well be that the interest of the European Commission and Parliament in harmonising contract law is caused by the emphasis legal academics have put on the importance of unification of contract law,[128] thus denying the marginal influence such uniformity may have on the decisions of contracting parties. The importance of other influences on parties' behaviour, like language, distance and culture, are thus not given their proper place.

4.6   The Economic Argument against Unification

Until now, the traditional argument in favour of harmonisation was considered. In this section, the argument *against* harmonisation still needs to be addressed. The survey of this argument can be much shorter than that of the argument in favour as discussed in section 4.2: it was already touched upon in the above and is also elaborately discussed in the contribution of Gerhard Wagner to this book. In view of the scope of this contribution, the argument against unification is best put in terms of *costs* of uniformity. Ribstein and Kobayashi[129] distinguish three types of such costs:

a. *Exit costs.* The classic argument in favour of diversity of law was brought forward by Tiebout.[130] The fact that people and firms can exit a jurisdiction they do not like, motivates national governments to reflect the preferences of the voters. Unified law decreases this exit opportunity and will thus lead to less efficient law. Put otherwise: competition of legal systems means that more preferences are satisfied.

b. *Reducing innovation and experimentation.* In case of diversity of law, more solutions to a problem are provided than in case of one uniform law. Experimentation with these several solutions may lead to some better laws than a uniform law can offer.

c. *Reducing local variation.* Uniform law does not only decrease experimentation and thus the possibility of finding the 'best' rules, it also may be the case that local variation produces rules that are best suited for particular localities.[131]

In short, this argument praises the virtues of competition.[132] The general economic idea is that if every individual pursues its own interests, this indi-

---

[128] Cf. Ogus (1999) 411.

[129] Ribstein and Kobayashi (1996) 140 ff.

[130] Tiebout (1956) 416. Also see Helmut Wagner, par. 3 (a) and Gerhard Wagner, par. III.2.

[131] Ribstein and Kobayashi (1996) 141.

[132] Cf. Wagner (2002) 999, the contribution of Gerhard Wagner to this volume and Ogus (1999).

vidual *and* society as a whole will be better-off. But individuals can only pursue their own preferences if there *is* something to choose. The chance that a national government can provide this possibility is not optimal. It is therefore best to also have competition among lawmakers, allowing several legal systems to exist next to each other. Tiebout therefore argued that if citizens have different preferences, only competition among several systems will lead to efficient outcomes.[133] This argument is further explored in the contribution of Gerhard Wagner to this book, who also gives examples of successful competition in family law and corporate law. The argument is subsequently looked at from the behavioural perspective by Heico Kerkmeester.

All this does not mean that diversity is always to be preferred above unification. It could well be that the costs of diversity as described in section 4.2 are larger than the costs of unification. Uniform law should thus still be adopted if the benefits of uniformity outweigh the costs.[134] When this is the case is, again, difficult to calculate. There is, however, a type of cost involved that is not mentioned by Ribstein and Kobayashi. These are the costs of transition of one legal system to another or, put differently, the transaction costs of eliminating national legal systems. Such costs are considerable. They include costs of political decision-making and the costs of effective realisation of the reform as well as the costs of adaptation to the new regime (such as the cost of amending contracts and of educating lawyers and judges).[135] When a new civil code was introduced in the Netherlands in 1992, it was estimated that the costs of this recodification amounted to almost 7 billion euro over a period of 20 years.[136] In his contribution to this book, Helmut Wagner explains that because of these transition costs *and* because of the costs identified by Ribstein and Kobayashi, full harmonisation is not recommendable.

5 Concluding Remarks

The aim of this contribution was to see whether the European Union is in need of uniform contract law. The criterion to assess this need is primarily the development of the internal market. But the above shows that it is difficult to establish the exact relationship between diversity of law and the enhancement of the economy through transfrontier contracting. Three conclusions can be drawn.

First, it seems impossible to calculate either the cost of legal diversity or the cost of uniform law: a quantitative analysis cannot provide the answer to the

---

[133] Tiebout (1956).

[134] Ribstein and Kobayashi (1996) 137 ff.

[135] Part of these costs originate from path dependence: see Smits (2002a).

[136] See Van Dunné, Luijten and Stein (1990).

question raised. This does not mean that the economic arguments set out in the above (sections 4.2 and 4.6) cannot play a role, but they should be put into perspective. The best way to address the question is probably to put it in terms of a comparison: would the savings in transaction costs through the removal of legal diversity be greater than the losses caused by the termination of competition of legal systems? This question cannot be provided with a definitive answer either, but phrasing it like this does allow to make an analysis on basis of the *quality* of the arguments. How these are appreciated depends on one's own preferences.

A second outcome is that it seems wrong to link legal certainty to uniform law. One of the most important arguments of proponents of unification is that legal diversity refrains businesses and consumers from contracting because of the legal uncertainty diversity brings with it. Economic analysis abundantly shows (as is apparent from in particular Helmut Wagner's contribution to this book) that legal uncertainty is indeed a barrier to trade, but there is no evidence that uniform law would create *more* legal certainty than diverse contract law regimes. Provided that enough information is available on the various regimes, the demands of legal certainty can also be satisfied.

The third conclusion that can be drawn from the above concerns the way to proceed with the development of uniform contract law. If one is uncertain about the effects of uniformity on international contracting, it is best to adopt a step-by-step approach. It means the time is not ripe for grand projects. Instead, one should adopt a model that allows corrections at an early stage and allows business and consumers to get acquainted with a new contract law regime. This points in the direction of drafting an optional contract code that parties can choose for if they find this code suits their interests best.

REFERENCES

ANTONIDES (1996)

G. Antonides, *Psychology in Economics and Business* (Dordrecht etc.: Kluwer Academic Publishers 1996)

ATRILL (2004)

S. Atrill, "Choice of Law in Contract: The Missing Pieces of the Article 4 Jigsaw?", 53 *International and Comparative Law Quarterly* (2004) 549-577

BACHE AND FLINDERS (2004)

I. Bache and M. Flinders (eds.), *Multi-level Governance* (Oxford: Oxford University Press 2004)

BADOSA COLL (2003)

F. Badosa Coll, "'... Quae ad ius Cathalanicum pertinet': the civil law of Catalonia, *ius commune* and the legal tradition", in: H.L. MacQueen, A. Vaquer and S. Espiau Espiau (eds.), *Regional Private Laws and Codification in Europe* (Cambridge: Cambridge University Press 2003) 136-163

BASEDOW (1996)

J. Basedow, "Rechtskultur – zwischen nationalem Mythos und europäischem Ideal", 3 *Zeitschrift für Europäisches Privatrecht* (1996) 379-381

BEALE AND DUGDALE (1975)

H. Beale and T. Dugdale, "Contracts between businessmen", 2 *British Journal of Law & Society* (1975) 45-60

BERTRAMS (1995)

R.I.V.F. Bertrams, *Enige aspecten van het Weens Koopverdrag* (Lelystad: Koninklijke Vermande 1995)

BROWN (2003)

W.M. Brown, "Overcoming distance, overcoming borders: comparing North American regional trade", available through http://www.statcan.ca (2003)

ENGEL (2003)

C. Engel, "Review of Sunstein (ed.), Behavioral Law and Economics", 67 *Rabels Zeitschrift für ausländisches und internationales Privatrecht* (2003) 406-407

ERA-FORUM (2002)

Special Issue European Contract Law, *ERA-Forum* (2002), vol. 2

ESPIAU ESPIAU (2003)

S. Espiau Espiau, "Unification of the European Law of Obligations and Codification of Catalan Civil Law", in: H.L. MacQueen, A. Vaquer and S. Espiau Espiau (eds.), *Regional Private Laws and Codification in Europe* (Cambridge: Cambridge University Press 2003) 180-198

EUROPEAN COMMISSION (2001)

European Commission, *Communication from the Commission to the Council and the European Parliament on European Contract Law*, COM (2001) 398 final

EUROPEAN COMMISSION (2003)

European Commission, *Communication from the Commission to the European Parliament and the Council. A More Coherent Contract Law – An Action Plan*, COM (2003) 68 final

EUROPEAN COMMISSION (2004)

European Commission, *Communication from the Commission to the European Parliament and the Council: European Contract Law and the Revision of the Acquis: the Way Forward*, COM (2004) 651 final

EVANS-JONES (1998)

R. Evans-Jones, "Receptions of Law, Mixed Legal Systems and the Myth of the Genius of Scots Private Law", 114 *The Law Quarterly Review* (1998) 228-249

GANDOLFI (2001)

G. Gandolfi (ed.), *Code européen des contrats: avant-projet, vol. 1* (Milano: Giuffrè 2001)

GISPERT I CATALÁ (2003)

N. de Gispert I Catalá, "The Codification of Catalan Civil Law", in: H.L. MacQueen, A. Vaquer and S. Espiau Espiau (eds.), *Regional Private Laws and Codification in Europe* (Cambridge: Cambridge University Press 2003) 164-171

GRAY (1986)

W. Gray, "E Pluribus Unum? A Bicentennial Report of Unification of Law in the United States", 50 *Rabels Zeitschrift für ausländisches und internationales Privatrecht* (1986) 111-145

GRUNDMANN (2001)

S. Grundmann, "The Structure of European Contract Law", 9 *European Review of Private Law* (2001) 505-528

GRUNDMANN AND STUYCK (2002)

S. Grundmann and J. Stuyck (eds.), An Academic Green Paper on European Contract Law (The Hague: Kluwer Law International 2002)

HAYEK (1973)

F.A. Hayek, *Law, Legislation and Liberty: A New Statement of the Liberal Principles of Justice and Political Economy* (London: Routledge 1973)

HESSELINK (2002)

M.W. Hesselink, *The New European Private Law* (The Hague: Kluwer Law International 2002)

HONNOLD (1999)

J.O. Honnold, *Uniform Law for International Sales under the 1980 United Nations Convention*, 3rd ed. (The Hague: Kluwer Law International 1999)

HUSA (2004)

J. Husa, "Classification of Legal Families Today: Is it Time for a Memorial Hymn?", *Revue Internationale de Droit Comparé* (2004) 11-38

JOLLS, SUNSTEIN AND THALER (1998)

C. Jolls, C. Sunstein and R. Thaler, "A Behavioral Approach to Law and Economics", 50 *Stanford Law Review* (1998) 1471-1550

JOLLS (2004)

C. Jolls, "State Legal Variation and Economic Outcomes: Identifying the Effects etc.", 94 *The American Economic Review* (2004) 447-453

KOROBKIN (2000)

R. Korobkin, "Behavioral Economics, Contract Formation, and Contract Law", in: C. Sunstein (ed.), *Behavioral Law and Economics* (Cambridge: Cambridge University Press 2000) 116-143

KOROBKIN AND ULEN (2000)

R.B. Korobkin and T.S. Ulen, "Law and behavioural science: Removing the rationality assumption from law and economics", 88 *California Law Review* (2000) 1051-1144

KOROBKIN (2001)

R. Korobkin, "A Multi-Disciplinary Approach to Legal Scholarship: Economics, Behavioral Economics, and Evolutionary Psychology", Research Paper 01-5 UCLA School of Law (Los Angeles 2001)

KRAUSS AND LEVY (2004)

M.I. Kraus & R.A. Levy, "Can Tort Reform and Federalism Coexist?", George Mason University School of Law Economics Working Paper Series 04-14

LANDO (1993)

O. Lando, "Is Codification Needed in Europe?", 1 *European Review of Private Law* (1993), 157-170

LANDO (2000)

O. Lando, "Optional or Mandatory Europeanisation of Contract Law", 8 *European Review of Private Law* (2000) 59-69

LANDO AND BEALE (2000)

O. Lando and H. Beale (eds.), *Principles of European Contract Law, Parts I and II* (The Hague etc.: Kluwer Law International 2000)

LANDO et al (2003)

O. Lando, E. Clive, A. Prüm and R.Zimmermann (eds.), *Principles of European Contract Law, Part III* (The Hague etc.: Kluwer Law International 2003)

LEGRAND (1996)

P. Legrand, "European Legal Systems are not Converging", 45 *International and Comparative Law Quarterly* (1996) 52-81

LEIBLE (1998)

S. Leible, "Aussenhandel und Rechtssicherheit", 97 *Zeitschrift für Vergleichende Rechtswissenschaft* (1998) 286-319

LEVITT (2001)

S. Levitt, "The Impact of Legalized Abortion on Crime", 116 *Quarterly Journal of Economics* (2001) 379-420

MACAULAY (1963)

S. Macaulay, "Non-contractual relations in business: a preliminary study", 28 *American Sociological Review* (1963) 55-70

MACQUEEN (2000)

H.L. MacQueen, *Scots Law and the Road to the New Ius Commune* (Ius Commune Lecture 1) (Maastricht : METRO 2000)

MACQUEEN, VAQUER AND ESPIAU ESPIAU (2003)

H. MacQueen, A. Vaquer and S. Espiau Espiau (eds.), *Regional Private Laws and Codification in Europe* (Cambridge: Cambridge University Press 2003)

MAHONEY (2001)

P.G. Mahoney, "The Common Law and Economic Growth: Hayek Might be Right", 30 *Journal of Legal Studies* (2001) 503-525

MATTLI (1999)

W. Mattli, *The Logic of Regional Integration: Europe and Beyond* (Cambridge: Cambridge University Press 1999)

MCCALLUM (1995)

J. McCallum, "National Borders Matter: Canada-US Regional Trade Patterns", 85 *American Economic Review* (1995) 615-623

MILLIMET AND OSANG (2004)

D.L. Millimet and T. Osang, "Do State Borders Matter for U.S. Intranational Trade? The Role of History and Internal Migration", available through http://faculty.smu.edu (May 2004)

NITSCH (2002)

V. Nitsch, *Border Effects and Border Regions: Lessons from the German Unification*, Discussion Paper Hamburg Institute of International Economics 203 (Hamburg 2002), available through http://www.hwwa.de (May 2004)

NORTH (1987)

D.C. North, "Institutions, Transaction Costs and Economic Growth", 25 *Economic Inquiry* (1987) 419-428

OGUS (1999)

A. Ogus, Competition between national legal systems: a contribution of economic analysis to comparative law, 48 *International and Comparative Law Quarterly* (1999) 405-418

OTT AND SCHÄFER (2002)

C. Ott and H.-B. Schäfer, "Die Vereinheitlichung des europäischen Vertragsrechts: Ökonomische Notwendigkeit oder akademisches Interesse?", in: C. Ott and H.-B. Schäfer (eds.), *Vereinheitlichung und Diversität des europäischen Zivilrechts in transnationalen Wirtschaftsräumen* (Tübingen: Mohr Siebeck 2002) 203-236

REICH (2004)

N. Reich, *Transformation of Contract Law and Civil Justice in New EU Member Countries*, Riga Graduate School of Law Working Papers nr. 21 (Riga 2004)

REIMANN (1996)

M. Reimann, "American Private Law and European Legal Unification – Can the United States be a Model?", *Maastricht Journal of European and Comparative Law* (1996) 217-233

RIBSTEIN AND KOBAYASHI (1996)

L.E. Ribstein and B.H. Kobayashi, "An Economic Analysis of Uniform State Laws", 25 *Journal of Legal Studies* (1996) 131-199

ROSTAIN (2000)

T. Rostain, "Educating *Homo Economicus*: Cautionary Notes on the New Behavioral Law and Economics Movement", 34 *Law & Society Review* (2000) 973-1006

RUBIN (1977)

P.H. Rubin, "Why is the Common Law Efficient?", 6 *Journal of Legal Studies* (1977) 51-63

RUBIN (2004)

P.H. Rubin, "Why Was the Common Law Efficient?", Law & Economics Research Paper Series, Emory School of Law, Working Paper 04-06, available through http://ssrn.com

SCHLECHTRIEM (2004)

P. Schlechtriem, *Kommentar zum einheitlichen UN-Kaufrecht*, 4th ed. (München: Beck 2004)

SMITS (2001)

J.M. Smits (ed.), *The Contribution of Mixed Legal Systems to European Private Law* (Antwerpen: Intersentia 2001)

SMITS (2002A)

J.M. Smits, "The Harmonisation of Private Law in Europe: Some Insights from Evolutionary Theory", 31 *Georgia Journal of International and Comparative Law* (2002) 79-99

SMITS (2002B)

J.M. Smits, "The Future of European Contract Law: on Diversity and the Temptation of Elegance", in: M. Faure, J. Smits and H. Schneider (eds.), *Towards a European Ius Commune in Legal Education and Research* (Antwerpen: Intersentia 2002) 239-256

SMITS AND HARDY (2002)

J.M. Smits and R.R.R. Hardy, "De toekomst van het Europees contractenrecht", *Weekblad voor Privaatrecht, Notariaat en Registratie* 6513 (2002) 827-833

SMITS AND HARDY (2003)

J.M. Smits and R.R.R. Hardy, "Het actieplan voor een coherenter Europees contractenrecht: een bespreking", *Weekblad voor Privaatrecht, Notariaat en Registratie* 6532 (2003) 385-389

STAUDENMAYER (2002)

D. Staudenmayer, "The Commission Communication on European Contract Law: What Future for European Contract Law?", 10 *European Review of Private Law* (2002) 249-260

STAUDENMAYER (2003)

D. Staudenmayer, "The Commission's Action Plan on European Contract Law", 11 *European Review of Private Law* (2003) 113-127

SUNSTEIN (2000)

C. Sunstein (ed.), *Behavioral Law and Economics* (Cambridge: Cambridge University Press 2000)

TEUBNER (1998)

G. Teubner, "Legal irritants: Good Faith in British Law or How Unifying Law Ends Up in New Divergences", 61 *Modern Law Review* (1998) 11-32

TIEBOUT (1956)

C. Tiebout, "A Pure Theory of Local Expenditures", 64 *Journal of Political Economy* (1956) 416-424

VAN DEN BERG (2001)

H. Van den Berg, *Economic Growth and Development* (Boston etc: McGraw 2001)

VAN DUNNÉ, LUIJTEN AND STEIN (1990)

J.M. van Dunné, E.A.A. Luijten and P.A. Stein, *Kosten en tekortkomingen van het Nieuw Burgerlijk Wetboek (boeken 3, 5 en 6): rapport uitgebracht aan de vaste Commissie voor justitie van de Tweede Kamer* (Arnhem: Gouda Quint 1990)

WAGNER (2002)

G.Wagner, "The Economics of Harmonization: The Case of Contract Law", 39 *Common Market Law Review* (2002) 995-1023

WEATHERILL (2001)

S. Weatherill, "The European Commission's Green Paper on European Contract Law: Context, Consent and Constitutionality", 9 *European Review of Private Law* (2001) 339-399

WEBLEY *et al* (2001)

P. Webley *et al, The Economic Psychology of Everyday Life* (Hove: Psychology Press 2001)

WHITE AND SUMMERS (2000)

J.J. White and R.S. Summers, *Uniform Commercial Code*, 5th ed. (St. Paul Minn.: West Group 2000)

ZIMMERMANN (2004)

R. Zimmermann, "Roman Law and the Harmonisation of Private Law in Europe", in: A. Hartkamp *et al* (eds.), *Towards a European Civil Code*, 3rd ed. (Nijmegen: Ars Aequi 2004) 21-42

ZIMMERMANN (1997)

R. Zimmermann, "The Civil Law in European Codes", in: D.L. Carey Miller and R. Zimmermann (eds.), *The Civilian Tradition and Scots Law: Aberdeen Quincentenary Essays* (Berlin: Duncker & Humblot 1997) 259-294

ZWEIGERT AND KÖTZ (1998)

K. Zweigert and H. Kötz, *An Introduction to Comparative Law*, 3rd ed. translated by Tony Weir (Oxford: Oxford University Press 1998)

Authors

Jaap Hage is Associate Professor of Legal Theory, Maastricht University

Heico Kerkmeester is Associate Professor of Law, Erasmus University Rotterdam

Jeffrey J. Rachlinski is Professor of Law, Cornell Law School

Jan Smits is Professor of European Private Law, Maastricht University

Gerhard Wagner is Professor of Private Law, Procedural Law, Private International Law and Comparative Law, University of Bonn

Helmut Wagner is Professor of Economics, University of Hagen

Thomas Wilhelmsson is Professor of Civil and Commercial Law, University of Helsinki